Penguin Education

Monetary Theory

Edited by R. W. Clower

Penguin Modern Economics Readings

General Editor

B. J. McCormick

Advisory Board

Monetary Theory

Selected Readings

Edited by R. W. Clower

Penguin Books

Penguin Books Ltd, Harmondsworth,
Middlesex, England
Penguin Books Inc., 7110 Ambassador Road,
Baltimore, Md. 21207, U.S.A.
Penguin Books Australia Ltd, Ringwood,
Victoria, Australia

First published by Penguin Books Ltd. 1969
First published by Penguin Books Inc 1970
This selection copyright © R. W. Clower, 1969
Introduction and notes copyright © R. W. Clower, 1969

Printed in the United States of America by
Kingsport Press, Inc.
Set in Monotype Times

Contents

Introduction

This volume is intended to provide a representative sample of traditional and modern thinking about the role of money in economic activity. Its central theme is the continuing quest for theoretical understanding of monetary phenomena. Other collections of readings on money, like standard textbooks on money and banking, convey a false impression of the authority of received doctrine. In truth, contemporary monetary theory is among the least-settled branches of economic analysis and no serious student of modern economics can afford to be ignorant of this fact – or of the reasons for it. With this thought in mind, I have purposely selected for inclusion in this volume a number of contributions that are concerned primarily with disputed issues. The result is a book the perusal of which may seem more like an excursion through uncharted seas than a guided tour through merely foreign territory. But such is the nature of contemporary monetary theory.

The literature of monetary theory overlaps or verges on virtually every other branch of economic analysis; yet it does not contain a single coherent characterization of two 'objects' the existence of which is the *sine qua non* of monetary theory itself, namely, *money commodity* and *money economy*. To attempt definitively to remedy these omissions in the space of the present introductory essay would be to confess myself a chronic sufferer from delusions of adequacy to which, in truth, I am only moderately prone. But it may be of some help to the reader, before he is confronted with a thematic analysis of the selections on monetary theory that appear in this volume, to have available at least one person's conception of the foundations of the subject.

Frontal attacks on the problem of defining the terms 'money commodity' and 'money economy' traditionally have produced more heat than light. Taking a hint from the experience of mathematicians, many of whose problems can be successfully attacked only by methods of indirect proof, let us attempt to

7

discover what money is and does by dealing first with an imaginary world in which monetary complications are non-existent – a barter economy where all exchange transactions entail simply a trade of goods for other goods.

To lend intuitive colour to our story, suppose that all individuals in our barter world live on a wooded island (perhaps in company with the odd snake or tiger) and must seek out other individuals as and when they wish to engage in commercial transactions. We need not conceive the society to be primitive in an anthropological sense; on the contrary, we may suppose that institutions for the protection of individual lives, limbs, property and the sanctity of exchange contracts, are as highly developed as might be desired by the most ardent believer in *laissez-faire*. We may further suppose that each individual is an enthusiastic trader, being impelled by talent and temperament to thirst for goods that he does not produce.

In the absence of established arrangements for organized trade, individuals will incur heavy costs (in terms of time and effort) in seeking out other individuals, establishing the existence of a double coincidence of wants (a necessary condition for barter exchange), and higgling and haggling over the terms at which proposed commodity trades shall be concluded. Accordingly, we may presume that no individual will engage in trade purely for pleasure; on the contrary, shopping expeditions will be set in motion as infrequently as can be contrived without the benefits of inaction being outweighed by psychological and other costs of having to consume one's own products.

The degree of trading inactivity of a representative individual will be reflected with fair reliability in the quantities of various goods that he holds as stocks – stocks of goods already produced and now awaiting disposal through trade, as well as stocks of goods destined for future consumption. Using some kind of weighted average of such stocks as a measure of the average length of the individual's *transaction period*, we now inquire more closely into the relation between the length of this period and total trading costs.

The total amount of time and effort that an individual spends in search and bargaining activity during any given interval of calendar time will depend directly on the length of the transaction period, for the work involved in any given shopping expedition will be much the same regardless of quantities traded; but the total amount of work required to move a given quantity of goods will be less if the individual engages in a few large transactions per unit of time than if he trades frequently in small amounts. Let us refer to this aspect of total trading expense – work devoted to search and bargaining activity – as *transaction costs*. In the nature of the case, transaction costs will vary *inversely* with the length of the transaction period.

If total trading costs consisted solely of transaction cost, rational behaviour might well induce some individuals to refrain from trade altogether – for transaction costs would surely bulk large in a world of simple barter. However, if an individual did not trade at all, he would have to consume his own produce – a subjectively abhorrent prospect, according to earlier hypothesis. And this is just an extreme case of a general principle: subjective costs are incurred by an individual when any desired commodity trade is postponed, whether the postponement is short or long. But unlike transaction costs, subjective costs associated with delays in trade vary *directly* with the length of the transaction period. Moreover, some costs of delay are objective, for longer transaction periods involve larger costs of commodity storage and also larger costs of foregone income on earning assets whose purchase is delayed. Let us refer to all these kinds of expense – subjective and objective consequences of delayed trading – as *waiting costs*. Since waiting costs vary directly with the length of the transaction period, whereas transaction costs vary inversely, we may be sure that somewhere between a transactions frequency of zero and a transactions frequency of infinity, there will occur a certain length of the transaction period that minimizes total trading costs per unit interval of calendar time.

The relation of transaction costs and of waiting costs to the length of the transaction period (both cost magnitudes being measured in subjectively valued units of 'work') is illustrated in Figure 1. In keeping with earlier remarks, we assume that trans-action costs (per unit of calendar time) are a strictly decreasing function of the length of the transaction period, while waiting costs are a strictly increasing function of the same variable. The precise form of the two relations will depend on the mixture and amounts of commodities traded, on the individual's preferences for present as compared with future goods, on the individual's initial endowment of resources and his technical knowledge, and on various environmental conditions (including the mixture and amounts of commodities traded by *other* individuals). In any given situation of 'taste and technology', however, we may suppose that both cost relations are well defined. At any given

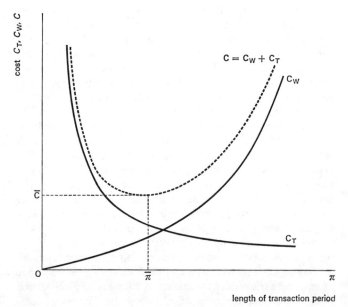

Figure 1

moment of time, therefore, we may suppose that there exists for each individual an *optimal transaction period* defined by the requirement that *total trading costs* (transaction costs plus waiting costs) be minimal. This will occur, of course, where *marginal* transaction costs are just equal to *marginal* waiting costs – for at this point ($\bar{\pi}$, $\bar{C}$ in Figure 1) *any* variation in the length of the transaction period will add more to one component of trading costs than it subtracts from the other.

In barter conditions, rates of exchange among commodities would have to be settled by individual bargaining. In principle, therefore, individual choice problems would be more complicated than in a world with organized markets. Under stationary conditions, however, a barter economy presumably would settle down eventually to a long-run equilibrium in which rates of exchange among commodities were uniform for all individuals. In such an equilibrium, the usual marginal equivalencies would have to hold: that is, marginal rates of return (objective or imputed) would be equal on all assets held by an individual; marginal personal and technical rates of substitution between any two commodities would be equal to their rate of exchange, and so forth. Out of this welter of conditions there would emerge for each individual a number representing the average time elapsing between successive bouts of trading activity – the length of the optimal transaction period. In a world of barter, as in a more advanced society, what appear outwardly to be institutionally determined patterns of timing in trading activity are determined in truth by individual choices.

Total trading costs would be enormous, of course, in an economy that had no institutional arrangements for organized trade. The term 'real balances' would be anything but a euphemism for 'purchasing power' – for real commodities are precisely what people would have to use as means of payment, stores of value and units of account. We need not attempt to trace through a mythical history of the development of techniques for eliminating some of the costs and complications of barter exchange. For our purposes, it suffices to note that search and bargaining activities in our island economy would be greatly facilitated by the establishment on the island of a 'community fairground', where individuals could meet other individuals desiring to engage in commodity trade. Transaction costs could then be reduced further by establishing within the fairground a separate 'trading post' for each distinct pair of commodities traded. If provision were made for *direct* trading of each good for every other good, however, a total of $\frac{1}{2}n(n-1)$ trading posts would be required to provide enough posts for n commodities. A more convenient way to allow for *ultimate* (indirect) pairwise trading of all commodities would be to establish trading posts for all commodities *except* one, the exceptional commodity being distinguished from all others by being tradeable at all posts.

The cost implications of each of the market arrangements outlined above are illustrated in Figure 2 (the curves in this figure

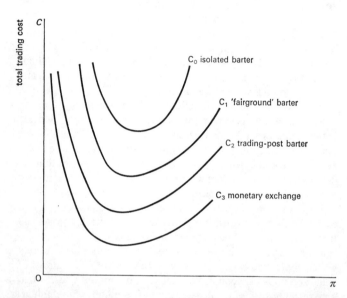

Figure 2

represent vertical sums of transaction cost and waiting cost curves such as those shown in Figure 1). We notice, first, that the total trading cost curve associated with each successive innovation lies *everywhere* below its predecessor; that is to say, there is an absolute (and possibly enormous) gap between trading costs in highly organized as compared with moderately or unorganized markets. Because market organization mainly affects transaction rather than waiting costs, however, the minimum point of each successive cost curve lies ever closer to the 'work' axis. This corresponds to a second and socially very important consequence of organized trading arrangements: transaction periods become shorter and holdings of commodity stocks become smaller as the degree of sophistication of market organization increases.

In the last of the innovations discussed above, the choice of commodities to be assigned to particular posts – hence the choice of an intermediary commodity – would be largely arbitrary. From the standpoint of minimizing transaction costs, what is important is that a prospective seller or buyer of any commodity should always be able to go to a particular trading post and know that all other individuals whose wants complement his own will sooner or later appear at the same place. However, it would evidently be wasteful of physical resources to choose as 'money' (as we may now call the intermediary commodity) a good that is a staple item of consumption. Even if such a good were chosen initially, arrangements would sooner or later be made whereby the commodity was diverted to other uses and its functions as an exchange intermediary were taken over by warehouse receipts or by socially sanctioned issues of fiat money, Giro cheques, etc. Would such 'nominal' money commodities be accepted and used? The answer is in the affirmative. The use of money in exchange transactions presupposes a certain degree of organization of trading activity. Such organization is socially beneficial because it enables individuals to channel into production or leisure labour and resources that would otherwise have to be devoted to search and bargaining activity. Barter would always be *possible* in a world with organized markets, but it would never in any circumstances be *efficient* as long as organized markets continued to function. Accordingly, we may say without hesitation that the technical characteristics of commodities chosen to serve as 'money' are of minor economic importance; what matters is the existence of social institutions condoned by either custom or law that enable individuals to trade efficiently *if they follow certain rules* – in particular, the rule that *one commodity traded in every exchange should be socially sanctioned as an exchange intermediary*. There are no specific trading rules in a world of barter; goods are simply

13

traded for goods, and that is all that can be said. In every money economy, however, there are fairly precise rules; *goods buy money, and money buys goods – but goods do not buy goods in any organized market.*

It would appear from the preceding discussion that an essential feature of a money economy is the existence of institutional arrangements whereby at least one commodity becomes universally acceptable in exchange for all other commodities. From the standpoint of economic efficiency, however, the particular devices that are used to give effect to these arrangements are of minor concern. From a logical standpoint, indeed, the physical characteristics of *money commodities* are no more relevant to the *institution* of money than different forms of courtship are revelant to the *institution* of marriage. Possession of many commodities is, so to speak, a passport for entry into the organized sector of a money economy. No passport, no entry – but the sector exists even if some individuals do not (or cannot) visit it. The *institution of money* is a valuable social resource, fully on a par with the most advanced machines of modern industry or the richest of natural-resource endowments. But *money commodities* are another matter. Arbitrary manipulation of these, in form or quantity, clearly cannot add significantly to (but may detract substantially from) the welfare of society.

We began this discussion by asking what money is and what money does. The materials for an answer are now assembled. We observe, firstly, that the market for 'money' is surely the least thin of all markets, because the 'market' for money consists of the set of all markets for other commodities. So 'money' is the ultimate in liquidity. Secondly, 'money' must be a store of value, because one of its functions is to enable individuals to delay transactions; hence it must serve as a temporary abode of purchasing power. But these characteristics, as also the characteristic of being a unit of account, are incidental to its third and primary function, which is to give effect to institutional arrangements for organized trading. All exchangeable commodities are media of exchange by virtue of the fact that they serve to pay for at least *one* other commodity; but only money commodities are means of payment for *all* other commodities. Money differs from other commodities in being universally acceptable as an exchange intermediary by virtue not of individual choice but rather by virtue of social contrivance.

Our characterization of 'money' might be thought to have some bearing on the question as to what objects should be considered money in the real world. But this is not so; for our 'definition' of money has precise meaning only in relation to other concepts such as 'commodity' and 'organized market' that are themselves open to a variety of different factual interpretations. All of these words are primitive (undefined) concepts of monetary theory in the same sense as the words 'point' and 'line' are primitive concepts of Euclidean geometry. Considered in isolation, 'money' is just a word – as 'point' is just a word, unless we are also told that 'points' have to do with diagrams rather than verbal or written debate. Intellectual understanding of observed monetary pheno-mena depends not on prior 'definition' of something called 'money' (such a definition could never be more than a picturesque description in any case); what is required is prior formulation of a coherent theory of monetary phenomena – which brings us to the content of the present book of readings.

The themes that underlie the several parts of this volume emerge in natural sequence from historical episodes in the development of monetary theory. The origins of contemporary theory are buried too deep in the past to admit of any but piecemeal excavation. The emergence everywhere of market arrangements that inhibit or preclude settlement of trading debts with any but a restricted range of socially sanctioned exchange intermediaries is no doubt attributable to private and social recognition of benefits to be realized from so organizing trading activity that only a short list of 'money commodities' are directly exchangeable for other commodities in established market-places. As such arrangements have developed, however, they have steadily eroded or altogether eliminated possibilities for engaging in trade of any kind without thereby engaging in the purchase or sale of commodities speci-fically designed to serve as means of payment. Thus practices that originally were matters of social convenience have hardened, with the passage of time, into legal and institutional restrictions; restrictions which ensure that virtually all market transactions involve two distinct operations – buying for money and selling for money – so that the holding of money balances for transactions purposes becomes a practical if not a physical necessity.

Early observers of this phenomenon naturally found it slightly paradoxical; for why should individuals find it advantageous to engage in *two* transactions where *one* would seem to accomplish the same final result more expeditiously? Much early writing on money was concerned directly or indirectly with analysing and resolving this paradox. To describe this literature as 'theory' would be a slight abuse of language; it might more accurately be described as systematized common sense. The scientific importance of the literature cannot be overemphasized, however, for it is from this cloth – sense evidence of the most direct and obvious kind – that the suit of formal monetary theory ultimately must be cut.

The selections in Part One (Money and the Mechanism of Exchange) are broadly representative of the descriptive stage in the development of monetary theory, though most of them are modern and some go well beyond systematized common sense in identifying what their authors regard as theoretically relevant aspects of the structure of a money economy. As will become apparent in later selections, formal theory has never managed to capture certain elements of everyday experience that 'common-sense' writers consider crucial. In all descriptive accounts of monetary exchange, for example, it is taken for granted that money commodities play a peculiar role as media of exchange – that money commodities are, in principle, distinguishable from other commodities by virtue of this role. No such distinction is logically admissible, however, within the framework of established price theory. On the contrary, the analytical (as contrasted with the verbal) content of the most general of modern statements of value and monetary theory (namely, Don Patinkin's *Money, Interest and Prices*) is logically indistinguishable from that of the most traditional theory of a barter economy. The failure of monetary theorists adequately to express in formal language this and other aspects of their own intuitive conception of the nature of 'monetary reality' no doubt is attributable more to the complexity of monetary phenomena than to the ignorance, oversight or 'wrong-headedness' of theorists. However, the considered view of keen observers of monetary phenomena merit serious and careful study, though the observers be utterly devoid of theoretical guile.

The theme of the selections in Part Two (Traditional Doctrine: The Quantity Theory of Money) is a natural outcome of the growing use of selected commodities as exchange intermediaries at the dawn of the Industrial Revolution. As noted earlier, money commodities are important from the standpoint of social welfare only as devices for facilitating exchange. Individuals acquire money commodities not because such commodities are directly useful but because they can later be used to purchase other commodities that are desired for their own sake. By virtue of these devices, practical effect is given to the institution of money; the establishment of organized markets enables individuals to channel into productive activity labour and other resources that would otherwise be devoted to search and bargaining activities. But money, as money, need not be intrinsically valuable, for what matters is not the particular commodity (or commodities) that serve as money, but rather the existence of social institutions that make monetary transactions feasible and efficient.

The unimportance of the 'stuff' of which money is made is obvious enough to people who live in a world of fiat currencies; but what is obvious today was not so clear to people whose money consisted largely of gold, silver and other intrinsically valuable materials. In those circumstances, many if not most people were easily persuaded to believe that money was wealth in the same sense as, say, a cow, a field or a piece of machinery. So we find that the earliest formal analyses of monetary phenomena are directed at dispelling this illusion by examining the consequences of a once-over change in the quantity of money commodities.

The *locus classicus* of all such analyses is an essay by David Hume entitled 'Of money'.

Money is nothing but the representation of labour and commodities, and serves only as a method of rating or estimating them. Where coin is in greater plenty – as a greater quantity of it is required to represent the same quantity of goods – it can have no effect, either good or bad, taking a nation within itself; any more than it would make an alteration in a merchant's books, if instead of the Arabian method of notation, which requires few characters, he should make use of the Roman, which requires a great many . . .

Notwithstanding this conclusion, which must be allowed just, it is certain that since the discovery of the mines in America, industry has increased in all the nations of Europe, except in the possessors of those mines; and this may justly be ascribed, among other reasons, to the increase of gold and silver. Accordingly, we find that in every kingdom, into which money begins to flow in greater abundance than formerly, everything takes on a new face; labour and industry gain life; the merchant becomes more enterprising, and even the farmer follows his plough with greater alacrity and attention . . .

To account then for this phenomenon, we must consider, that though the high price of commodities be a necessary consequence of the increase of gold and silver, yet it follows not immediately upon that increase; but some time is required before the money circulates through the whole state, and makes its effect be felt on all ranks of people. At first, no alternation is perceived; by degrees the price rises, first of one commodity, then of another; till the whole at last reaches a just proportion with the new quantity of specie which is in the kingdom. In my opinion, it is only in this interval or intermediate situation, between the acquisition of money and the rise of prices, that the increasing quantity of gold and silver is favourable to industry. (1, pp. 292–4.)

Hume's essay provides a nicely balanced account of what has since become known as the *quantity theory of money*. Later writers have not always stated or interpreted the theory so judiciously. As construed by some writers, indeed, the propositions advanced by Hume were made to assert that the 'real' work money has to perform is determined simply by the amount of goods and services that have to be traded; hence that money, as money, is merely a 'veil', explicit consideration of which obscures the working of those *truly* important forces (and Calvinist virtues) of productivity and thrift that are the ultimate determinants of social welfare.

This bowdlerized version of Hume, or something very like it, has occupied a prominent place in the thinking of professional economists through much of modern history. It underlies what today is referred to as the *naive quantity theory*, the central proposition of which is that the total quantity of means of payment governs the absolute scale of money prices but does not affect real rates of exchange among other commodities. On this reckoning, the determination of real rates of exchange, and of quantities traded, is the business not of monetary but of value theory. Monetary theory is seen as a trivial addendum to conventional demand-and-supply analysis rather than a subject deserving systematic study in its own right.

The dichotomy thus established between monetary and value theory ultimately produced two relatively distinct breeds of economist to which some wag later assigned the descriptive labels 'curve benders' and 'curve stretchers'. The selections of Part Two sketch the story of this dichotomy from its origin up to very recent times. The end – or apparent end – of the story is unfolded in the selections appearing in Parts Three and Four (Contemporary Theory: Neo-Walrasian Equilibrium Analysis; and Monetary Theory and Keynesian Economics).

There plainly is much to be said for Hume's version of the quantity theory as an *ad hoc* description of the factors that mainly govern the determination of the general level of money prices *in the long run*. Looking at the problem of price behaviour from a theoretical point of view, however, one finds it difficult to see how any significant role can be assigned to money in the long run unless money also is assumed to play an important role in short-run events; and if money is assigned an important role in short-run economic analysis, then a *separate* long-run theory of money should not be necessary. Long-run conclusions should follow from short-run assumptions. However that may be, the fact is that until the appearance in 1936 of John Maynard Keynes' *General Theory of Employment, Interest and Money*, most professional economists took it for granted that all economic problems of any practical importance could be adequately handled using established techniques of demand-and-supply analysis, thereby presupposing that money was as much a 'veil' in the short run as it was in the long – for at no stage in pre-Keynesian economics was any serious attempt made to build peculiarly monetary assumptions into the micro-foundations of economic analysis.

The closest approach to such an attempt was initiated by Leon Walras (1834–1910) in his pioneering treatment of general equilibrium analysis; but it involved little more than a mechanical application of quantity theory ideas to a conceptual model, the analytical structure of which precluded assignment of a specialized role to money as a means of payment. A less formal, but ultimately more influential attack on the same problem was later undertaken by J. R. (now Sir John) Hicks in his famous 'Suggestion for simplifying the theory of money', the central theme of which was that money could be assigned a natural place in established demand-and-supply analysis by treating it as a special kind of asset. The effect of both attempts was to strengthen the already prevalent notion that economics could do without a separate theory to describe short-run price and quantity behaviour in a money economy.

Keynes' *General Theory* temporarily dispelled this illusion, firstly by raising doubts about the theoretical generality of traditional value theory and its relevance for describing *on-going* as contrasted with *virtual* economic processes; secondly by proposing an alternative scheme of analysis certain implications of which seemed inconsistent with received doctrine. I say 'temporarily dispelled' because subsequent developments in economic theory, associated mainly with the writings of Hicks, Lange, Modigliani, Samuelson and Patinkin, gradually have persuaded many and perhaps most economists that the Keynesian revolution, however beneficial may have been its *practical effects* on a nearly decadent science, added nothing novel or worthwhile to the *theoretical foundations* of economic science. As concerns monetary theory, in particular, contemporary opinion – as indicated by the selections in Part Three – appears strongly to favour what might be described as a 'neo-Walrasian quantity theory' to the effect that money matters only slightly in the short run, and not at all in the long. No other conclusion is possible, indeed, if one adopts the conception of a money economy implicit in recent statements of the general equilibrium theory of money and prices. In all such neo-Walrasian models, money appears as just one among many analytically indistinguishable commodities in a world where trading activities are costlessly co-ordinated by a central market authority in such a manner that all feasible trades ultimately can be carried out directly, without the use of exchange intermediaries. Money indeed *is* a cipher in such a world as this, for its only apparent function is to serve as a store of value – a function that would appear to be better served by assets that have a positive income yield.

Such is the stage that monetary theory had reached by 1960.

Developments since then have raised some interesting questions, generated occasional heat and produced a modicum of light on doctrinal and other issues. As a consequence, it now seems clear that neo-Walrasian monetary models are little if any better than the most orthodox of classical barter models for analysing short-run movements in economic activity. What is not yet clear, however, is how the shortcomings of accepted theory can be remedied. Most economists who are not specialists in money appear to take the view that the problem is not all that serious. The theoretical rockets that accompanied the development of neo-Walrasian and Keynesian monetary theory have long since vanished, leaving behind them wispy trails of wisdom that are quite disproportionate to the original sound and fury.

Monetary specialists generally take a more serious view of the inadequacies of existing theory, but few of them have any concrete suggestions for improvement. Failing suggestions by others, they have tended to turn either to econometric study of observed behaviour (measurement with so little theory that it really does not matter), or to consciously academic exercises in the dynamics of monetary growth (theory with so little reality that it does not matter either). The literature on monetary econometrics is too extensive and technical on the one hand, and too devoid of analysis on the other, to offer much usable material for a volume such as this. The literature on monetary growth, however, has considerable intellectual appeal, and it may even afford some useful insights into the working of inflationary and deflationary processes. Accordingly, a small but provocative sample of this literature is presented in Part Five (Money and Economic Growth).

Reference
1. D. HUME, 'Of money', *Essays*, Oxford University Press, 1750.

Part One Money and the Mechanism of Exchange

The ubiquity of money in everyday commerce is a major obstacle to clear understanding of those features of a money economy that distinguish it from a world of barter. The selections that follow are intended to lessen if not eliminate this obstacle. Each draws largely on commonplace knowledge yet manages to identify and illuminate aspects of economic organization that lend money a special role in economic activity. But it is one thing to assert how and why 'money matters' and another to express these assertions in an intellectually satisfying manner. As later theoretical selections show, there is no clear link between generally accepted facts of experience and their logical interpretation. Money may play an obvious role in actual life, but its position in accepted monetary theory is anything but transparent.

1 W. S. Jevons

Barter

W. S. Jevons, 'Barter', *Money and the Mechanism of Exchange*, Kegan Paul, 23rd edn, 1910, ch. 1, pp. 1–7.

Some years since, Mademoiselle Zélie, a singer of the *Théâtre Lyrique* at Paris, made a professional tour round the world, and gave a concert in the Society Islands. In exchange for an air from *Norma* and a few other songs, she was to receive a third part of the receipts. When counted, her share was found to consist of three pigs, twenty-three turkeys, forty-four chickens, five thousand cocoa-nuts, besides considerable quantities of bananas, lemons and oranges. At the Halle in Paris, as the *prima donna* remarks in her lively letter, printed by M. Wolowski, this amount of livestock and vegetables might have brought four thousand francs, which would have been good remuneration for five songs. In the Society Islands, however, pieces of money were very scarce; and as Mademoiselle could not consume any considerable portion of the receipts herself, it became necessary in the meantime to feed the pigs and poultry with the fruit.

When Mr Wallace was travelling in the Malay Archipelago, he seems to have suffered rather from the scarcity than the super-abundance of provisions. In his most interesting account of his travels, he tells us that in some of the islands, where there was no proper currency, he could not procure supplies for dinner without a special bargain and much chaffering upon each occasion. If the vendor of fish or other coveted eatables did not meet with the sort of exchange desired, he would pass on, and Mr Wallace and his party had to go without their dinner. It therefore became very desirable to keep on hand a supply of articles, such as knives, pieces of cloth, arrack or sago cakes, to multiply the chance that one or other article would suit the itinerant merchant.

In modern civilized society the inconveniences of the primitive method of exchange are wholly unknown, and might almost seem to be imaginary. Accustomed from our earliest years to the use of money, we are unconscious of the inestimable benefits which it confers upon us; and only when we recur to altogether different states of society can we realize the difficulties which arise in its absence. It is even surprising to be reminded that barter is actually the sole method of commerce among many uncivilized races. There is something absurdly incongruous in the fact that a joint-stock company, called 'The African Barter Company Limited', exists in London, which carries on its transactions upon the West Coast of Africa entirely by bartering European manufactures for palm oil, gold dust, ivory, cotton, coffee, gum and other raw produce.

The earliest form of exchange must have consisted in giving what was not wanted directly for that which was wanted. This simple traffic we call *barter* or *truck*, the French *troc*, and distinguish it from sale and purchase in which one of the articles exchanged is intended to be held only for a short time, until it is parted with in a second act of exchange. The object which thus temporarily intervenes in sale and purchase is money. At first sight it might seem that the use of money only doubles the trouble, by making two exchanges necessary where one was sufficient; but a slight analysis of the difficulties inherent in simple barter shows that the balance of trouble lies quite in the opposite direction. Only by such an analysis can we become aware that money performs not merely one service to us, but several different services, each indispensable. Modern society could not exist in its present complex form without the means which money constitutes of valuing, distributing and contracting for commodities of various kinds.

Want of Coincidence in Barter

The first difficulty in barter is to find two persons whose disposable possessions mutually suit each other's wants. There may be many people wanting, and many possessing those things wanted; but to allow of an act of barter, there must be a double coincidence, which will rarely happen. A hunter having returned from a successful chase has plenty of game, and may want arms and ammunition to renew the chase. But those who have arms may happen to be well supplied with game, so that no direct exchange is possible. In civilized society the owner of a house may find it unsuitable and may have his eye upon another house exactly fitted to his needs. But even if the owner of this second house wishes to part with it at all, it is exceedingly unlikely that he will exactly reciprocate the feelings of the first owner and wish to barter houses. Sellers and purchasers can only be made to fit by the use of some commodity, some *marchandise banale*, as the French call it, which all are willing to receive for a time, so that what is obtained by sale in one case, may be used in purchase in another. This common commodity is called a *medium of exchange*, because it forms a third or intermediate term in all acts of commerce.

Within the last few years a curious attempt has been made to revive the practice of barter by the circulation of advertisements. The *Exchange and Mart* is a newspaper which devotes itself to making known all the odd property which its advertisers are willing to give for some coveted article. One person has some old coins and a bicycle, and wants to barter them for a good concertina. A young lady desires to possess *Middlemarch* and offers a variety of old songs, of which she has become tired. Judging from the size and circulation of the paper, and the way in which its scheme has been imitated by some other weekly papers, we must assume that the offers are sometimes accepted and that the printing press can bring about, in some degree, the double coincidence necessary to an act of barter.

Want of a Measure of Value

A second difficulty arises in barter. At what rate is any exchange to be made? If a certain quantity of beef be given for a certain quantity of corn, and in like manner corn be exchanged for cheese, and cheese for eggs, and eggs for flax and so on, still the question will arise – how much beef for how much flax, or how much of any one commodity for a given quantity of another? In a state of barter the price-current list would be a most complicated document, for each commodity would have to be quoted in terms of every other commodity, or else complicated rule-of-three sums would become necessary. Between one hundred articles there must exist no less that 4950 possible ratios of exchange and all these ratios must be carefully adjusted so as to be consistent with each other, else the acute trader will be able to profit by buying from some and selling to others.

All such trouble is avoided if any one commodity be chosen and its ratio of exchange with each other commodity be quoted. Knowing how much corn is to be bought for a pound of silver and also how much flax for the same quantity of silver, we learn without further trouble how much corn exchanges for so much flax. The chosen commodity becomes *a common denominator* or *common measure of value*, in terms of which we estimate the values of all other goods, so that their values become capable of the most easy comparison.

Want of Means of Subdivision

A third, but it may be a minor inconvenience of barter, arises from the impossibility of dividing many kinds of goods. A store of corn, a bag of gold dust, a carcase of meat, may be portioned out, and more or less may be given in exchange for what is wanted. But the tailor, as we are reminded in several treatises on political economy, may have a coat ready to exchange, but it much exceeds in value the bread which he wishes to get from the baker, or the meat from the butcher. He cannot cut the coat up without destroying the value of his handiwork. It is obvious that he needs the medium of exchange, into which he can temporarily convert the coat, so that he may give a part of its value for bread, and other parts for meat, fuel and daily necessaries, retaining perhaps a portion for future use. Further illustration is needless; for it is obvious that we need a means of dividing and distributing value according to our varying requirements.

In the present day barter still goes on in some cases, even in the most advanced commercial countries, but only when its inconveniences are not experienced. Domestic servants receive part of their wages in board and lodging; the farm labourer may partially receive payment in cider, or barley, or the use of a piece of land. It has always been usual for the miller to be paid by a portion of the corn which he grinds. The *truck* or barter system, by which workmen took their wages in kind, has hardly yet been extinguished in some parts of England. Pieces of land are occasionally exchanged by adjoining landowners; but all these are comparatively trifling cases. In almost all acts of exchange, money now intervenes in one way or other, and even when it does not pass from hand to hand it serves as the measure by which the amounts given and received are estimated. Commerce begins with barter and in a certain sense it returns to barter; but the last form of barter, as we shall see, is very different from the first form. By far the greater part of commercial payments are made at the present day in England apparently without the aid of metallic money; but they are readily adjusted, because money acts as the common denominator, and what is bought in one direction is balanced off against what is sold in another direction.

2 A. C. Pigou

Money, a Veil?

Excerpt from A. C. Pigou, 'Money, a veil?', *The Veil of Money*, Macmillan, 1941, ch. 4, pp. 20–27.

To every community there are available at any time certain resources provided by nature, which the classical economists compendiously called land; a certain accumulation of objects made by man, with the help perhaps of other like objects, called capital; and a certain population of men, women and children endowed with various types of skill. Out of this population the workers, brain workers and hand workers together, or rather those of them who are at the time employed, co-operate with land and capital to produce a great variety of goods and direct services, including, as a rule, some net addition to the stock of capital. This inventory of objects is commonly called the community's 'real income'. If the community is in contact with other communities a part of the process of production may be indirect, one community producing one set of things to be exchanged with other communities for another set, which then enters, while the things exchanged away do not enter, into its real income. All the things entering into that real income are distributed among the members of our community in one way or another. The amount of work that people do, the way in which this work is allocated among different occupations, between the production of consumer's goods and of capital goods and among the various kinds of each, the amount and kinds of the goods and services that result, and the variations in all these elements that take place from time to time, are for the economist the essential things and the primary object of his study.

One aspect of this reality can be displayed by way of an instantaneous photograph. In such a photograph no indication will appear of any process of movement. The picture will comprise, not flows at all, only stocks. Thus there will be seen, in part rooted to the ground, such-and-such a physical equipment of fixed capital, including houses, such-and-such stocks of raw materials, of partly grown crops and partly manufactured goods, standing in what has been called the machine of process; such-and such stocks of physically finished goods standing in what we may call the machine of distribution, i.e. in the hands of wholesalers, transporting agents and retail dealers; such-and-such stocks of completed goods, including motor-cars and other forms of consumer's capital, standing in people's homes; and, lastly, such-and-such a stock of human beings of various ages and capacity.

An instantaneous picture is, however, of much less interest than a moving one; because the wheel of our economy is not at rest, but in continuous revolution. The term 'stationary state', as used by economists, is, indeed, not linguistically apt. The idea that it was meant to convey is not, as the word suggests, that of non-motion but that of rotation at a constant speed, neither accelerating nor decelerating. Consider then an economy in a stationary state in that sense, or, what comes to the same thing, in *any* state restricted to a time interval short enough to allow such accelerations or decelerations as may be taking place to be ignored. In a moving picture of this all the several stocks described in the last paragraph remain constant in size. No additions to or subtractions from any of them take place, which implies that there is no net investment or disinvestment and no change in the size of the population of working age. The shape of the waterfall is unvarying, but the place occupied at one moment by this drop is the next moment occupied by that one. Parts of the stock of fixed capital are continuously being worn out and replaced. Raw materials and partly manufactured goods move continuously forward through the machine of process, passing into the machine of distribution and, through that again, into the hands of the final holders; corresponding quantities of material being fed into the machine of process by an intake pipe and worked up inside in such wise as exactly to balance the outflow. Of what flows to the final holders a part replaces wear and tear of consumer's capital – motor-cars, furniture, clothes, crockery and so on; a part, after a momentary stay in larders and kitchens, is literally consumed in the bodies of the people; a part, such as the services rendered by

31

doctors, teachers and musicians, passes directly into consumption without any mediating machine.

The final holders, to whom all these goods flow out, are all the time, with the help of the stock of capital equipment, performing the work by means of which new materials are continuously pushed through the intake pipe into the machine of process and operated upon inside it. The goods which finally emerge in any time interval are the result of efforts scattered over a prior period, the centre of gravity of which stands, so to speak, for each sort of good, a specifiable number of days backward in time. For all sorts of goods that enter into real income taken together this number of days must obviously bear to 365 the same ratio that the stock of goods in process and distribution – working capital – bears to annual income. For this country there is reason to believe that the ratio is in the neighbourhood of half. That, however, from the present standpoint, is a secondary matter. The essential fact, to put it paradoxically, is that our economic machine is a perpetual motion machine, whose movement generates the fuel which keeps the movement going.

Thus far of the so-called stationary state. But in actual life the wheel does not rotate at constant velocity, the waterfall does not retain a constant shape or size. If, instead of restricting ourselves to a very short length of moving-picture reel, we run through a moderately long one, this becomes at once apparent. The several stocks we have distinguished change in volume and in the form of their content from time to time. We might imagine for ourselves if we wished – and for some purposes this would prove a convenient imagining – an economy growing continuously in all its parts at one and the same constant geometrical rate.[1] In actual life we do not find economies moving in steady progress of any

1. It would be impossible for all its parts to grow at the same constant *arithmetical* rate. For if the flow of consumption goods is to increase at a constant arithmetical rate, the stock of equipment must (on obviously plausible assumptions) increase at that constant arithmetical rate, and this implies that apart from the need for replacements, the output of the industries making equipment is not increasing at all. It should be noted that there is no general *a priori* reason for believing it to be possible for all the parts of a whole to increase even at one and the same *geometrical* rate. If a pet elephant this year contains twice the volume of flesh and bone that it did last, it will contain much less than twice the area of skin.

sort, but rather as successive curlings and uncurlings, after the manner of a caterpillar. The waterfall may on the whole be increasing (or decreasing) in size, but in some time intervals of given length the increase is much larger than in others, while in some there may be actual decreases. Moreover, the shape of the waterfall neither remains constant nor varies in a constant manner, while the drops that were originally water alter from time to time, consisting now perhaps of wine, now of vinegar, The total outflow of goods and services, the types of these, the total quantity of work people finding employment, their various qualities, the total quantity of equipment at work and its various kinds, all these things continuously shift and change, and all the shifts and changes our long strip of film faithfully records.

Over against the real facts and happenings thus roughly outlined there stand monetary facts and happenings. There is not indeed any *a priori* necessity about this. In primitive conditions small groups of neighbours, or even families, were in great part self-sufficing. A farm family grew its own food, made its own clothes, kept its own house in repair. A substantial part of the work that a man did and of the services that he rendered yielded their product directly to himself. Now, in the main this is not so. With the division of labour carried so far as it has been, it could not be so. In general, a man receives as real income only a small extent of those things which his own particular work has contributed in producing. By far the predominant part of his real income he obtains by exchanging, and exchanging against money, so that money income, which is the obverse of money expenditure by final buyers – not, of course, by intermediaries – is the purchase price, or value, of the community's real income. It is in connexion with this exchanging that monetary facts and happenings come into being. They differ from 'real' facts and happenings in that, unlike these they have no *direct* significance for economic welfare. Take the real facts and happenings away and the monetary facts and happenings necessarily vanish with them, but take money away and, whatever else might follow, economic life would *not* become meaningless – there is nothing absurd about the conception of a self-sufficing family, or village group, without any money at all. In this sense money clearly *is* a veil. It does not comprise any of the essentials of economic life.

But this is not to say that monetary facts and happenings are unimportant to economic life. The body is more than raiment, but raiment greatly affects the comfort of the body. Thus money – the institution of money – is an extremely valuable social instrument, making a large contribution to economic welfare. Under any conditions other than the most primitive, people find it, as we have seen, economically advantageous to carry on a great deal of interchange among various sorts of goods and services. Such interchange by way of direct barter, if not entirely impracticable would, as is abundantly illustrated in the textbooks, be extremely inconvenient and costly in time and trouble; so much so that, if there were no generally accepted money, many of these transactions would not be worth undertaking, and as a direct consequence the division of labour would be hampered and less services and goods would be produced. Thus not only would real income be allocated less satisfactorily, from the standpoint of economic welfare, among different sorts of goods, but it would also contain smaller amounts of many, if not of all sorts. Obviously then money is not *merely* a veil or a garment or a wrapper. Like the laws of property and contract, it constitutes at the least a very useful lubricant, enabling the economic machine to function continuously and smoothly; a railway through the air, the loss of which would inflict on us the same sort of damage as we should suffer if the actual railways and roads, by which the different parts of the country are physically linked together, were destroyed.

So far everyone would be agreed. But now an important distinction must be drawn. The *institution* of money is, as we have seen, a powerful instrument promoting wealth and welfare. But the *number of units of money* embodied in that instrument is, in general, of no significance. It is all one whether the garment, or the veil, is thick or thin. I do not mean, of course, that it is immaterial whether the number of units of money is held constant, or is variable in one manner, or is variable in another manner in relation to other economic happenings. I mean that if, other things being equal, over a series of months or years the stock of money contains successively mx_1, mx_2, mx_3, . . . units, it makes no difference what the value of m is. A doubled value of m throughout means simply doubled prices throughout of every type of goods – subject, of course, to the rate of interest not being reckoned for this purpose as a price – and all real happenings are exactly what they would have been with a value of m half as large. The reason for this is that, money being only useful *because* it exchanges for other things, a larger quantity does not, as with other things, carry more satisfaction on its back than a smaller quantity, but the same satisfaction. As we are dealing in similes, a new one, to clinch this argument, may be allowed us. Money then, let us say, is a key, by means of which productive energies, that would otherwise have been imprisoned, can be released; but, provided only it fits the lock, it is of no significance whether the key contains a great deal of metal or very little.

So far everything is clear. If then we were confronted in the actual world with the steadily rotating state, inaptly called stationary, of economic fiction, there would be no further question to ask and nothing more to say. But the fact of change destroys this convenient simplicity. The economic body alters, and the veil that shrouds, or the garment that enwraps it, alters also. How are these alterations related? At one time it was the practice of an important school of writers to assert that psychical happenings were mere epiphenomena of physical happenings; that they were wholly an effect of these latter happenings and in no degree reacted upon them. Pressure on the heart caused mental distress, but mental distress could not cause pressure on the heart; laughter caused pleasurable emotion, not, as the layman might suppose, pleasurable emotion laughter. In like manner, it might be argued, all changes which occur in the money garment result from changes initiated in the body, and these changes in the garment do not react in any way on the body; just as if the number of persons travelling in a railway train were recorded by an enterprising spy, the record would be a mere epiphenomenon. The similes of the garment, the veil and the wrapper suggest that this is in fact so. But the suggestion is wrong. Many important changes that occur in the garment are, indeed, effects of changes initiated in the body. But, in general, these in turn react in a greater or less degree on the state of the body. *What* changes in the garment result from given changes initiated in the body and what reactions they, or the lack of them, in turn produce depends on how the garment is constructed. Besides these induced changes that occur in the garment there are, or may be, other changes that are autonomous, originating in the garment itself. These too have effects on the body. What they are and what their effects again depends on how the garment is constructed.

3 L. B. Yeager

The Medium of Exchange

L. B. Yeager (1968) 'Essential properties of the medium of exchange', *Kyklos*, vol. 21, no. 1, pp. 45–68.

I Liquidity and Money

The *Radcliffe Report* and many writings on nonbank financial intermediaries urged more attention to the total liquidity position of a developed economy and less to money in the old narrow sense. This advice met widespread skepticism. Something remains to be said, though, about what facts justify this skepticism and why they are crucial although banally familiar. The actual medium of exchange remains distinctive in ways seldom fully appreciated. The differences between it and other elements of liquidity may be unimportant to the individual, yet they are crucial to the system. An individual holder might consider certain near-moneys practically the same as actual money because he could readily exchange them for it whenever he wanted. But micro-exchangeability need not mean ready exchangeability of aggregates. (Although gold and paper moneys under the gold standard meant practically the same thing to an individual holder, for example, they did not have the same functions and significance in the national economy, especially not at a time of balance-of-payments trouble.) The sound precept of 'methodological individualism' prizes information gained by considering the decisions of the individual economic unit, but it does not insist on generalizing from the individual point of view *alone*. The famous fallacy of composition warns against that.

An excess demand for actual money shows itself to individual economic units less clearly than does an excess demand for any other thing, even the nearest of near-moneys. It eliminates itself more indirectly and with more momentous macroeconomic consequences. The present paper, building up to its main conclusion in Section V, tries to explain how. It gives new support to the diagnosis of depression as an essentially monetary disorder.

One familiar approach to the definition of money scorns any supposedly *a priori* line between money and near-moneys. Instead, it seeks the definition that works best with statistics. One strand of that approach seeks clues to substitutabilities among assets – to how similar or different their holders regard them – by studying how sensitively holdings of currency, demand deposits and other liquid assets have depended on income, wealth and interest rates.[1] Another strand seeks the narrowly or broadly defined quantity that correlates most closely with income in equations fitted to historical data. Information obtained from such studies can be important for some purposes. But it would be awkward if the definition of money accordingly had to change from time to time and country to country. Furthermore, even if money defined to include certain near-moneys does correlate somewhat more closely with income than money narrowly defined, that fact does not necessarily impose the broad definition. Perhaps the amount of these near-moneys depends on the level of money income and in turn on the amount of medium of exchange through the gearing process described in Section III below. More generally, it is not obvious why the magnitude with which some other magnitude correlates most closely deserves overriding attention; it might be neither the most interesting nor the most controllable one. The number of bathers at a beach may correlate more closely with the number of cars parked there than with either the temperature or the price of admission, yet the former correlation may be less interesting or useful than either of the latter. The correlation with national income might be closer for either consumption or investment than for the quantity of money; yet the latter correlation could be the most interesting one to the monetary authorities.

Of course, a broad definition of money is not downright 'wrong', since many definitions can be self-consistent. But no mere definition should deter us, when we are trying to understand the flow of spending in the economy, from focusing attention on

1. Statistical demand-for-money studies are examples of 'individual experiments', as distinguished from 'market experiments' (1, pp. 11–12, 387–94).

the narrow category of assets that actually get spent. It is methodological prejudice to dismiss as irrelevant, without demonstrating their irrelevance, such facts as these: Certain assets do and others do not circulate as media of exchange. No reluctance of sellers to accept the medium of exchange hampers anyone's spending it. The medium of exchange can 'burn holes in pockets' in a way that near-moneys do not. Supply creates its own demand (in a sense specified later) more truly for the medium of exchange than for other things. These are observed facts, or inferences from facts, not mere *a priori* truths or tautologies.

In comparing the medium of exchange with other financial assets, we must go beyond asking what determines the *amount* of each that people demand to hold. We must also consider the *manner* in which people acquire and dispose of each asset and implement a change in their demand for it. This is presumably what W. T. Newlyn meant in urging a 'functional' distinction between money and near-money according to 'operational effects in the economy rather than [just] according to asset status from the point of view of the owner' (2, pp. 327–46).

To recognize how nonmonetary liquidity affects total demands for money and for goods and services, we need not blur the definition of money so badly as to subvert measurement and control of its quantity. We need not blur the distinctions between supplies of and demands for assets and between influences on supply and influences on demand. We can define the supply of money narrowly, as a measureable quantity, and see it confronted by a demand for cash balances – a demand influenced, to be sure, by the availability and attractiveness of other assets.

This approach keeps two concepts of 'liquidity' distinct. The first, a vague one, corresponds roughly to what Newlyn has called 'financial strength' – the total purchasing power that firms and individuals consider available in their asset-holdings and their possibilities of borrowing. This 'essentially . . . *ex-ante* concept . . . reflects "the amount of money people think they can get hold of"'. What they could in fact get hold of all at once is something else again. In a second sense, liquidity means the amount of medium of exchange in existence (or perhaps, as Newlyn implies, the relation between that amount and the volume of transactions to be performed).[2] Given a fixed stock of actual medium of exchange, widespread attempts to sell liquid assets or borrow to mobilize supposed 'financial strength' for spending would partially frustrate each other through declines in the prices of financial assets, higher interest rates, tighter credit rationing, and the like.

II The Example of Claims on Nonbank Intermediaries

To highlight the properties of the medium of exchange by contrast, let us focus on the liquid liabilities of nonbank financial intermediaries. (Doing so is an expository device only; most of the disputes over the intermediaries do not, in their own right, concern us here.) James Tobin has restated some of the issues raised by Gurley and Shaw in a helpfully clear and forceful way (3, pp. 408–19). He questions the traditional story of how banks create money by expanding credit. If other intermediaries are mere brokers in loanable funds, then so are the banks. A savings and loan association is a creditor of the mortgage borrower and at the same time a debtor to the ultimate saver who holds its shares; similarly, the commercial bank can be a creditor because it is in debt to its depositors. Only ultimate savers can provide loanable funds. If in some sense both types of institution do create credit by issuing their own liquid liabilities, they are alike in that respect. Bank demand deposits are unique in being actual media of exchange, Tobin concedes; but since each type of claim on a financial intermediary has its own brand of uniqueness, there is nothing unique about being unique. It is 'superficial and irrelevant' to insist 'that a bank can make a loan by "writing up" its deposit liabilities, while a savings and loan association . . . cannot satisfy a mortgage borrower by crediting him with a share account'. Whether or not money spent by a borrower from a bank stays in the banking system as a whole depends not on how the loan was initially made but on 'whether somewhere in the chain of transactions initiated by the borrower's outlays are found depositors who wish to hold new deposits equal in amount to the new loan. Similarly, the outcome for the savings and loan industry depends on whether in the chain of transactions initiated by the

2. The quotation comes from (2, p. 342) where Newlyn quotes the *Radcliffe Report*, para. 390.

mortgage are found individuals who wish to acquire additional savings and loan shares' (3, pp. 412–13).

Tobin would extend our doubts in this last case to bank deposits also. He envisages 'a natural economic limit to the scale of the commercial banking industry'. Given their wealth and asset preferences, people will voluntarily hold additional demand deposits only if the yields thereby sacrificed on other assets fall. But beyond some point, lower yields would make further lending and investing unprofitable for the banks. 'In this respect the commercial banking industry is not qualitatively different from any other financial intermediary system' (3, p. 414). Even with no reserve requirements, bank credit and deposits could not expand further when no further loans and investments were available at yields high enough to cover the costs (among others) of attracting and holding deposits.

In so arguing, Tobin slights some familiar contrasts. The banking system as a whole *can* expand credit and deposits so far as reserves permit. There is no problem of lending and spending new demand deposits into existence. No one need be persuaded to invest in them before they can be created.[3] No one will refuse

---

3. Yet Lyle E. Gramley and Samuel B. Chase, Jr, praise and adopt Tobin's 'new view' (4, see especially pp. 1381 n., 1385, 1389–90). They work with a model in which 'the quantity of deposits a bank sells depends on the willingness of the public to purchase its deposits. Since this is true for each and every bank in the system, the constraint on bank deposits – and hence on bank asset holdings – is derived from the public's desire to hold bank deposits'. They dismiss as 'confusion' the view (as they paraphrase it from J. M. Culbertson, 5) that 'the public has no choice but to acquire' any newly created demand deposits. Apparently they intend more than the old point – see the next footnote – that withdrawal of reserve funds into hand-to-hand circulation can limit bank expansion.

In mentioning possible offsets to expansionary open-market operations by the central bank, Gramley and Chase are in effect merely saying that throwing more logs on the fire could fail to warm a room if at the same time its doors and windows were flung open to the January air.

According to the authors, 'open market operations alter the stock of money balances if, and only if, they alter the quantity of money *demanded* by the public'. This statement is misleading because it pretends to be more than the near-truism it is. Actually, a change in the stock of money *does* alter the quantity of money demanded – through the familiar process mentioned in the next paragraph of the present text. The quoted statement is analogous to portentously announcing that a price cut intended to expand

the routine medium of exchange for fear of being stuck with too much. Unwanted savings and loan shares, in contrast, would not be accepted and so could not be created in the first place. (And if anyone did find himself somehow holding unwanted shares, he would simply cash them in for money and so make them go out of existence. He would still cash them even if he did not want to *hold* the money instead, since money is the intermediary routinely used in buying all sorts of things.)

A holder of unwanted money exchanges it *directly* for whatever he does want, without first cashing it in for something else.[4] Nothing is more ultimate than money. Instead of going out of existence, unwanted money gets passed around until it ceases to be unwanted. Supply thus creates it own demand (both expressed as nominal, not real, quantities of course). To say this is not to assert that there is no such thing as a demand function for money or that the function always shifts to keep the quantities demanded and in existence identical.[5] Rather, an initial excess supply of

sales of some commodity will not work unless the quantity of the commodity demanded increases. True enough, but a sufficient price cut *will* increase the quantity demanded.

4. One qualification is minor in this context: when demand deposits are cashed in for currency, the drain on reserves limits banks' assets and deposits. But this limitation works on the supply-of-money side, not the demand side. If the authorities that create 'high-powered dollars' and the banks, taken together, want to expand the money supply, they can do so, unhampered by any unwillingness of the public to accept or hold money.

Another minor qualification concerns commercial-bank time deposits. A shift in the public's preferences to them from demand deposits does tend to shrink the latter if the same kind of reserve money, fixed in total amount, is held against both types of deposit. The shrinkage is the smaller, the smaller the reserve ratio for time deposits is in comparison with the ratio for demand deposits. Anyway, the decline in reserves available to support demand deposits is an occurrence affecting the *supply* of demand deposits. By providing enough reserves to support them, the monetary authorities can maintain any desired amount of demand deposits in existence.

5. J. G. Gurley and E. S. Shaw intimated that J. M. Culbertson harbored some such idea (18).

The argument about how the supply of money creates its own demand applies to the aggregate of all types of the medium of exchange and not, of course, to dimes alone or currency alone or demand deposits alone. The necessary proviso about suitable proportions of different kinds and denominations of money in their total does not impair the contrast in question between money and near-moneys.

money touches off a *process* that raises the nominal quantity demanded quite *in accordance with* the demand function. Initially unwanted cash balances 'burn holes in pockets', with direct or indirect repercussions on the flow of spending in the economy, in a way not true of near-moneys. Although anyone holding near-money has *chosen* to hold it as a store of value at least temporarily and has not just routinely received it in payment for goods or services sold, people do receive money in this way. A person accepts money not necessarily because he chooses to continue holding it but precisely because it is the routine intermediary between his sales and his purchases or investments and because he knows he can get rid of it whenever he wants. People's actions to get rid of unwanted money make it ultimately wanted by changing at least two of the arguments in the demand function for money – the money values of wealth and income rise through higher prices or fuller employment and production, and interest rates may move during the adjustment process.

No such process affects near-moneys and other nonmoneys. For an ordinary asset, a discrepancy between actual and desired holdings exerts direct pressure on its price (or on its yield or similar terms on which it is acquired and offered). If the supply and demand for an asset are out of balance, 'something has to give'. If the something is specific and 'gives' readily, the adjustment can occur without widespread and conspicuous repercussions. But the medium of exchange has no single, explicit price of its own in terms of a good other than itself, nor does it have any explicit yield of its own that can 'give' readily to remove an imbalance between its supply and demand. Widespread repercussions (described in Section V) occur instead.

Like nonmoney assets, borrowing privileges that people do not care to use also fail to touch off any such process. (I refer to the famous idea that unexhausted overdraft privileges are an important type of liquidity.) A magical doubling of all lines of credit, unaccompanied by monetary expansion, would hardly 'burn holes in pockets' in the same way a doubled money supply would. And as we have seen, people's initial unwillingness to *hold* all newly created actual money would not keep them from accepting it and would not prevent its creation.

Tobin's idea (already cited) that a decline in interest rates on

43

loans and investments will limit profitable expansion of bank credit and deposits, even if reserves permit, forgets Wicksell's 'cumulative process'. As money expansion raises prices and incomes, the dollar volume of loans demanded at given interest rates rises also. Yields on bank loans and investments need *not* keep falling. The great inflations of history disprove any 'natural limit' posed by falling interest rates.

III Asymmetrical Asset Preferences

Let us suppose that the nonbank intermediaries, at their own initiative, somehow issue more claims against themselves to acquire earning assets. (Never mind what makes people acquire these claims in the first place.) As people find themselves holding more and more near-moneys relative to both money and non-liquid assets, they exercise what Gurley and Shaw have called a 'diversification demand' for actual money (6, especially pp. 525–6). People have some idea of appropriate compositions of their portfolios and will not keep on indefinitely accumulating securities or near-moneys unaccompanied by additional money. And even if, understandably, people did not want additional money as a store of value, they would nevertheless want more of it to lubricate transactions in the other components of their expanded portfolios. Asset preferences thus limit the expansion of near-moneys if the money supply is constant; exclusive attention to the low (and voluntary) reserve ratios typical of nonbank intermediaries exaggerates their scope for multiple expansion.[6] Conceivably, though, this limit could be a rubbery one if asset preferences were highly sensitive to interest rates (a question noted again toward the end of Section IV).

Besides a portfolio-balancing or 'diversification' demand and a portfolio-transactions demand for actual money, a transactions demand connected with ordinary income and expenditure would come into play. It would, anyway, if in some implausible way issuers did expand the stock of near-moneys at their own initiative, inflating prices and incomes. People would want larger

6. For a comparison of how the public's asset preferences and their own reserve ratios restrain the nonbank intermediaries, see Donald Shelby, 'Some implications of the growth of financial intermediaries' (19).

holdings of the shrunken money units and might cash in some of their near-moneys as one way to get money.

Asset preferences work asymmetrically. Because of them, a constant supply of actual money can restrain the expansion of near-moneys. But no such restraint works the other way around; not even some sort of ceiling on near-moneys could keep the monetary authorities from creating as much money as they wished. In the absence of a ceiling, near-moneys tend to gear themselves to the money supply. When monetary expansion has inflated prices or incomes, the desired nominal amounts of borrowing on the one hand and of saving and financial investment on the other hand will have grown more or less in step and so, therefore, will the amounts of securities and financial intermediation in existence.[7] To dramatize the asymmetry, however, let us suppose that some official ban on the expansion of near-moneys thwarts this gearing. As the quantity of money expanded beyond what people initially wanted to hold, competition for the fixed supply of near-moneys would drive their yields low enough to keep people indifferent at the margin between them and money. But nothing would keep prices or money incomes from rising until people desired to hold all the new money.

7. Cf. R. W. Clower and M. L. Burstein, 'On the invariance of demand for cash and other assets' [Reading 11 of this volume], and M. L. Burstein, *Money* (7, pp. 208, 734–6, 781 [see Reading 8]). With evident approval Roy Harrod describes as a piece of 'old orthodoxy' the proposition that bank-credit expansion will promote additional nonbank lending as well (8, p. 5).

It follows that given unchanged 'wants, resources and technology', the existence of securities, near-moneys and financial intermediation does not invalidate the comparative-static propositions of the quantity theory. (However, these things presumably do keep a change in the money supply from affecting equilibrium prices in such a direct, quick and tight way as otherwise.)

Although Burstein and Harrod recognize the gearing stressed in the present paper, their discussions leave doubt whether they recognize the asymmetry also.

Contradicting the principle of gearing, James Tobin and William C. Brainard (9, especially pp. 391–2; and 4, p. 1381 n.) have envisaged a tendency, operating through asset yields, for the quantity of near-moneys to adapt *inversely* to the quantity of money. Their idea apparently is that a change in the quantity of one thing causes opposite changes in the demand for and thus in the equilibrium quantities of its close substitutes.

Much of the contrast developed so far boils down to saying that 'the most important proposition in monetary theory' (10, p. 609) holds true of the actual medium of exchange only. Individual economic units are free to hold as much or as little money as they see fit in view of their own circumstances; yet the total of their freely chosen cash balances is identical with the money supply, which the monetary authorities can make as big or as small as they see fit. The process that resolves this paradox has no counterpart for claims on nonbank intermediaries; instead, unwanted holdings go out of existence. The proposition also fails for other near-moneys, such as securities; but instead of shrinking in actual amount to the desired level, an excessive quantity shrinks in the market appraisal of its total money value.

Expansion of claims on nonbank intermediaries promotes economy in holding cash balances – or so post-war American experience seems to illustrate. Though not entirely wrong, this proposition is loosely phrased. The rise of nonbank intermediaries is not an autonomous change to which asset holders simply respond. Near-moneys, unlike money, cannot expand unless either monetary expansion or changes in 'wants, resources or technology' make people decide to accumulate more of them. Except as reflected in the yields or other advantages that various assets offer him, the individual does not care about their total amounts in existence. If savings and loan associations, for example, have contributed to the post-war rise in the velocity of actual money, the cause is not the sheer growth in their outstanding shares; instead, it comprises whatever changes have underlain a shift of asset preferences in their favor. These underlying changes presumably include not only the 1950 improvement in insurance features and the post-war uptrend in interest rates, permitting higher rates on savings-and-loan shares, but also whatever other factors have underlain the opening of new offices in convenient places, paid and word-of-mouth advertising and a cumulative familiarity. Savings-and-loan growth has not unambiguously helped *cause* a rise in monetary velocity; both, rather, have *resulted* from more ultimate changes. Much the same is true of expansion in the amounts of other near-moneys.

IV Functional Contrasts

An imaginary experiment will further distinguish near-moneys from money. Suppose the government gives each citizen a newly printed \$1000 treasury bill.[8] It resolves not to create money to pay off the bills as they come due; instead it will sell new ones at whatever interest rate may be necessary. People do not want to continue holding the entire addition to their wealth in the form they receive it in – treasury bills. They sell some, which raises their yield enough to find voluntary holders for the entire increased amount. Generalized by arbitrage, higher interest rates tend somewhat to restrain the spur that the increased private wealth gives to demands for consumer and investment goods. On the other hand, the higher rates tend to restrain people in demanding larger cash balances to lubricate transactions in goods and services at increased prices. Whether prices do rise, however, is not certain; for the new private nominal wealth given out by the government tends to raise the demand for cash balances relative to income and expenditure. The greater the role wealth plays in the demand function for cash balances, the less far-fetched is the possibility that the outcome of the whole experiment might be *de*flation on balance.[9] That possibility would be even less far-fetched if the government had given out long-term bonds rather than short-term bills and would not be far-fetched at all if it had given out consumer and investment goods magically conjured into existence. As these examples suggest, the outcome depends on how complementary or substitutable at the margin people regard the new securities given them, other securities, actual money and commodities. It also depends on how wealth-elastic and interest-elastic the demands for these things are. The actual

8. We drop savings-and-loan shares as our standard example of near-money because it is hard to suppose that they, being private liabilities as well as private assets, are simply donated into existence.

9. With similar considerations in mind, Allan Meltzer and Karl Brunner have dropped a thought-provoking hint about how a government budget deficit financed by bond issues rather than by new money could conceivably have an eventually deflationary influence. 'The place of financial intermediaries in the transmission of monetary policy' (20). Richard H. Timberlake, Jr, alludes to a similar possibility, though without necessarily claiming realism for it, in 'The stock of money and money substitutes' (21).

values of these complementarities, substitutabilities and elasticities in particular countries and periods need not concern us here. What highlights the contrast in question is that an increment of near-moneys could *conceivably* cause deflation, while the result of expanding the actual money supply could hardly be doubtful.

Newlyn develops his 'neutrality' or 'functional' distinction between money and nonmoney by inquiring whether a payment financed from a holding of an asset does or does not tend to change either its total quantity or its price (by changing the relation between supply and demand of loans or securities at the old interest rate). He classifies an asset as money (medium of exchange) if the effect of disposing of some of it to make a payment is 'neutral', neither changing the total amount of that sort of asset in existence nor disturbing the loan market. A nonneutral effect occurs when the person making a payment either (i) sells some asset or (ii) draws his claims on a financial intermediary, causing 'a reduction in the aggregate of such claims and a consequential sale of an asset by the intermediary' (2, p. 336).[10]

Currency changes hands in Newlyn's most obvious example of a 'neutral' payment; interest rates feel no *direct* effect. A payment by check, transferring ownership of demand deposits, does cause a fully loaned-up drawee bank to shrink its loans or sell securities, true enough; but another bank gains reserves and can expand its credit; so this payment is also neutral in Newlyn's sense. (Financing a payment by drawing down a commercial-bank time deposit would be neutral only if reserve ratios were the same against demand and time deposits.) Cashing a savings-and-loan account wipes it out and is obviously *not* neutral. Similarly, selling a treasury bill to finance a payment tends to depress the aggregate money value of the bills in existence.

Although Newlyn does not classify a traveler's check, we may gain further insight into his neutrality criterion by trying. When

10. Harold Rose has made some brief remarks anticipating Newlyn's criterion (11).

In principle, any decision to buy goods or services by parting with money or any other financial asset does have *some* general interdependence effect on everything in the economy, including the loan market and interest rates. But such effects are more indirect and feeble and even less dependable in direction than the unambiguous direct effects that Newlyn presumably has in mind.

its holder spends a check, he starts it on its way back to the issuer. The issuer obtains funds to honor it by selling securities from his portfolio (assuming, of course, a significant total of check encashments). The resulting upward pressure on interest rates, as well as the shrinkage in the total amount of checks in existence, disqualifies a nonbank traveler's check from counting as a medium of exchange.[11]

As this example reminds us, a seller of goods or services may sometimes accept payment in nonmoney to get his customer's business. In effect he serves as an agent who converts the nonmoney into cash afterwards, sparing his customer the trouble of doing so in the first place. Such accommodation does not mean that the asset in question has become a medium of exchange. Things would be different if the custom developed of endorsing traveler's checks in blank and circulating them indefinitely – if each payee accepted them with the intention of passing them along to others and without anyone's asking the issuer to redeem them. (Any reader who thinks that this view of the matter makes the distinction between money and nonmoney ridiculously slight is asked to suspend judgement until the last section of this paper.)

Since payments prepared for by unloading near-moneys tend to shrink the amount in existence or raise interest rates in a way not true of payments of actual money, decisions to buy goods and services stimulate total spending less when the purchases are to be financed from holdings of near-money than from cash balances. A decision to spend from actual money already held raises velocity directly; instead of merely representing an increase in the desired flow of spending relative to an unchanged cash balance, it represents an autonomous absolute drop in the demand for cash balances. As a matter of arithmetic, an individual's decision to finance expenditure from a holding of near-money also implies a rise in velocity – of his unchanged actual cash balance. Of

11. But Boris P. Pesek and Thomas R. Saving (12, especially pp. 184, 187, 190, 196–7), assume, with practically no argument, that traveler's checks *are* a medium of exchange, along with currency and demand deposits. In general, however, they insist on the distinctiveness of the medium of exchange even in contrast with close near-moneys. The considerations they stress – the net-wealth character of money and its role in the real-balance or wealth effect – are different from but not inconsistent with the arguments of the present paper.

course, he could not succeed in unloading near-money unless someone else were induced somehow (perhaps by increased interest rates) to part with cash. Even so, the rise in velocity does not necessarily imply a decline, or even constancy, in the economy-wide total amount of cash balances eventually desired. On the contrary, the total of cash balances desired for transactions purposes would even increase if spending could rise beyond a certain level. For this reason, any expansion in the total flow of spending on goods and services would meet some restraint, given the actual quantity of money, from the increase that would otherwise occur in the transactions balances desired even by individuals and firms other than those whose decisions had touched the expansion off.

Decisions to spend on goods and services are presumably still less expansionary when the buyers unload holdings of bonds rather than near-money. The questions relevant to this comparison concern different effects on the term structure of increased interest rates and the influences of interest rates both on choices between cash and other financial assets and on decisions about saving and investment. Intuitively, also, it makes sense that decisions to spend should be less expansionary when the financing is to come from unloading less money-like rather than more nearly money-like assets. The extreme example in this direction would be a desire to finance buying some commodities by unloading an inventory of other commodities. Well, just as it makes a difference whether purchases are financed by unloading commodities or unloading bonds, or by unloading bonds or unloading near-moneys, so it makes a difference whether near-money or actual money is to be unloaded. Partly for reasons still to be explained, the last distinction is the most noteworthy of all.

Desired shifts from bonds or near-moneys into goods and services could raise the velocity of money through raising interest rates. How strongly interest rates influence desired cash balances on the one hand and saving and investment on the other is too vast an issue for review here. Still, its relation to the main topic of this paper is worth mentioning. Conceivably (as noted in Section II), portfolio preferences could shift between actual money and near-moneys with extreme sensitivity to interest rates, causing important inflationary or deflationary effects even with the money supply constant. Especially because the available statistical evidence appears contradictory, some general considerations telling against such sensitivity are worth attention. A. J. L. Catt reaches a skeptical conclusion by analysing the responses of different types of asset-holder, particularly the small unsophisticated saver at one extreme and the large corporation always anxious to keep its funds at work at the other extreme. Similarly, Lawrence Ritter reasons that interest-rate levels and expectations are more relevant to choices between bonds and near-moneys, subject to much and little price fluctuation, respectively, than to choices between the medium of exchange and other financial assets (13, 14). Furthermore, developments that may promote a long-run trend toward greater and greater economy in holding actual cash balances by no means necessarily imply a short-run two-way sensitivity of cash-holdings to interest rates.

V Excess Demand for the Medium of Exchange

Some further functional contrasts between the medium of exchange and near-moneys bear on the essentially monetary nature of depressions. By Walras' law, any aggregate excess demand for or supply of currently produced goods and services, valued at prevailing prices, must be matched by an aggregate excess supply of or demand for all other things. Demand for current output cannot be excessive or deficient unless, at the same time, the opposite is true of the medium of exchange in particular: at not-yet-changed levels of income and prices, people must be wanting to hold less or more money than exists.[12]

Exceptions hinging on excess demands for non-currently produced goods other than money are not inconceivable but would be economically unrealistic. In the *General Theory*, Keynes remarks that a deficiency of demand for current output might be matched by an excess demand for assets having three 'essential properties': (a) their supply from private producers responds slightly if at all to an increase in demand for them; (b) a tendency to rise in value will only to a slight extent enlist substitutes to help meet a strengthened demand for them; (c) their liquidity advan-

12. In this context it is unnecessary to dwell on the distinction between flow and stock disequilibriums.

tages are large relative to the costs of holding them. Another point that Keynes notes by implication belongs explicitly on the list: (d) their values are 'sticky' and do not adjust readily to remove a disequilibrium.

Money is the most obvious asset having these properties. Keynes asks, however, whether a deficiency of demand for current output might be matched by an excess demand for other things instead, perhaps land or mortgages. Other writers have asked, similarly, about other securities, works of art and jewelry.[13]

My answer is no. Such things might be in excess demand *along with* but not *instead of* money. Money itself would also be in excess demand. One reason is that all other exchangeable things trade against money in markets of their own and at their own prices expressed in money. (This is true even of claims against financial intermediaries if their interest rates count as corresponding, inversely, to prices.) An excess demand for a good or a security tends to remove itself through a change in price or yield. If, however, interest rates should resist declining below the floor level explained by Keynes and Hicks, people would no longer prefer additional interest-bearing assets to additional money, and any further shift of demand from currently produced goods and services to financial assets would be an increase in the excess demand for actual money in particular. (If stickiness or arbitrary controls should keep prices and yields of financial assets from adjusting and clearing the market, the situation would be essentially the same as in the case of price rigidity of other assets, considered in the next and later paragraphs.) The monetary interpretation of deficient demand for current output thus does not depend on any precise dividing line between money and other assets (even though the present paper does draw such a line); if money broadly defined is in excess demand, money narrowly

13. Keynes (15, especially pp. 230–32) puts his own emphasis on how an asset with the properties in question might hold the interest rate above the level at which investment would be adequate for full employment; he does not specifically draw the Walras'-law implications of an excess demand for money or some such thing. For an illuminating interpretation of Keynes' chapter 17, see Abba P. Lerner, 'The essential properties of interest and money' (16). For an example of concern with possible excess demand for nonmonetary assets, see Harold Loeb, *Full Production without War* (17, pp. 93–4).

defined must be in excess demand also. Unlike other things, money has no single definite price of its own[14] that can adjust to clear a market of its own; instead, its market value is a reciprocal average of the prices of all other things. This 'price' tends to be sticky for reasons almost inherent in the very concept of money (16, pp. 188, 190–93).

Shares of stock and nonreproducible goods like land and 'old masters' even more obviously than bonds and near-moneys, do not account for depressions by being in excess demand instead of money. Flexibility in their individual prices would clear their individual markets. But suppose controls or market imperfections hold down the price of some such asset despite a strengthened demand for it. How do its frustrated buyers behave, and with what consequences? They might turn to demanding something else as a second-best, leaving the outcome operationally much the same as if they had not wanted the rigidly priced good in the first place. Alternatively, they might continue waiting for an opportunity to buy what they want, meanwhile holding and thus demanding cash balances. While the demand for the medium of exchange would in a sense have strengthened passively or by default, its distinctiveness would still come to the fore.

This point deserves restatement. Demand for an asset other than money, even if one not currently produced, is either equilibrated with its supply (by adjustment in its price if not in its production) or is frustrated. If frustrated, the demand must turn elsewhere. If it turns to other goods, it causes no deficiency of demand for current output. A shift toward leisure, reducing the supply of current goods and services, certainly could not account for an excess supply of these things. A shift toward money could occur, however, with the usual far-reaching consequences.

Not only must the medium of exchange thus be one of the things whose excess demand matches a deficiency of demand for current output, but this excess demand causes more pervasive disruption than excess demand for even the nearest of near-

14. This is true when the same kind of money serves as both unit of account and medium of exchange. The present paper ignores the far-fetched but theoretically challenging concept of a system in which the two functions are split, with the actual medium of exchange fluctuating in price in terms of the separate unit in which ordinary goods and services are also priced.

moneys. People demand money to *hold*, true enough, but they are continually adding to and drawing on their holdings and want them of the right size in relation to the flows through them. Because money – unlike even the nearest of near-moneys – is the one thing routinely exchanged against all sorts of things, an excess supply of or demand for it does not appear on any particular market or in connexion with any particular disequilibrium price. Monetary disequilibrium does not show up as any specific frustration. An individual meets frustration trying to buy or sell various particular goods and services but sees no difficulty attached to money itself. Whatever he might be trying to buy with or sell for money, he does not find money generally unacceptable or generally unobtainable.[15] An unemployed person perceives a deficiency of demand for his labor, not an excess demand for money. He does not want money just to add it permanently to his cash balance, anyway; he wants to earn and spend it.

This divergence between individual and overall viewpoints is crucial to the macroeconomic consequences of monetary disequilibrium. An over-all excess demand for money does not manifest itself as such to the individual. Unlike frustrated demand for an ordinary good or service or financial asset, it does not either cause a market-clearing adjustment in one particular price or else force individuals to decide what available things to acquire instead. This peculiarity of monetary disequilibrium is connected with the above-mentioned fundamental proposition: everyone can individually hold as much or as little money as he effectively demands, even though the total supply is fixed. To get it, the individual need only curtail his spending or lending relative to his inflow of income and other receipts, just as someone with more cash than he wants can do the opposite. An economy-wide excess demand for money shows up not as specific frustration in buying money but as dispersed, generalized frustration in selling things and earning incomes. Furthermore, the persons who experience

15. A qualification about suppressed inflation might seem necessary. The frustration would attach, however, to purchases of the individual goods and services subject to the price controls. Money could still be freely spent on uncontrolled goods. And in so far as practically everything was subject to effective price ceilings, the former money would cease to serve as a general medium of exchange (as in Germany before June 1948). All the analysis here relates to an *actual* medium of exchange.

this frustration most keenly are not necessarily those who had wanted to build up their cash balances. Conceivably, the persons who want more money can get it, while those who part with it are those whose reduced incomes keep them from demanding cash balances as large as before.

For the individual, the flow of income and expenditure through his cash balance is less readily adjustable than the balance he holds.[16] But for the economy as a whole (excluding the monetary authorities), the money stock is a datum to which flows adjust. If total cash balances demanded exceed the money stock, the flow of money shrinks in the aggregate and for the typical or average economic unit. This happens as the typical unit shrinks its spending, thereby cutting others' receipts and spurring greater and more widespread efforts to shrink spending into line.[17] Efforts to build up or conserve cash balances make the flow of income and expenditure shrink precisely because money is what routinely flows to accomplish the exchange of goods and services. The shrinkage continues until, from the individual and over-all points of view alike, stocks of money no longer are inadequate in relation to the shrunken flows. Eventually, the cash balance effect stops the decline.

No other excess demand could be as pervasively disruptive as an excess demand for money. The contrast with anything else, ranging from 'old masters' to the nearest of near-moneys, is instructive. Because a nonmoney does not have a routine *flow* to *be* interrupted or shrunken in the first place, efforts to hold more

16. His flows are more nearly but not entirely a datum, since adjusting them is, after all, how he adjusts his balance. In a sense, though, he can adjust his balance more sensitively: an adjustment in the sustained level of either his inflow or outflow would mean continuing growth or shrinkage of his balance, while an adjustment of his balance would require only a temporary modification of flows.

17. What difference does it make if some units try to accumulate cash by pushing their own sales harder rather than by cutting their purchases? If their price cuts and intensified sales efforts take customers away from other sellers, but without prices in general being flexible enough to make the real quantity of money meet the demand for it, the incomes that the others have to spend decline; and the analysis continues much the same as in the text. The key point is that people can try to build up or conserve cash balances by cutting purchases of each other's outputs, with a chain of repercussions that hinges on money's role as medium of exchange.

of the asset than exists cannot cause such pervasive trouble. People cannot try to accumulate old masters or treasury bills or savings-and-loan shares by mere passive restraint in spending income, since they do not routinely receive income in any such form. Instead, people must take action to acquire such things on the specific markets where they are sold, and at their own prices (or yields). For a nonmoney, excess demand hits its own market specifically. The frustrated demand either is removed by a rise in the thing's price (or fall in its yield, or increase in its production) or else is diverted onto other things. Its own market, by being disrupted, and its own price, by coming under pressure, serve as buffers limiting the contagion of the imbalance to the rest of the economy – unless the frustrated excess demand for the non-money is diverted onto money itself. Because a nonmoney is not a medium of exchange with which other things are routinely bought, no excess demand for it can persist, unaccompanied by an excess demand for money and yet show up as deficiency of demand for other things in general.

For the medium of exchange, however, excess demand is neither removed directly nor diverted. Because money is traded on all markets and on none specifically its own, and because it has no single price of its own to come under specific pressure, an imbalance between its supply and demand has far-reaching consequences. Its excess demand appears as a deficiency of demand for other things because demand for it can be exercised by mere restraint in spending it. Although money has many close substitutes as a store of value, not even the nearest of near-moneys shares with it the simple but momentous characteristic of routine exchange and circulation.

This peculiarity underlines the main theme of this paper: in analysing the demands for money and other liquid assets, we must go beyond investigating what determines *how much* of each asset people demand to hold. We must also consider *in what way* people go about giving effect to their demands.

An excess demand for money tends to remove itself in a distinctive and unpleasant way. Despite the over-all excess demand, anyone can gratify his demand for cash balances simply by keeping part of his income in the form in which he routinely receives it. The routine flow of money income and expenditure shrinks.

Anything that shrinks the flow of money interferes – barring complete price flexibility – with the exchange of goods and services. In an advanced economy, people specialize as producers and depend on exchange for the opportunity to do so. Any interference with the process of exchange on the market narrows opportunities for worthwhile production of goods to be exchanged. A fall in the flow of money thus damages production and employment. An inadequate quantity of even the nearest near-money could not do the same pervasive damage.[18]

A general deficiency of demand for goods and services must thus be a specifically monetary disorder involving an excess demand for the actual medium of exchange. To emphasize this, let us suppose that all prices are 'right' relative to each other but are 'too high', in the same proportion, relative to the quantity of money. Everybody is willing to exchange his goods for other people's goods at the ratios implied by their existing money prices. Yet shortage of the medium of exchange interferes. Since people have been trying to build up their cash balances, they initially are failing to spend all the money received by selling their goods and labor. And since others are doing the same, the typical economic unit has trouble earning income. The depression of income is what chokes off the demand for cash balances below what it would be at full employment.[19]

18. Admittedly, an inadequate supply of an important near-money – or perhaps, strictly speaking, the resulting unattractiveness of its yield – could make the demand for actual money stronger than otherwise. But the macroeconomic difficulties *would* then involve an excess demand for money, not merely an excess demand for something else *instead*. Furthermore, a sufficient increase in the supply of money could satiate the excess demand for it, even if the quantity of the near-money did not increase.

19. Conceivably, an autonomous upward push on wages and prices could be what kept tending to make an existing or even a growing money supply inadequate for a full-employment level of activity. While monetary in nature, the disorder would not be monetary in origin.

A deficiency of money is not the only *conceivable* impediment to the flow of spending and the production and exchange of real income. Relative prices, including wages, could conceivably be wrong. A capricious system of ceilings and floors, for example, could make some prices too low and others too high, yet leave the general purchasing power of money, calculated somehow, correct for the quantity of money in existence. Wrong exchange ratios would hamper production by keeping desires to exchange various goods from meshing. Some goods would be in excess demand and others

VI Transactions Costs

Momentous consequences seem to follow from apparently slight differences between close near-moneys and actual media of exchange. Whether or not a thing serves as a general medium of exchange might even seem a mere matter of degree, as the example of traveler's checks might suggest. If sellers of goods and services become willing to accommodate buyers by accepting payment in a near-money and if this practice reaches the point where everyone accepts it with no intention of cashing it in because he knows he can simply pass it along to someone else, who in turn will not want to cash it in, then the thing has become an actual medium of exchange.

At some point, apparently, the shading or drift from the properties of close near-moneys toward those of money becomes a jump from a difference in degree to a difference in kind. Embarrassingly enough, we seem to have something like the Hegelian–Marxian 'jump of quantity into quality'. Yet this really may be the way things are with money. Several assets may have low transactions costs, but the asset with the *lowest* costs of all is unique in that respect.[20] Having the lowest transactions costs

---

in excess supply. For each, of course, only the smaller of the desired supply and demand quantities would be the quantity actually exchanged. With exchange impeded, production and real incomes and real purchasing power would suffer also. Like decreed ceilings and floors, mere rigidities in prices and wages might similarly block the continuous clearing of markets and choice of production techniques and patterns compatible with full employment after a change in 'wants, resources or technology'. The change proving disruptive in the face of price rigidity would not *necessarily* have to be an increase in the propensity to save or in liquidity preference. This point is one of the main themes of W. H. Hutt, *Keynesianism – Retrospect and Prospect* (22).

While 'structural' or 'frictional' difficulties are thus conceivable, the trouble would not be a *general* deficiency of demand for goods and services. In the real world, such difficulties are less characteristic of depression than is monetary disequilibrium.

20. Transactions costs may take the form of time and trouble, of course. Ambiguity about the lowest transactions costs could explain the coexistence of two or more varieties of medium of exchange. Currency has the lowest transactions costs – loosely speaking, it is the most convenient medium of exchange – in some types of transactions, and demand deposits have the

and being the medium of exchange are properties so related that even a slight disturbance to existing institutions or practices could conceivably be self-reinforcing. Perhaps the shifting of a ship's cargo offers an analogy. Minor causes can sometimes have major consequences.

If savings-and-loan shares had transactions costs no higher than those of money, the associations could grant loans in the form of their own shares, confident that the borrowers would be able to spend them directly. The essence of being merely a near-money is that people have to be *persuaded* to take it – persuaded by its yield (or by the prospect of losing a sale if the seller did not thus accommodate his customer). For assets on the borderline, what would be adequate persuasion for some takers might not be adequate for others. Hence an asset cannot be a *generally* acceptable means of payment if some inducement is required not merely to persuade people to hold it for some time but even to persuade them to accept payment in that particular form in the first place.

Fortunately, our economy has no assets just on a borderline between serving and not serving as media of exchange. Not even traveler's checks circulate indefinitely without being presented for redemption. So far as this paper has any direct implications at all for policy, and not just for theory – beyond the obvious warning against confusion over a nebulous general liquidity – it warns against blurring the crucial though possibly slight distinctions that keep an awkwardly large variety of assets from coming into routine circulation. Policy should avoid creating incentives to broaden the range of such assets, as it might do if it attached excessive disadvantages to the use of money and to the demand-deposit business. Policy should beware of the institutional instability that could arise from instability in or doubt about the relative lowness of the transactions costs of different assets.

References

1. D. PATINKIN, *Money, Interest and Prices*, 2nd edn, Harper & Row, 1965.
2. W. T. NEWLYN, 'The supply of money and its control', *Economic Journal*, vol. 74, 1964, pp. 327–46.

lowest costs in others. But no other asset has lower transactions costs than currency and demand deposits, respectively, in the types of transaction in which each predominates.

3. J. Tobin, 'Commercial banks as creators of money', *Banking and Monetary Studies*, Deane and Carson (eds.), Irwin, 1963, pp. 408–19.
4. L. E. Gramley and S. B. Chase, 'Time deposits in monetary analysis', *Federal Reserve Bulletin*, vol. 51, 1965, pp. 1380–404.
5. J. M. Culbertson, 'Intermediaries and monetary theory: a criticism of the Gurley–Shaw theory', *American Economic Review*, vol. 48, 1958, pp. 119–31.
6. J. G. Gurley and E. S. Shaw, 'Financial aspects of economic development', *American Economic Review*, vol. 45, 1955, pp. 515–38.
7. M. L. Burstein, *Money*, Schenkman, 1963.
8. R. F. Harrod, 'Is the money supply important?', *Westminster Bank Review*, November 1959, pp. 1–6.
9. J. Tobin and W. C. Brainard, 'Financial intermediaries and the effectiveness of monetary controls', *American Economic Review*, vol. 53, May 1963, pp. 383–400.
10. M. Friedman, Hearings before the Joint Economic Committee, U.S. Congress, Part 4, *Employment, Growth and Price Levels*, U.S. Govt Printing Office, May 1959, p. 609.
11. H. Rose, 'Money still under review', *The Banker*, vol. 3, February 1961, pp. 105–6, and April 1961, pp. 289–90.
12. B. P. Pesek and T. R. Saving, *Money, Wealth and Economic Growth*, Macmillan, 1967.
13. A. J. L. Catt, 'Idle balances and the motives for liquidity', *Oxford Economic Papers*, n.s. vol. 14, June 1962, pp. 124–37.
14. L. S. Ritter, 'The structure of financial markets, income velocity and the effectiveness of monetary policy', *Schweizerische Zeitschrift für Volkswirtschaft und Statistik*, 1962, no. 3, pp. 276–89.
15. J. M. Keynes, *The General Theory of Employment, Interest and Money*, Harcourt Brace, 1935, ch. 17, pp. 222–44.
16. A. P. Lerner, 'The essential properties of interest and money', *Quarterly Journal of Economics*, vol. 66, May 1952, pp. 172–93.
17. H. Loeb, *Full Production without War*, Princeton University Press, 1946.
18. J. G. Gurley and E. S. Shaw, 'Reply to the criticism of J. M. Culbertson', *American Economic Review*, vol. 48, March 1958, pp. 135–6.
19. D. Shelby, 'Some implications of the growth of financial intermediaries', *Journal of Finance*, vol. 13, pp. 527–41.
20. A. Meltzer and K. Brunner, 'The place of financial intermediaries in the transmission of monetary policy', *American Economic Review*, vol. 53, May 1963, p. 381.
21. R. H. Timberlake, 'The stock of money and money substitutes', *Southern Economic Journal*, vol. 30, January 1964, p. 255.
22. W. H. Hutt, *Keynesianism – Retrospect and Prospect*, Regnery, 1963.

4 M. L. Burstein

The Index-Number Problem

Excerpt from M. L. Burstein (1963), *Money*, Schenkman, ch. 1, pp. 12–14.

What is meant by the 'purchasing power' of money (or any other good)? In order to answer this question, construct an imaginary world in which the only categories of goods are food, clothing and transportation. Food includes pork, beef and vegetables. Clothing includes woollens and cottons. Transportation services are provided by automobiles and horses. Consider these alternative sets of prices (in dollars – money of account):

Table 1

	Set I	*Set* II	*Set* III
Food			
1 lb pork	0·20	5·00	15·00
1 lb beef	2·00	0·10	10·00
1 lb vegetables	0·50	10·00	0·20
Clothing			
1 yd wool	10·00	1·00	40·00
1 yd cotton	0·50	20·00	0·25
Transportation			
Rental: 1 auto for 1 day	3·50	30·00	30·00
Rental: 1 horse for 1 day	30·00	0·50	0·80

Now consider the following three types of persons: (a) Mohammedans who love proteins, are allergic to cotton and live in a country without highways; (b) Hindus, allergic to horses, living in a country with good roads and a warm climate; (c) vegetarian seventh-day adventists who are allergic to wool. For type (a) persons, *Set* II offers a low cost of living (high purchasing power of money); *Set* I is a nightmare. But *Set* II would be a severe test of the faith of the most devout Hindu; for a Hindu (or Buddhist if you insist) *Set* I conditions are a veritable Nirvana. Type (c) persons would count their blessings under *Set* III prices and would rue the day they were born under *Set* II prices – except when they had occasion to travel. Imagine the reaction of a vegetarian seventh-day adventist, faced with *Set* II prices contemplating ebullient Mohammedans, also on horseback (at the frontier), full of praise of the golden sixties and *Set* II prices.

It is abundantly clear that alternative sets of prices cannot ordinarily be considered independently of the tastes and habits of the persons involved when one ranks purchasing powers of money. This can be stated more elegantly and concretely, if the price level is defined (where the price of the *numéraire* good is unity) as

$$P = w_1 p_1 + w_2 p_2 + \ldots + w_n p_n.$$

The ps show the quantities (the number of standard units) of the *numéraire* good (here the $n+1$th) that must be surrendered in order to obtain unit quantities of the first, second, . . . and nth other goods. (We use *numéraire* and *numéraire good* interchangeably.) The ws are weights. $w_1 + w_2 + \ldots + w_n = 1$. We have seen, rather fantastically, that alternative sets of weights lead to different rankings of alternative sets of prices – P depends on the ws as well as the ps. In order to see this more clearly, let us suggest weights that would be appropriate for Type (a) and Type (b) persons, examining outcomes for *Price Sets* I and II. Transition

Table 2

Good	Type (a) Weight	Type (b) Weight	I/a	I/b	II/a	II/b
Pork	0·00	0·15				
Beef	0·45	0·00				
Vegetables	0·05	0·35				
Wool	0·30	0·10				
Cotton	0·00	0·25				
Autos	0·00	0·15				
Horses	0·20	0·00				
P Calculation			9·93	1·86	0·95	13·85

from *Price Set* I to *Price Set* II finds *P* less than a tenth of its original value – using (a) weights. (This is to specify a correspon- ding rise in the purchasing power of money.) However, if one uses (b) weights, *P* rises more than eightfold when we move from I to II prices

Of course, to deny that the purchasing power of a good *must* unambiguously have increased, decreased or stayed the same, is not to deny that there can be unambiguous statements. Thus, if we could be sure that *relative* prices twenty years from now would be the same as today, and if the number and quality of available goods were unchanged, the hypothetical IOU could be precise in its 'real' meaning if it read:

> I promise to pay John Everyman legal tender twenty years from this date (16 July 1961) such that its purchasing power, using the set of weights classified as Type (a), will equal that of legal tender valued at 100 dollars on this date.

It really would not matter what were the constituent weights *if* relative prices remained the same; if all nominal prices changed by the factor *k*, repayment of $k \times 100$ dollars in 1981 would leave the parties in precisely the real position created by repayment of 100 dollars in 1981 where all nominal prices remained the same (again subject to the *caveat* of the next paragraph). On the other hand, a shift in relative prices could very substantially alter the real positions of the parties if their tastes differed. Thus, if the debtor were a Mohammedan and the creditor a Hindu, and if *Set* I prices prevailed in 1961 and *Set* II prices in 1981, the revised IOU would ruin the creditor – he would receive back less than ten dollars in circumstances in which he would have to receive more than 800 dollars in order to continue to purchase his 1961 budget in 1981.

There are difficulties in longer-run comparisons of the pur- chasing power of money transcending differences in habits and tastes among people. These concern technological change and innovation, changes in supply conditions and uniform changes in taste over time. They can be exemplified by problems arising from comparison of the cost of living in the United States in 1900 and in 1961. No doubt prices of whalebone corset stays, patent-leather pumps, carriages and lard had increased very substantially. On the other hand, television sets, helicopters, radios, electric refrigerators, penicillin, Cadillacs and water-skis did not exist in 1900. How would you propose to write a constant-purchasing-power clause into a 1900 instrument promising to pay $100 to bearer in 1961 even if you knew in 1900 what 1961 would look like? Would your 1961 price-index number be based on the number of dollars required in 1961 to purchase a basket of 1900 goods (leaving aside the fact that the dollar is defined differently in 1961 than in 1900)? Obviously, you cannot sensibly ask what a basket of 1961 goods would have cost in 1900. The matter need not be pushed further; there are very substantial *a priori* difficulties preventing precise comparisons of purchasing power of money (or of any other good) over time; precise measures for real deferred payments are logically impossible in other than a completely static world.

Part Two Traditional Doctrine: The Quantity Theory of Money

The notion that there is a simple and direct relation between the quantity of money and the general level of commodity prices has intrigued thoughtful men for centuries. But the precise nature of the relation has yet to be established, for except on assumptions that reduce the problem to a trivial exercise in comparative statics, there appears to be no middle ground between brute empiricism and full-scale theoretical specification of dynamical interrelations between monetary magnitudes and other aspects of economic activity. What Senior had to say on the subject more than a century ago is nearly as penetrating as anything that has been written since. Indeed, the difficulty of asserting anything that is both interesting and non-obvious runs like a red thread through the whole of the literature on the quantity theory of money, becoming especially prominent in those writings that attempt to assign money an independent role as a causal factor in economic fluctuations. The essay of Professor Friedman is particularly instructive in the latter respect. Marshall speaks with a firmer voice only because he carefully omits all but incidental reference to dynamical complications. As matters presently stand, the quantity theory of money is interesting more for doctrinal than for substantive reasons.

5 N. W. Senior

The Value of Money

N. W. Senior, 'On the quantity and value of money', *Three Lectures on the Value of Money*, 1829, lecture 1, pp. 5–31.[1]

The general doctrine is, that the value of money depends partly on its quantity, and partly on the rapidity of its circulation.

It is not difficult to perceive [says Mr Mill] that it is the total amount of the money in any country which determines what portion of that quantity shall exchange for a certain portion of the goods or commodities of that country.

If we suppose that all the goods of the country are on one side, all the money on the other, and that they are exchanged at once against one another, it is obvious that one-tenth, or one-hundredth, or any other part of the goods, will exchange against one-tenth, or any other part of the whole of the money; and that this tenth, etc. will be a great quantity or small, exactly in proportion as the whole quantity of the money in the country is great or small. If this were the state of the facts, therefore, it is evident that the value of mon ey would depend wholly upon the quantity of it.

It will appear that the case is precisely the same in the actual state of the facts. The whole of the goods of a country are not exchanged at once against the whole of the money; the goods are exchanged in portions, often in very small portions, and at different times during the course of the whole year. The same piece of money which is paid in one exchange today, may be paid in another exchange tomorrow. Some of the pieces will be employed in a great many exchanges, some in a very few, and some, which happen to be hoarded, in none at all. There will in all these varieties be a certain average number of exchanges, the same which if all the pieces had performed an equal

1. This reading is taken from a privately printed copy of the lectures available at the University of Essex from the library of John Strachey. This is the B. Fellowes, Ludgate Street, London 1840 edition. The lectures were published in 1931 by the London School of Economics and Political Science (University of London) as no. 4 in the Series of Reprints of Scarce Tracts in Economics and Political Science.

number would have been performed by each: that average we may suppose to be any number we please; say, for example, ten. If each of the pieces of money in the country perform ten purchases, that is exactly the same thing as if all the pieces were multiplied by ten, and performed only one purchase each. As each piece of the money is equal in value to that which it exchanges for, if each performs ten different exchanges to effect one exchange of all the goods, the value of all the goods in the country is equal to ten times the value of all the money.

This, it is evident, is a proposition universally true. Whenever the value of money has either risen or fallen (the quantity of goods against which it is exchanged, and the rapidity of circulation, remaining the same), the change must be owing to a corresponding diminution or increase of the quantity, and can be owing to nothing else. If the quantity of goods diminish while the quantity of money remains the same, it is the same thing as if the quantity of money had been increased; and if the quantity of goods be increased while the quantity of money remains unaltered, it is the same thing as if the quantity of money had been diminished.

Similar changes are produced by any alteration in the rapidity of circulation. By rapidity of circulation is meant, of course, the number of times the money must change hands to effect one sale of all the commodities (1).

Mr Mill does not say in so many words that the value of money is decided by causes differing from those which decide the value of other commodities; but such is, in fact, the result of the statement which I have just read, if it be compared with his section on exchangeable value. In that section he states, that 'the relative values of commodities, in other words, the quantity of one which exchanges for a given quantity of another, depends entirely upon cost of production'. He does not mention rapidity of circulation; or, in other words, a frequent change of masters; or alteration of actual quantity, except for short periods, as among the actual elements of value. And if they are not the principles which regulate the value of other things, what reason is there for supposing that they regulate the value of money?

Unless it be maintained that the attributes of gold and silver are changed the instant the metals are divided into portions of a given weight and fineness, and authenticated by a stamp, it must be admitted that their value is governed by the same rules as those which govern the value of all other commodities, produced under similar circumstances. Now the circumstances under which all metals are produced are those of competition, but competition in which the competitors have unequal advantages. They are obtained from alluvial deposits, and mines, all of unequal productiveness. The value of every portion that is produced must, therefore, be sufficient to pay the wages and profits of those who use the least fertile mine, or sift the most poorly impregnated sand, that can be worked without loss. If the value were to rise higher, mines and streams still less productive would be resorted to. If it were to fall lower, the worst now in use would be abandoned. When these principles are applied to native commodities we at once recognize their justice. If I were to ask why one bushel of wheat will in general exchange for two bushels of barley, anyone who had thought on the subject would at once reply, 'because, speaking generally, it costs about as much (or, in my nomenclature, requires the same sum of labour and abstinence) to produce two bushels of barley as one of wheat'. But we are not accustomed to consider money as a thing annually produced, and depending for its value on the cost of its production. We talk of it as if nature, or some other equally unknown cause, had diffused a certain amount of it through the country; and, consistently with such an opinion, ascribe its value solely to its quantity. It appears to me that the only mode of acquiring clear ideas on the subject is to inquire how the value of the precious metals would be fixed under the simplest state of circumstances: and we shall afterwards find that the same causes do, in fact, fix their value under the complicated relations of European society.

It will be necessary, however, to preface this inquiry by some remarks on the causes which determine the quantity of money which a community shall possess.

It is obvious, in the first place, that the whole quantity of money in a community must consist of the aggregate of all the different sums possessed by the different individuals of whom it is constituted.

And what this quantity shall be must depend partly on the number of those individuals; partly on the value in money of the aggregate of their respective incomes; and partly on the average proportion of the value of his income which each individual habitually keeps by him in money.

The two first of these causes do not require much explanation. It is clear, *ceteris paribus*, that two millions of people must possess more money than one million. It is also clear that, *ceteris paribus*, a nation, the value of whose average aggregate income amounts to a hundred million pounds sterling a year, must possess more money than one whose annual income is only fifty million pounds.

But the causes which determine what proportion of the value of his income each individual shall habitually retain in money require to be considered at some length.

Briefly, it may be said to depend, first, on the proportion to his income of his purchases and sales for money; and secondly, on the rapidity with which they succeed one another: but such a statement is too concise to be intelligible without further explanation.

Exchange, as it is the principal cause, is also one of the principal effects of improvement. As men proceed from a primitive to a refined state of society, as they advance from hunters to shepherds, from shepherds to agriculturists, from villagers to townspeople, and from being inhabitants of towns, depending for their supplies on the adjacent country, to be the citizens of a commercial metropolis, using the whole world as one extensive market; at each of these stages man becomes more and more a dependent being, consuming less and less of what he individually produces until at last almost every want, and every gratification, is supplied by means of an exchange. Our ancestors lived on their own estates, fed their households from the produce of their own lands, and clothed them with their own flax and wool, manufactured within their own halls. Food and clothing were the wages of their domestic servants; and their tenants, instead of paying rents in money, were bound to cultivate the lord's demesne, to supply him certain quantities of corn or livestock, and to serve under his banner in public or private war. The services of the church were obtained by allowing the priest a tenth of the annual produce, and the demands of the state were limited to the maintaining of roads and bridges, defence of castles, and attendance in war, for forty days, with adequate provisions. Under such circumstances, the barons and their dependents – and these two classes comprised the bulk of the community – might pass years without having to make a sale or a purchase. Exchanges they made, where one party gave services or produce, and the other party food, clothing, shelter or land; but these were all made by barter. The yeoman, who cultivated his own land, and used the manufactures of his own family, might, in fact, live without even an exchange; nor could the serf, though he received maintenance in return for labour, be said to make an exchange, since he had no more power to enforce, or even to require, any stipulation, than any other domestic animal.

The same circumstances must, however, have occasioned what money there was in the country to circulate very slowly; or, in other words, to change hands very infrequently. A man, who, in such a state of society, received a sum, might not find for a long time an advantageous opportunity of spending it. And he would have many reasons for not parting with it, even on what might appear advantageous terms. Where property and person are so insecure, as they were among our ancestors, every one must feel anxious to have some means of support, if he should be forced to quit his home, or to witness the destruction of his less portable property. Again, the demands for money, when they did come, were great, and unforeseen. The knight was in constant danger of having to pay a ransom; the tenant of having to assist in raising that ransom; and the crown, from time to time, required a subsidy or an escuage.

Under such circumstances it is probable that each individual, or, to speak more correctly, each person managing his own concerns, might on an average receive in money one-fiftieth part of the value of his annual income. But it is likewise probable that what he did so receive he might retain at an average for four years. Such a sum would not exceed a month's income; a very moderate hoard, where the motives for hoarding were so powerful. I am inclined to think that the average proportion of their incomes, which our ancestors hoarded during the first two or three centuries after the Conquest, was much larger. It is impossible otherwise to account for the importance attached to treasure trove, which seems to have formed a material portion of the royal revenue, and now probably does not afford, except from ancient deposits, ten pounds a year. The whole money of the country would, under such circumstances, change hands only once in four years. If we now add to these suppositions that of a given number of families (meaning by that word, either single persons managing their own affairs, or small knots of persons managing their affairs together, as a man and his wife and their infant children), and suppose the average income of each, we shall have data from which the whole amount of money in the country may be inferred. I will suppose, therefore, 500 000 families, having at an average an annual income a-piece of ten pounds sterling: making the value of the whole annual income of the community £5 000 000 sterling. Each independent person or head of a family is supposed to receive one-fiftieth part of his annual income in money, being four shillings, and to keep it in his possession for four years; sixteen shillings therefore would be the average sum possessed by each family; and as there are 500 000 families, sixteen times 500 000, or 8 000 000 shillings, or £400 000 sterling, would be the whole quantity of money possessed by the community.

It is probable that in this supposition, which is not without resemblance to the state of England under the Norman and Plantagenet lines, I have stated the extremes both of absence of exchange and of slow circulation of money that could take place in a community entitled to be called civilized. We will now suppose the country to be at peace, and secure within and without, and all the peculiar motives for hoarding to be removed. Instead of a month's income, each family might retain only a week's, or four shillings instead of sixteen shillings. Instead of once in four years, the whole money of the country would change hands every year; and £100 000 would perform all the offices of money as well as £400 000 did before. I shall, at a future period, endeavour to show the means by which the stock of money would be diminished to meet the altered state of things; but that it would be diminished must, I think, be at once acknowledged.

Having examined into the causes which determine the quantity of money in any community, I now proceed to inquire into those which determine its value; assuming, what I suppose will not be questioned, that the value of the precious metals, as money, must depend ultimately on their value as materials of jewellery and plate; since, if they were not used as commodities, they could not circulate as money.

I will suppose an insulated society of 10 000 families, having an abundance of land of such fertility, and using manufactures so rude, that the trifling capital employed by them may be disregarded; and so equal in fortune and rank, that the relations of landlord and tenant, and capitalist and workman, shall not exist. I will suppose gold alone to be their money, and that it is obtained by washing alluvial deposits without any expensive machinery or skill, and always in the same ratio to the labour employed.

The cost of producing gold would, under these circumstances, always remain the same, and its value in labour, or, in other words, the amount of labour which a certain quantity of it could purchase, would always correspond with its cost of production, except for short intervals, when any sudden increase or diminution in the demand for it should occasion the existing supply to be for a time relatively excessive or deficient. Under such circumstances the value of all other things would be estimated by comparing their cost of production with that of gold. If the labour of a family employed for a year could gather from the washing places fifty ounces of gold, and by equal exertion gather from the spontaneous produce of the fields fifty quarters of rice, the rice and the gold would be of equal value, and a single quarter of rice would be worth an ounce of gold. If the same labour could produce in the same time one hundred ounces of gold instead of fifty, a quarter of rice would be worth two ounces instead of one; or if the same labour could gather one hundred quarters of rice instead of fifty, a quarter of rice would be worth only half an ounce instead of a whole ounce; but while a year's labour could produce just fifty ounces of gold, the yearly income of each family, however employed, supposing their diligence, strength, and skill equal, would be of the value of precisely fifty ounces of gold.

The quantity of gold produced would depend partly on the quantity wanted for plate, including under that word all use of gold except as money, and partly on the quantity wanted for money. The quantity wanted for plate would of course depend on the prevailing fashions of the country: the quantity wanted for money would depend, as we have seen, partly on the value in money of the incomes of all the inhabitants, and partly on the average proportion of the value of his income which each person habitually kept in his possession in money.

If each family cultivated its own land, and prepared its own manufactures, and thus provided for its wants almost without the intervention of exchange, each family would receive in money a very small proportion of the value of its income, and a very small amount of money would be sufficient.

On the other hand, if we suppose each family to be as dependent as an English citizen's on exchange; to part with all its own produce, and to live altogether on what it obtained in return, and at the same time to effect almost all these exchanges, either by means of barter or of accounts regularly kept, and from time to time settled by being balanced against one another, a very small amount of money would again be sufficient.

A much larger quantity would of course be necessary, if we suppose the same prevalence of exchange, but at the same time, the absence of barter and of the balancing of accounts; and consequently suppose the actual use of money in every exchange, and each person to receive in money the whole of his income.

The quantity wanted in that case would depend partly on the cost of producing gold, and partly on the rapidity of its circulation. The rapidity of circulation being given, it would depend on the cost of production. It is obvious that twice as much money would be required to effect every exchange, if a day's labour could obtain from the washing places 34 grains of gold, as would be necessary if a day's labour could obtain only 17. And the cost of production being given, the quantity of money wanted would depend on the rapidity of its circulation.

I have supposed 10 000 families of equal incomes. I will now suppose the cost of producing gold to be such, that a family could gather 118 grains, or what we call a guinea, per week, or about 17 grains per day. Now if the habits of the country were such, that each family lived from hand to mouth, and purchased every day the day's consumption (an impossible supposition, but one which may be used in framing what may be called an intellectual diagram), it is obvious that no family would at an average possess more or less than 17 grains of gold. 170 000 grains, therefore, would be the precise quantity wanted for the purposes of money. And all the money would change hands every day. Let us now consider what would be the consequence if their custom were to make their purchases half-yearly instead of daily. At first sight, we might think that the rapidity of circulation would be retarded in the proportion of 1 to 182½; and, consequently, that rather more than 182 times as much money would be necessary. Such would be the case if each family were on one and the same day to make all their purchases for the ensuing half a year's consumption. But if we suppose them to lay in their stocks of different articles at different times, and at an average to make their purchases and sales, and of course to receive their incomes, on thirty-six different days during each year, the quantity of money wanted, instead of being 182 times, would not be much more than ten times the former quantity. Each family would, at an average, instead of 17, possess rather more than 170 grains of gold, the whole quantity wanted would rather exceed 1 700 000 grains of gold, and would change hands nearly ten times in a year. But though any alteration in the rapidity of circulation would much affect the quantity wanted, it would not, except during short periods, affect the value of money while the cost of production remained unaltered. Whether 170 000 or 1 700 000 grains were wanted, still while a day's labour could produce neither more nor less than 17 grains of gold, 17 grains of gold would, except during comparatively short intervals, be the price of every commodity produced by the labour of a day.

I say 'except during comparatively short intervals' because though the causes which limit the supply of gold are supposed to be unalterable, those which give it utility, or, in other words, which create the demand for it, might be increased or diminished; and during the interval between the diminution or increase of the demand, and the increase or diminution of the supply in the market, the value might rise above, or sink below, the cost of production.

The primary cause of the utility of gold is, as I have already observed, its use as the material of plate. The secondary cause is its use as money. And in the absence of any disturbing cause, the labour employed in producing gold would be just enough to supply the annual loss and wear of the existing stock of plate and money. Suppose now a change of fashion to occasion a sudden demand for an increased quantity of plate: the introduction, for instance, of the Roman Catholic forms of worship, and a belief in the meritoriousness of adorning every altar with golden candlesticks. That demand would be supplied, partly by melting and converting into candlesticks some of the existing plate, and some of the existing money, and partly by employing on plate all the current supply of gold, a part of which would otherwise have been used as money. The whole quantity of money being diminished, the average quantity possessed by each family must be diminished. A less portion would be offered on every purchase, all prices (except that of plate) would fall, and the monied incomes of all persons, except the gatherers of gold, would be diminished. This of course would occasion much more labour to be employed in gathering gold until the former amount of money were replaced.

If, after this had taken place, the use of plate should suddenly diminish; if, for instance, protestant forms of worship should supplant the catholic, the consequences would of course be precisely opposite. The candlesticks would be melted down, and the sudden supply of gold would sink its value. Part of that additional supply would probably be used as plate, of which each family could afford to use a little more; the rest would be turned into money. The whole quantity of money being increased, each family would have rather more; rather more would be offered on every exchange; all prices (except the price of plate) would rise, and the money incomes of all persons, except the gatherers of gold, would be increased. The gathering of gold would, of course, cease until the gradual loss and wear of plate and money, uncompensated by any annual supply, should reduce the quantity of gold below the amount necessary to supply the existing demand for plate and money. On the occurrence of that event, it would again become profitable to gather gold, and the price of everything would again depend on the proportion of the labour necessary to its production, compared with the labour necessary to obtain a given quantity of gold.

Similar and equally temporary consequences would follow from any causes which should increase or diminish the demand for gold by diminishing or increasing either the use of money in exchange or the rapidity of its circulation.

I will suppose the daily amount of gold that a family can obtain from the washing places to be ten grains, and, consequently, the daily money income of each of the ten thousand families to be 10 grains. Now if such were the habits of the country, as that each family should habitually keep in their possession, at an average, 20 days' income, or 200 grains, the total amount of money in the country would be 2 000 000 grains, and it would change hands about eighteen times every year. If a banker should establish himself, and offer to take charge of that portion of each man's income which was not necessary for immediate use, it is possible that half the money of the country might be deposited with him. Each family might think it safer in his custody than in their own, and would feel the convenience of being able to make payments by drawing on him, and avoiding the trouble of carrying about sums of money. Many exchanges in which money was previously used would now be effected by a mere transfer of credit. A seller would often receive from a purchaser a cheque, and pay it to the banker, and instead of receiving money for it, merely occasion a certain sum to be taken from the account of the purchaser and placed to that of the seller. If, however, the banker were to keep in his chests all the money deposited with him, one-half of the money would become absolutely stagnant, and the rate of circulation of the whole money in the country might be said to be retarded by one-half; this would precisely balance the effect of the diminution of exchanges for money, and the same quantity of money would be required as before.

We will adopt, however, the more probable supposition, that the banker would keep in his coffers only enough to answer the utmost probable demands of his customers, and employ the remainder either in making purchases himself, or in loans to persons desirous of obtaining commodities or labour, but without sufficient funds of their own. If we suppose him to have received in deposits 1 000 000 grains, or half the money of the country, to retain in his coffers 500 000, and to issue again, in purchases or loans, the remaining 500 000, the effect would be the same as if the existing money of the country were increased by one-fourth. In the first place, there would remain in circulation the 1 000 000 grains undeposited; secondly, there would be the banker's cheques acting as money, and supplying, as instruments of exchange, the million grains deposited; and lastly, there would be 500 000 grains of deposits reissued. The consequence would be, a rise in the price of every commodity except plate, and in the wages of all labourers, except the gatherers of gold. The use of plate would probably be somewhat increased, and the gathering of gold would cease, until the loss and wear of money and plate had reduced the stock of plate to its former amount, and the stock of money to three quarters of its former amount. If the banker should find the public ready to take his written promise to pay as of equal value with actual payment, and should venture to issue, in purchases and loans, the whole of the 500 000 grains, which we have supposed him to reserve to answer the demands of his customers, this would have the effect of adding a quarter more to the currency of the country. Prices would again rise, and would not gradually subside to their former level until the unsupplied loss and wear of the gold should have reduced the quantity of money to one half of what had been its amount when the banker began his operations.

If, by this time, it should be discovered that the banker had no reserve to meet the demands of his customers, and the drafts upon him, which before had passed as cash, should become valueless, the same effects would be produced as would have been produced before his establishment, if half the money of the country had been destroyed – had been put, for instance, on board a vessel, and lost at sea. All prices, except the price of plate, and all incomes, except the incomes of the gold gatherers, would fall one half. Plate would be melted into money, and additional labour employed in gathering gold, till the former stock of plate and money were replaced.

My principal object in this long discussion has been to show that the value of money, so far as it is decided by intrinsic causes, does not depend *permanently* on the quantity of it possessed by a given community, or on the rapidity of its circulation, or on the prevalence of exchanges, or on the use of barter or credit, or, in short, on any cause whatever, excepting *the cost of its production*.

Other causes may operate for a time, but their influence wears away as the existing stock of the previous metals within the country accommodates itself to the wants of the inhabitants. As long as precisely 17 grains of gold can be obtained by a day's labour, every thing else produced by equal labour will, in the absence of any natural or artificial monopoly, sell for 17 grains of gold; whether all the money of the country change hands every day, or once in four days, or once in four years; whether each individual consume principally what he has himself produced, or supply all his wants by exchange; whether such exchanges are effected by barter or credit, or by the actual intervention of money; whether there be 1 700 000 or 170 000 grains in the country.

In these respects, my insulated community of 10 000 families is a miniature of the whole world. The whole world may be considered as one community, using gold and silver as money, and ascertaining the value of other commodities by comparing their cost of production with the cost of obtaining gold and silver. And though many causes may alter the quantity of the precious metals possessed by any single nation, nothing will permanently alter their value, so far as that value depends on intrinsic causes, unless it affect their cost of production.

Reference
1. J. S. MILL, *Elements of Political Economy*, 3rd edn, section 7.

6 A. Marshall

The Total Currency Needed by a Country

Excerpt from A. Marshall (1924), *Money, Credit and Commerce*, Macmillan, ch. 4, pp. 38–50.

I Functions of a Currency

Money or 'currency' is desired as a means to an end; but yet it does not conform to the general rule that, the larger the means towards a certain end, the better will that end be attained. It may indeed be compared to oil used to enable a machine to run smoothly. A machine will not run well unless oiled, and a novice may infer that the more oil he supplies, the better the machine will run; but in fact oil in excess will clog the machine. In like manner an excessive increase of currency, causes it to lose credit and perhaps even to cease to be 'current'.

This analogy may seem at first sight to be rather forced. But it is to be observed that:

A. Money is not desired mainly for its own sake, but because its possession gives a ready command of general purchasing power, in a convenient form. A railway ticket is desired for the sake of the journey over which it gives control. If a railway company adjusted its tickets to the lengths of the corresponding journeys, a long ticket might be more desirable than a short one; but if the lengths of all the tickets were doubled, the increase of lengths would merely cause a little inconvenience. In like manner an increase in the volume of a country's currency, other things being equal, will lower proportionately the value of each unit. In fact, if that increase threatens to be repeated, the value of each unit may fall more than in proportion to the increase already made.

B. As a railway ticket is valued in accordance with the length of the journey to which it gives access, so currency is valued in accordance with the amount of ready purchasing power over which it gives command. If an extension of the advantage thus gained could be acquired without cost, everyone would keep a large command of ready purchasing power on hand in the form of currency. But currency held in the hand yields no income; therefore everyone balances (more or less automatically and instinctively) the benefits, which he would get by enlarging his stock of currency in the hand, against those which he would get by investing some of it either in a commodity – say a coat or a piano – from which he would derive a direct benefit; or in some business plant or stock-exchange security, which would yield him a money income. Thus the total value of the currency which a nation holds is kept from falling considerably below, or rising considerably above, the amount of ready purchasing power, which its members care to hold in hand. If then the discovery of new mines, or any other cause, increases considerably the stock of currency, its value must fall, until its fall makes the acquisition of increased supplies of gold unprofitable. That is, the value of a gold coin, freely minted, will tend to be held rather close to the cost of attainment of the gold which it contains.

A country's demand is not for a certain amount of metallic (or other) currency; but for an amount of currency which has a certain purchasing power. Her stock of gold at any time tends to be equal to the amount, which (at that value) equals the purchasing power that the people care to keep in the form of gold either in their own custody or in their banks, together with the amount that the industrial arts of the country will absorb at that value.

If she has gold mines of her own, her stock of gold is governed by cost of production, subject to indirect influences of changes in demand for exportation, etc. If she has no gold mines, her stock tends to be such that she can absorb it at about the rate of cost at which she can make and export commodities which gold-producing countries will accept in exchange for it; the manner in which this adjustment is effected will be considered later on.

If her stock of gold were fixed by nature's decree, gold being used by her only for currency, all her other media of exchange being in effect orders for certain quantities of gold; then the total value of that gold would be the same whatever its amount. But gold generally passes from one country to another with perfect freedom; and therefore the stock of it, which each country holds, adjusts itself to her demand for it as currency and in other uses.

Its purchasing power within her territory must bear such a relation to its purchasing power in other countries, that neither her importers nor her exporters find a considerable advantage in substituting gold on a large scale for other goods. Therefore her stock of gold never diverges for any considerable time far from that amount which keeps her general level of prices in accord with that of other countries, allowance being made where necessary for costs of transport and frontier taxes.

Of course the total demand for each precious metal is made up of the demand for it for use in currency, and the demand for it in industrial and personal uses. These uses include for instance the service of silver in spoons and silver-plated spoons, and the service of gold in watch-chains and in gilding picture frames and so on. Each of these various demands has its own law of variation. The more difficult of attainment the silver is, the less use of it is likely to be made in each industry; but its power of enabling a person to make considerable purchases would be increased by a rise in its value. Many people habitually carry on their persons and keep in store at home a greater weight of silver than of bronze coin, because not many of their needs can be satisfied by the expenditure of only a few bronze coins.[1]

II

In early times it was commonly said that the values of gold and silver are 'artificial'. But in fact they are governed on the side of supply by cost of attainment, and on the side of demand by the needs of people for ready purchasing power based on gold and silver, together with the demand for these metals for the purposes of industry and display.

Observations that the value of a coin often rose above that of the metal contained in it, suggested the notion that the value of currency generally is 'artificial'; that is, due to convention, custom or other inclination of the mind. Many centuries passed before general attention was given to the dependence of the value of each unit of a currency of given volume on the quantity of

1. These matters are discussed in some detail in the present writer's *Principles of Economics*, III, VI; and the notes in the mathematical appendix, attached to it (1).

work which the currency had to do. But a little progress of thought in this direction was often made, when either the inconstancy of nature's supply of the precious metals, or exceptional recklessness on the part of those responsible for the quality of the currency, had caused or threatened great changes in general prices. Discussions on the value of money were eager, though not well-informed, in England when Henry VIII debased the currency; and again when the mines of the New World sent their first large deliveries to Europe: and they rose again to a high level in the seventeenth century, when commerce was demanding more exact systems of coinage than before and thought was becoming more patient and solid.

At last it was seen that the conditions of the country at any time governed the amount of ready purchasing power, which was then required for the convenient discharge of the country's business. To use a shorter phrase, the general conditions of the country imposed a certain amount of work on her currency. Therefore the greater the quantity of her currency the less work there would be for each part of it to perform; the less therefore would be the effective demand for each coin, and the lower its value. The next step was to take account also of the way in which the work to be done by money itself could be lightened by the aid of credit.[2]

It was not, however, till the beginning of the last century that the study of the causes which govern the value of money was taken quite seriously. Men's thoughts were then much occupied with the economic basis of political security as well as of general well-being. Again, the violent disturbances of public credit and prices, which were caused by the devastations and the alarms of the Napoleonic wars, set a singularly able and well-informed group of students and men of affairs at work on the problem, and

2. Thus Petty (*Taxes and Contributions*, 1667), considered how the title deeds of land, under a good system of registry, and warrants issued by 'depositories of metals, cloth, linen, leather and other usefuls' together with 'credit in Lombards or money-banks' will make 'less money necessary to drive the trade.' He meant of course less money at its previous purchasing power, and equal money at a lower purchasing power. Good work was done by Locke; and by that reckless, and unbalanced but most fascinating genius, John Law. Harris, and the acute though little known Cantillon, together with others, led the way up to Hume and Adam Smith.

they left very little to be added as regards fundamentals by their successors.[3]

The *Bullion Report* of 1810 states that 'the effective currency of the country depends upon the quickness of circulation, and the number of exchanges performed in a given time, as well as upon its numerical amount; and all the circumstances, which have a tendency to quicken or to retard the rate of circulation, render the same amount of currency more or less adequate to the wants of trade. A much smaller amount is required in a high state of public credit, than when alarms make individuals call in their advances, and provide against accidents by hoarding; and in a period of commercial security and private confidence, than when mutual distrust discourages pecuniary arrangements for any distant time. But, above all, the same amount of currency will be more or less adequate, in proportion to the skill which the great money-lenders possess in managing and economizing the use of the circulating medium. . . . The improvements, which have taken place of late years in this country and particularly in the District of London with regard to the use and economy of money among bankers, and in the mode of adjusting commercial payments . . . consist principally in the increased use of bankers' drafts in the common payments of London; the contrivance of bringing all such drafts daily to a common receptacle, where they are balanced against each other; the intermediate agency of bill-brokers; and several other changes in the practice of London bankers, are to the same effect, of rendering it unnecessary for them to keep so large a deposit of money as formerly.' This terse statement carries far.

The stocks of gold and silver in the western world are known to have increased rapidly during recent decades, though no definite statistics in regard to them are available. But it seems that the annual production of silver increased about tenfold since the middle of last century. The stock of gold increased nearly tenfold

3. Ricardo held a chief place among them; and his high prestige has perhaps tended to throw the work of others into the shade. Professor Hollander (2) has shown that nearly every part of Ricardo's doctrine was anticipated by some one or other of his predecessors; but his masterly genius, like that of Adam Smith, was largely occupied with the supreme task of building up a number of fragmentary truths into coherent doctrine. Such a doctrine has constructive force, because it is an organic whole.

between 1840 and 1855: but slowly for the next forty years: latterly its increase has been rapid.[4]

Meanwhile the use of gold in the arts of production has increased fast; and that considerable part of it which takes the form of gilding unfits the gold used for further employment. It is possible therefore, that in the course of a few centuries the stock of gold may become small and its purchasing power may be liable to great changes from small causes. In that case there may be strong arguments in favour of basing all long-term obligations on authoritative standards of general purchasing power.

In England a large purchase is generally effected, not by transfer of currency itself, but by transfer of a cheque (or other document) that gives command over currency. For that reason the demand for currency in England is not representative of general conditions even in the western world: but we may ignore for the present the influences on prices which are exerted by cheques and other private documents; something will be said about them later.

III

The total value of a country's currency, multiplied into the average number of times of its changing hands for business purposes in a year, is of course equal to the total amount of business transacted in that country by direct payments of currency in that year. But this identical statement does not indicate the causes that govern the rapidity of circulation of currency: to discover them we must look to the amounts of purchasing power which the people of that country elect to keep in the form of currency.

The main facts are then: (a) every change in the rapidity of circulation of goods tends to cause a corresponding change in the rapidity of circulation of currency and substitutes for currency; and (b) the chief of these substitutes are cheques, and – in some cases – bills of exchange. But the motives that govern the rapidity of circulation of money are not obvious; let us look for them.

It will appear, on consideration, that changes in the rapidity of circulation of money are themselves incidental to changes in the

4. Professor Lexis (3) says, in the article on 'Gold' in the *Handwörterbuch der Staatswissenchaften*, that four-fifths of the production of gold between the years 1801 and 1908 belongs to the last sixty years of the period.

amount of ready purchasing power which the people of a country find it advantageous to keep in their own holding. This amount is governed by causes, the chief of which can be seen with but little trouble. It is true that comparatively few people analyse their own motives in such matters; but implicit suggestions of their motives are contained in such observations as: 'I have kept a larger stock of money than I really need; I might have used some of it in purchases for personal use, or invested it.' Opposite reflections occur, when a man has spent or invested nearly all the money which he commands, and has in consequence failed to take advantage of a good bargain which came within his reach. Or he may have been forced to buy from retailers who charged him high prices and delivered inferior goods, being fortified by the knowledge that if he raised objections, he could be brought into subjection by a hint that he must pay up quickly. The customer might indeed obtain leave to overdraw his account at a bank; but this resource is not always available.[5]

This preliminary statement indicates the general nature of a country's demand for ready purchasing power in the form of currency; or, at least, of immediate command over currency, such as is derived from keeping a considerable sum of money on current account in a bank.

To give definiteness to this notion, let us suppose that the inhabitants of a country, taken one with another (and including therefore all varieties of character and of occupation) find it just worth their while to keep by them on the average ready purchasing power to the extent of a tenth part of their annual income, together with a fiftieth part of their property; then the aggregate

5. It is obvious that a private person, who buys on long credit without special cause, must pay dearly for his purchases in one way or another; for the trader looks to get profit on his capital, and the private person can seldom get more than a rather low rate of interest on his. It is not always to traders' advantage to have attention called to this fact; partly because, when customers are much in arrears, they are not in a position to complain against faults in the things sent to them. The total costs which they thus throw upon traders, in addition to those incurred in dealings for cash, vary with the amount of extra book-keeping involved, the risk of bad debts and other circumstances. In some cases the workman, who is but a single week behind with his payment, is in effect mulcted in interest at the rate of at least a halfpenny in the shilling for that week; that is, at 200 per cent per annum, counting simple interest only.

value of the currency of the country will tend to be equal to the sum of these amounts. Let us suppose that their incomes aggregate in value to five million quarters of wheat (in a normal year) and their property to twenty-five millions. Then the total value of the currency will be a million quarters of wheat; for at that rate everyone will be able to have as much ready purchasing power at command as he cares to have, after balancing one against another the advantages of a further ready command, and the disadvantages of putting more of his resources into a form in which they yield him no direct income or other benefit. If then the currency contains a million units, each will be worth a quarter of wheat; if it contains two million, each will be worth half a quarter.

Thus the position is this. In every state of society there is some fraction of their income which people find it worthwhile to keep in the form of currency; it may be a fifth, or a tenth, or a twentieth. A large command of resources in the form of currency renders their business easy and smooth, and puts them at an advantage in bargaining; but, on the other hand, it locks up in a barren form resources that might yield an income of gratification if invested, say, in extra furniture; or a money income, if invested in extra machinery or cattle. In a primitive state of society, even in one as far advanced as that of India, only the rich care to have much of their resources in the form of currency. In England all but the very poor keep a good deal; the lower middle classes keep a relatively very large quantity, while the very rich who pay all their tradesmen by cheques use relatively little. But, whatever the state of society, there is a certain volume of their resources which people of different classes, taken one with another, care to keep in the form of currency; and if everything else remains the same, then there is this direct relation between the volume of currency and the level of prices, that if one is increased by 10 per cent, the other also will be increased by 10 per cent. Of course, the less the proportion of their resources which people care to keep in the form of currency, the lower will be the aggregate value of the currency, that is, the higher will prices be with a given volume of currency.

This relation between the volume of the currency and the general level of prices may be changed permanently by changes, firstly in population and wealth, which change the aggregate income; secondly, by the growth of credit agencies, which substitute other means of payment for currency; thirdly, by changes in the methods of transport, production and business generally, which affect the number of hands through which commodities pass in the processes of making and dealing, and it may be temporarily modified by fluctuations of general commercial confidence and activity.[6]

Of course the total value of currency needed by the business of England is relatively small. For her middle and upper classes discharge most of their considerable obligations by cheques; and few of these cheques are presented for payment in cash. Most of them merely transfer command over currency from one banking account to another.

As has already been noted, the precious metals (whether in bulk or in the form of coin) used to be commonly hoarded in order to make provision against the needs of the future, known and unknown. This practice still prevails among the peasants of a large part of the world. But in 'western' countries even peasants, if well-to-do, incline to invest the greater part of their savings in government, or other familiar stock-exchange securities, or to commit them to the charge of a bank; and especially among Anglo-Saxon peoples, by far the greater part of the currency, which is held in private hands, is designed as provision against some occasion for its use as direct purchasing power in the not very distant future.

IV

Influences exerted by occupation and temperament on the amounts of currency, which people with similar incomes are likely to keep under their immediate control.

The improvidence of a particular weekly wage receiver may cause the gold and silver coins which come into his possession to circulate on the average quickly away from him; but as, unless he

6. The above statement is reproduced from my answers to Questions 11 759–11 761 put by the Indian Currency Committee in 1899. In fact a considerable part of the present discussion of the problems of money and credit may be found in my answers to Questions 11 757–11 850 put by that committee; and my answers to Questions 9623–10 014 and 10 121–10 126 put by the Gold and Silver Commission in 1887–8.

is exceptionally reckless, he keeps on hand at least a shilling to the end, he probably does not pay away his bronze coins much more quickly than other people. In like manner the improvidence of one whose salary is paid quarterly may raise the average rapidity of circulation of the gold coins which come into his possession; but, as he will seldom be without a pound's worth of money, it will not materially affect the rapidity with which silver and bronze coins pass in and out of his possession.

The large trader holds relatively little currency in a modern country in which nearly all considerable payments are made by cheques. But, in the absence of any credit auxiliaries to currency, every trader is dependent on the stock of purchasing power which he holds in the form of money, for the means of making good bargains when they offer. By instinct and experience he balances the benefit against the loss of a large holding. He knows that if he keeps too little purchasing power at his command, he will be frequently brought into straits; and that if he keeps an inordinate quantity, he will diminish the material sources of his income, and yet may find but few occasions on which he can turn the whole of his ready purchasing power to any great advantage.

To sum up – the rule for one man may not serve well for another in similar conditions; but, as Petty said, 'The most thriving men keep little . . . money by them, but turn and wind it into various commodities to their great profit.'[7]

7. Petty thought that the money 'sufficient for' the nation is 'so much as will pay half a year's rent for all the lands of England and a quarter's rent of the Houseing, for a week's expense of all the people, and about a quarter of the value of all the exported commodities.' (*Quantulumcunque*, Queries 23 and 25: see also his *Political Arithmetic*, ch. IX and *Verbum Sapienti*, ch. VI.) Locke estimated that 'one-fiftieth of wages and one-fourth of the landowner's income and one-twentieth part of the broker's yearly returns in ready money will be enough to drive the trade of any country.' Cantillon (1755), after a long and subtle study, concludes that the value needed is a ninth of the total produce of the country; or, what he takes to be the same thing, a third of the rent of the land. Adam Smith has more of the scepticism of the modern age and says: 'it is impossible to determine the proportion,' though 'it has been computed by different authors at a fifth, at a tenth, at a twentieth and at a thirtieth part of the whole value of the annual produce.'

V

Although the purchasing power of a unit of a currency varies, other things being equal, inversely with the number of the units; yet an increased issue of inconvertible paper currency may lower its credit, and therefore lessen the amount of ready purchasing power which the people care to hold. That is, it may lower the value of each of the units more than in proportion to the increase of their number.

So far no account has been taken of the influence which the credit of a currency exerts on the willingness of the population to hold much of their resources, either directly in the form of cash in hand and at a bank; or indirectly in the form of debentures and other stock-exchange securities, which yield fixed incomes in terms of currency. But the influence may become important, if the credit of the currency is impaired. In fact an ill-considered increase in the volume of an inconvertible currency is likely to lower the value of each unit more than in proportion to the increase; for it will lower the credit of the currency, and incline everyone to hold a rather smaller share of his resources in that form than he otherwise would. Each unit of the increased currency will therefore command a smaller part of that smaller share of his resources; and its value will thus suffer a double diminution. The total value of an inconvertible paper currency therefore cannot be increased by increasing its quantity: *an increase in its quantity, which seems likely to be repeated, will lower the value of each unit more than in proportion to the increase.*

This notion that the amount of ready purchasing power required by the population of a country at any time is a definite quantity, in any given state of her industry and trade, is implied, even when not explicitly stated, in the now familiar doctrine that the value of a unit of a currency varies, other things being equal, inversely with the number of the units and their average rapidity of circulation.

This 'quantity doctrine' is helpful as far as it goes; but it does not indicate what are the 'other things' which must be assumed to be equal in order to justify the proposition; and it does not explain the causes which govern 'rapidity of circulation'.

It is almost a truism; for if one column of a ledger recorded accurately all the transactions for money in a year with their values, while another column specified the number of the units of money employed in each transaction; then the two columns when added up would balance. The second column would of course represent the aggregate value of the total number of changes of ownership of all the units of money; and that is the same thing in other words as the total value of the money multiplied by the average changes of ownership (otherwise than by free gift, theft, etc.) of each unit.

The other things that must remain equal for the purposes of this statement, include (a) the population, (b) the amount of business transacted per head of the population, (c) the percentage of that business which is effected directly by money and (d) the efficiency (or average rapidity of circulation) of money. Only if these conditions are reckoned in, can the doctrine come under investigation; and if they are reckoned in the doctrine is almost a truism.

VI

Currency differs from other things in that an increase in its quantity exerts no direct influence on the amount of the service it renders. Inconvertible paper currencies.

The exceptional character of this 'quantity' statement in regard to the value of currency has been described in many ways. But the central fact in the account now submitted is that *an increase in the amount of money in a country does not increase the total services which it performs*. This statement is not inconsistent with the fact that an increase in amount of the gold in a country's currency increases her means of obtaining goods by exporting gold, and also gives her a power of converting some of her currency into articles of ornament. It merely means that the purpose of a currency is firstly to facilitate business transactions; and for this purpose, it needs to be clearly defined and generally acceptable. Next, it needs to command a stable purchasing power; such stability can be attained by an inconvertible paper currency, so long as the government (a) can prevent forged notes from getting into circulation, and (b) can make the people absolutely certain that genuine notes will not be issued in excess. Gold coins may indeed be regarded as currency based on the belief that nature will not countenance a violent increase in the currency drawn from her stores. If there were discovered (in spite of the opinion of geologists and mineralogists that no such thing is physically possible) a mine of gold ore with contents as large in volume as those of a vast coal mine, then gold coins would cease to serve any good purpose.[8]

Of course the stability of value of a gold coinage owes something to the stability of the demand for gold for ornament and for some industrial uses; but the discovery – if it were possible – of a vast deposit of gold would make it difficult to find good uses for it. We can conceive a planet, of different construction from ours, in which enough iron ore to make a good saw has a higher exchange value than a pound of gold.[9]

If an inconvertible currency is controlled by a strong government, its amount can be so regulated that the value of a unit of it is maintained at a fixed level. The level may be such that (a) the average level of prices, as evidenced by a trustworthy index number, remains unchanged; or (b) that this average level adjusts itself to general changes of prices, in countries whose currencies are firmly based on the precious metals; or (c) that the government of the country in question sets up a carefully framed list of general prices within its territory, and so adjusts the amount of her currency, that (say) a thousand units of it command, on average, uniform amounts of commodities in general.

'Convertible' notes – that is, notes for which gold (or other standard metallic) currency will *certainly* be given in exchange on demand – exert nearly the same influence on national price levels, as would be exerted by standard coins of equal nominal value. Of

8. The elaborate and careful printing of paper currencies makes plausible imitations of them very expensive, and yet liable to prompt detection. Forgery of Bank of England notes is well known to be prevented by exceptional arrangements and methods.

9. This consideration can be extended. If diamonds became abundant, they would revolutionize and extend branches of industry in which hard steel is not hard enough; but they would need to be used with great caution for personal ornament. On the other hand, if a fall in the price of wool, or almost any other serviceable commodity, caused a greater quantity of it to be consumed at a less aggregate cost, there would be a nearly proportional increase in the real wealth of the world; the rich would gain only a little, but the poor would be more warmly clad.

course, if even a small doubt arises as to their full convertibility into standard coins, men will be shy in regard to them; and if they cease to be fully convertible they will fall in value below the amounts of the gold (or silver) which they profess to represent.

It will be noted that this chapter is concerned with the demand for currency only when general credit is in a normal condition. When credit is shaken, it may be advisable to adopt abnormal, and (so to speak) medicinal measures in regard to the supply of currency.

References

1. A. MARSHALL, *Principles of Economics*, 5th edn., Macmillan, 1907.
2. J. H. HOLLANDER, 'The development of the theory of money from Adam Smith to David Ricardo', *Quarterly Journal of Economics*, vol. 25, 1911, pp. 429–70.
3. W. LEXIS, 'Gold', *Handwörterbuch der Staatswissenschaften*, Conrad (ed.), Jena, 1890–97.

7 M. Friedman

The Quantity Theory of Money: A Restatement

M. Friedman (1956), 'The quantity theory of money: a restatement', excerpt from *Studies in the Quantity Theory of Money*, Friedman (ed.), Chicago University Press, pp. 3–21.

The quantity theory of money is a term evocative of a general approach rather than a label for a well-defined theory. The exact content of the approach varies from a truism defining the term 'velocity' to an allegedly rigid and unchanging ratio between the quantity of money – defined in one way or another – and the price level – also defined in one way or another. Whatever its precise meaning, it is clear that the general approach fell into disrepute after the crash of 1929 and the subsequent Great Depression and only recently has been slowly re-emerging into professional respectability.

[. . .] Chicago was one of the few academic centers at which the quantity theory continued to be a central and vigorous part of the oral tradition throughout the 1930s and 1940s, where students continued to study monetary theory and to write theses on monetary problems. The quantity theory that retained this role differed sharply from the atrophied and rigid caricature that is so frequently described by the proponents of the new income–expenditure approach – and with some justice, to judge by much of the literature on policy that was spawned by quantity theorists. At Chicago, Henry Simons and Lloyd Mints directly, Frank Knight and Jacob Viner at one remove, taught and developed a more subtle and relevant version, one in which the quantity theory was connected and integrated with general price theory and became a flexible and sensitive tool for interpreting movements in aggregate economic activity and for developing relevant policy prescriptions.

To the best of my knowledge, no systematic statement of this theory as developed at Chicago exists, though much can be read between the lines of Simons' and Mints' writings. And this is as it should be, for the Chicago tradition was not a rigid system, an unchangeable orthodoxy, but a way of looking at things. It was a theoretical approach that insisted that money does matter, that any interpretation of short-term movements in economic activity is likely to be seriously at fault if it neglects monetary changes and repercussions and if it leaves unexplained why people are willing to hold the particular nominal quantity of money in existence.

The purpose of this introduction is not to enshrine – or, should I say, inter – a definitive version of the Chicago tradition. To suppose that one could do so would be inconsistent with that tradition itself. The purpose is rather to set down a particular 'model' of a quantity theory in an attempt to convey the flavor of the oral tradition which nurtured the remaining essays in this volume. In consonance with this purpose, I shall not attempt to be exhaustive or to give a full justification for every assertion.

1. The quantity theory is in the first instance a theory of the *demand* for money. It is not a theory of output, or of money income, or of the price level. Any statement about these variables requires combining the quantity theory with some specifications about the conditions of supply of money and perhaps about other variables as well.

2. To the ultimate wealth-owning units in the economy, money is one kind of asset, one way of holding wealth. To the productive enterprise, money is a capital good, a source of productive services that is combined with other productive services to yield the products that the enterprise sells. Thus the theory of the demand for money is a special topic in the theory of capital; as such, it has the rather unusual feature of combining a piece from each side of the capital market, the supply of capital (points 3 through 8 that follow), and the demand for capital (points 9 through 12).

3. The analysis of the demand for money on the part of the ultimate wealth-owning units in the society can be made formally identical with that of the demand for a consumption service. As in the usual theory of consumer choice, the demand for money (or any other particular asset) depends on three major sets of factors: (a) the total wealth to be held in various forms – the analogue of the budget restraint; (b) the price of and return on this form of wealth and alternative forms; and (c) the tastes and preferences

of the wealth-owning units. The substantive differences from the analysis of the demand for a consumption service are the necessity of taking account of intertemporal rates of substitution in (b) and (c) and of casting the budget restraint in terms of wealth.

4. From the broadest and most general point of view, total wealth includes all sources of 'income' or consumable services. One such source is the productive capacity of human beings, and accordingly this is one form in which wealth can be held. From this point of view, *the* rate of interest expresses the relation between the stock which is wealth and the flow which is income, so if Y be the total flow of income, and r, *the* interest rate, total wealth is

$$W = \frac{Y}{r}. \qquad\qquad 1$$

Income in this broadest sense should not be identified with income as it is ordinarily measured. The latter is generally a 'gross' stream with respect to human beings, since no deduction is made for the expense of maintaining human productive capacity intact; in addition, it is affected by transitory elements that make it depart more or less widely from the theoretical concept of the stable level of consumption of services that could be maintained indefinitely.

5. Wealth can be held in numerous forms, and the ultimate wealth-owning unit is to be regarded as dividing his wealth among them (point 3a), so as to maximize 'utility' (point 3c), subject to whatever restrictions affect the possibility of converting one form of wealth into another (point 3b). As usual, this implies that he will seek an apportionment of his wealth such that the rate at which he *can* substitute one form of wealth for another is equal to the rate at which he is just willing to do so. But this general proposition has some special features in the present instance because of the necessity of considering flows as well as stocks. We can suppose all wealth (except wealth in the form of the productive capacity of human beings) to be expressed in terms of monetary units at the prices of the point of time in question. The rate at which one form can be substituted for another is then simply $1.00 worth for $1.00 worth, regardless of the forms involved. But this is clearly not a complete description, because the holding of one form of wealth instead of another involves a difference in

the composition of the income stream, and it is essentially these differences that are fundamental to the 'utility' of a particular structure of wealth. In consequence, to describe fully the alternative combinations of forms of wealth that are available to an individual, we must take account not only of their market prices – which except for human wealth can be done simply by expressing them in units worth $1.00 – but also of the form and size of the income streams they yield.

It will suffice to bring out the major issues that these considerations raise to consider five different forms in which wealth can be held: (i) money M, interpreted as claims or commodity units that are generally accepted in payment of debts at a fixed nominal value; (ii) bonds B, interpreted as claims to time streams of payments that are fixed in nominal units; (iii) equities E, interpreted as claims to stated pro-rata shares of the returns of enterprises; (iv) physical non-human goods G; and (v) human capital H. Consider now the yield of each.

(i) Money may yield a return in the form of money, for example, interest on demand deposits. It will simplify matters, however, and entail no essential loss of generality, to suppose that money yields its return solely in kind, in the usual form of convenience, security, etc. The magnitude of this return in 'real' terms per nominal unit of money clearly depends on the volume of goods that unit corresponds to, or on the general price level, which we may designate by P. Since we have decided to take $1.00 worth as the unit for each form of wealth, this will be equally true for other forms of wealth as well, so P is a variable affecting the 'real' yield of each.

(ii) If we take the 'standard' bond to be a claim to a perpetual income stream of constant nominal amount, then the return to a holder of the bond can take two forms: one, the annual sum he receives – the 'coupon', the other, any change in the price of the bond over time, a return which may of course be positive or negative. If the price is expected to remain constant, then $1.00 worth of a bond yields r_b per year, where r_b is simply the 'coupon' sum divided by the market price of the bond, so $1/r_b$ is the price of a bond promising to pay $1.00 per year. We shall call r_b the market bond interest rate. If the price is expected to change, then the yield cannot be calculated so simply, since it must take account of the return in the form of expected appreciation or depreciation of the bond, and it cannot, like r_b, be calculated directly from market prices (so long, at least, as the 'standard' bond is the only one traded in).

The nominal income stream purchased for $1.00 at time zero then consists of

$$r_b(0) + r_b(0) \frac{d}{dt}\left(\frac{1}{r_b(t)}\right) = r_b(0) - \frac{r_b(0)}{r_b^2(t)} \frac{d}{dt} r_b(t), \qquad \mathbf{2}$$

where t stands for time. For simplicity, we can approximate this functional by its value at time zero, which is

$$r_b - \frac{1}{r_b} \frac{dr_b}{dt}. \qquad \mathbf{3}$$

This sum, together with P already introduced, defines the real return from holding $1.00 of wealth in the form of bonds.

(iii) Analogously to our treatment of bonds, we may take the 'standard' unit of equity to be a claim to a perpetual income stream of constant 'real' amount; that is, to be a standard bond with a purchasing-power escalator clause, so that it promises a perpetual income stream equal in nominal units to a constant number times a price index, which we may, for convenience, take to be the same price index P introduced in (i).[1] The nominal return to the holder of the equity can then be regarded as taking three forms: the constant nominal amount he would receive per year in the absence of any change in P; the increment or decrement to this nominal amount to adjust for changes in P; and any change in the nominal price of the equity over time, which may of course arise from changes either in interest rates or in price levels. Let r_e be the market interest rate on equities defined analogously to r_b, namely, as the ratio of the 'coupon' sum at any time (the first two items above) to the price of the equity, so $1/r_e$ is the price of an equity promising to pay $1.00 per year if the price level does not change, or to pay

$$\frac{P(t)}{P(0)}. \qquad \mathbf{1}$$

1. This is an oversimplification, because it neglects 'leverage' and therefore supposes that any monetary liabilities of an enterprise are balanced by monetary assets.

if the price level varies according to $P(t)$. If $r_e(t)$ is defined analogously, the price of the bond selling for $1/r_e(0)$ at time 0 will be

$$\frac{P(t)}{P(0)\, r_e(t)}$$

at time t, where the ratio of prices is required to adjust for any change in the price level. The nominal stream purchased for \$1.00 at time zero then consists of

$$r_e(0)\,\frac{P(t)}{P(0)} + \frac{r_e(0)}{P(0)}\,\frac{d}{dt}\left(\frac{P(t)}{r_e(t)}\right) = r_e(0)\,\frac{P(t)}{P(0)}$$

$$+ \frac{r_e(0)}{r_e(t)}\,\frac{1}{P(0)}\,\frac{dP(t)}{dt} - \frac{P(t)}{P(0)}\,\frac{r_e(0)}{r_e^2(t)}\,\frac{d}{dt}\,r_e(t). \qquad \textbf{4}$$

Once again we can approximate this functional by its value at time zero, which is

$$r_e + \frac{1}{P}\,\frac{dP}{dt} - \frac{1}{r_e}\,\frac{dr_e}{dt}. \qquad \textbf{5}$$

This sum, together with P already introduced, defines the 'real' return from holding \$1.00 of wealth in the form of equities.

(iv) Physical goods held by ultimate wealth-owning units are similar to equities except that the annual stream they yield is in kind rather than in money. In terms of nominal units, this return, like that from equities, depends on the behavior of prices. In addition, like equities, physical goods must be regarded as yielding a nominal return in the form of appreciation or depreciation in money value. If we suppose the price level P, introduced earlier, to apply equally to the value of these physical goods, then at time zero,

$$\frac{1}{P}\,\frac{dP}{dT} \qquad \textbf{6}$$

is the size of this nominal return per \$1.00 of physical goods.[2]

2. In principle, it might be better to let P refer solely to the value of the services of physical goods, which is essentially what it refers to in the preceding cases, and to allow for the fact that the prices of the capital goods themselves must vary also with the rate of capitalization, so that the prices of services and their sources vary at the same rate only if the relevant interest rate is constant. I have neglected this refinement for simplicity; the neglect can perhaps be justified by the rapid depreciation of many of the physical goods held by final wealth-owning units.

Together with P, it defines the 'real' return from holding \$1.00 in the form of physical goods.

(v) Since there is only a limited market in human capital, at least in modern non-slave societies, we cannot very well define in market prices the terms of substitution of human capital for other forms of capital and so cannot define at any time the physical unit of capital corresponding to \$1.00 of human capital. There are some possibilities of substituting non-human capital for human capital in an individual's wealth holdings, as, for example, when he enters into a contract to render personal services for a specified period in return for a definitely specified number of periodic payments, the number not depending on his being physically capable of rendering the services. But in the main, shifts between human capital and other forms must take place through direct investment and disinvestment in the human agent, and we may as well treat this as if it were the only way. With respect to this form of capital, therefore, the restriction or obstacles affecting the alternative compositions of wealth available to the individual cannot be expressed in terms of market prices or rates of return. At any one point in time there is some division between human and non-human wealth in his portfolio of assets; he may be able to change this over time, but we shall treat it as given at a point in time. Let w be the ratio of non-human to human wealth or, equivalently, of income from non-human wealth to income from human wealth, which means that it is closely allied to what is usually defined as the ratio of wealth to income. This is, then, the variable that needs to be taken into account so far as human wealth is concerned.

6. The tastes and preferences of wealth-owning units for the service streams arising from different forms of wealth must in general simply be taken for granted as determining the form of the demand function. In order to give the theory empirical content, it will generally have to be supposed that tastes are constant over significant stretches of space and time. However, explicit allowance can be made for some changes in tastes in so far as such changes are linked with objective circumstances. For example, it seems reasonable that, other things the same, individuals want to hold a larger fraction of their wealth in the form of money when they are moving around geographically or are subject to

unusual uncertainty than otherwise. This is probably one of the major factors explaining a frequent tendency for money holdings to rise relative to income during wartime. But the extent of geographic movement, and perhaps of other kinds of uncertainty, can be represented by objective indexes, such as indexes of migration, miles of railroad travel, and the like. Let u stand for any such variables that can be expected to affect tastes and preferences (for 'utility' determining variables).

7. Combining equations **4**, **5** and **6** along the lines suggested by equation **3** yields the following demand function for money:

$$M = f\left(P, r_b - \frac{1}{r_b}\frac{dr_b}{dt}, r_e + \frac{1}{P}\frac{dP}{dt} - \frac{1}{r_e}\frac{dr_e}{dt}, \frac{1}{P}\frac{dP}{dt}; w; \frac{Y}{r}; u\right). \quad 7$$

A number of observations are in order about this function.

(i) Even if we suppose prices and rates of interest unchanged, the function contains three rates of interest: two for specific types of assets, r_b and r_e, and one intended to apply to all types of assets, r. This general rate r is to be interpreted as something of a weighted average of the two special rates plus the rates applicable to human wealth and to physical goods. Since the latter two cannot be observed directly, it is perhaps best to regard them as varying in some systematic way with r_b and r_e. On this assumption, we can drop r as an additional explicit variable, treating its influence as fully taken into account by the inclusion of r_b and r_e.

(ii) If there were no differences of opinion about price movements and interest-rate movements, and bonds and equities were equivalent except that the former are expressed in nominal units, arbitrage would of course make

$$r_b - \frac{1}{r_b}\frac{dr_b}{dt} = r_e + \frac{1}{P}\frac{dP}{dt} - \frac{1}{r_e}\frac{dr_e}{dt}, \quad 8$$

or, if we suppose rates of interest either stable or changing at the same percentage rate,

$$r_b = r_e + \frac{1}{P}\frac{dP}{dt}, \quad 9$$

that is, the 'money' interest rate equal to the 'real' rate plus the percentage rate of change of prices. In application the rate of change of prices must be interpreted as an 'expected' rate of change and differences of opinion cannot be neglected, so we cannot suppose equation 9 to hold; indeed, one of the most consistent features of inflation seems to be that it does not.[3]

(iii) If the range of assets were to be widened to include promises to pay specified sums for a finite number of time units – 'short-term' securities as well as 'consols' – the rates of change of r_b and r_e would be reflected in the difference between long and short rates of interest. Since at some stage it will doubtless be desirable to introduce securities of different time duration,[4] we may simplify the present exposition by restricting it to the case in which r_b and r_e are taken to be stable over time. Since the rate of changes in prices is required separately in any event, this means that we can replace the cumbrous variables introduced to designate the nominal return on bonds and equities simply by r_b and r_e.

(iv) Y can be interpreted as including the return to all forms of wealth, including money and physical capital goods owned and held directly by ultimate wealth-owning units, and so Y/r can be interpreted as an estimate of total wealth, only if Y is regarded as including some imputed income from the stock of money and directly owned physical capital goods. For monetary analysis the simplest procedure is perhaps to regard Y as referring to the return to all forms of wealth other than the money held directly by ultimate wealth-owning units, and so Y/r as referring to total remaining wealth.

8. A more fundamental point is that, as in all demand analyses resting on maximization of a utility function defined in terms of 'real' magnitudes, this demand equation must be considered independent in any essential way of the nominal units used to measure money variables. If the unit in which prices and money income are expressed is changed, the amount of money demanded should change proportionately. More technically, equation 7 must be regarded as homogeneous of the first degree in P and Y, so that

$$f\left(\lambda P, r_b, r_e, \frac{1}{P}\frac{dP}{dt}; w; \lambda Y; u\right) = \lambda f\left(P, r_b, r_e, \frac{1}{P}\frac{dP}{dt}; w; Y; u\right) \quad \textbf{10}$$

3. See Reuben Kessel, 'Inflation: theory of wealth distribution and application in private investment policy' (unpublished doctoral dissertation, University of Chicago).

4. See point 23 [of the complete paper].

where the variables within the parentheses have been rewritten in simpler form in accordance with comments 7 (i) and 7 (iii).

This characteristic of the function enables us to rewrite it in two alternative and more familiar ways.

(i) Let $\lambda = 1/P$. Equation 7 can then be written

$$\frac{M}{P} = f\left(r_b, r_e, \frac{1}{P}\frac{dP}{dt}; w; \frac{Y}{P}; u\right). \qquad 11$$

In this form the equation expresses the demand for real balances as a function of 'real' variables independent of nominal monetary values.

(ii) Let $\lambda = 1/Y$. Equation 7 can then be written

$$\frac{M}{Y} = f\left(r_b, r_e, \frac{1}{P}\frac{dP}{dt}, w, \frac{P}{Y}, u\right)$$

$$= \frac{1}{v\left(r_b, r_e, \frac{1}{P}\frac{dP}{dt}, w, \frac{Y}{P}, u\right)} \qquad 12$$

or

$$Y = v\left(r_b, r_e, \frac{1}{P}\frac{dP}{dt}, w, \frac{Y}{P}, u\right) \cdot M. \qquad 13$$

In this form the equation is in the usual quantity theory form, where v is income velocity.

9. These equations are, to this point, solely for money held directly by ultimate wealth-owning units. As noted, money is also held by business enterprises as a productive resource. The counterpart to this business asset in the balance sheet of an ultimate wealth-owning unit is a claim other than money. For example, an individual may buy bonds from a corporation, and the corporation use the proceeds to finance the money holdings which it needs for its operations. Of course, the usual difficulties of separating the accounts of the business and its owner arise with unincorporated enterprises.

10. The amount of money that it pays business enterprises to hold depends, as for any other source of productive services, on the cost of the productive services, the cost of substitute productive services and the value product yielded by the productive service. Per dollar of money held, the cost depends on how the corresponding capital is raised – whether by raising additional

capital in the form of bonds or equities, by substituting cash for real capital goods, etc. These ways of financing money holdings are much the same as the alternative forms in which the ultimate wealth-owning unit can hold its non-human wealth, so that the variables r_b, r_e, P and $(1/P)$ (dP/dt) introduced into equation 7 can be taken to represent the cost to the business enterprise of holding money. For some purposes, however, it may be desirable to distinguish between the rate of return received by the lender and the rate paid by the borrower; in which case it would be necessary to introduce an additional set of variables.

Substitutes for money as a productive service are numerous and varied, including all ways of economizing on money holdings by using other resources to synchronize more closely payments and receipts, reduce payment periods, extend use of book credit, establish clearing arrangements, and so on in infinite variety. There seem no particularly close substitutes whose prices deserve to be singled out for inclusion in the business demand for money.

The value product yielded by the productive services of money per unit of output depends on production conditions: the production function. It is likely to be especially dependent on features of production conditions affecting the smoothness and regularity of operations as well as on those determining the size and scope of enterprises, degree of vertical integration, etc. Again there seem no variables that deserve to be singled out on the present level of abstraction for special attention; these factors can be taken into account by interpreting u as including variables affecting not only the tastes of wealth-owners but also the relevant technological conditions of production. Given the amount of money demanded per unit of output, the total amount demanded is proportional to total output, which can be represented by Y.

11. One variable that has traditionally been singled out in considering the demand for money on the part of business enterprises is the volume of transactions, or of transactions per dollar of final products; and, of course, emphasis on transactions has been carried over to the ultimate wealth-owning unit as well as to the business enterprise. The idea that renders this approach attractive is that there is a mechanical link between a dollar of payments per unit time and the average stock of money required to effect it – a fixed technical coefficient of production, as it were.

It is clear that this mechanical approach is very different in spirit from the one we have been following. On our approach, the average amount of money held per dollar of transactions is itself to be regarded as a resultant of an economic equilibrating process, not as a physical datum. If, for whatever reason, it becomes more expensive to hold money, then it is worth devoting resources to effecting money transactions in less expensive ways or to reducing the volume of transactions per dollar of final output. In consequence, our ultimate demand function for money in its most general form does not contain as a variable the volume of transactions or of transactions per dollar of final output; it contains rather those more basic technical and cost conditions that affect the costs of conserving money, be it by changing the average amount of money held per dollar of transactions per unit time or by changing the number of dollars of transactions per dollar of final output. This does not, of course, exclude the possibility that, for a particular problem, it may be useful to regard the transactions variables as given and not to dig beneath them and so to include the volume of transactions per dollar of final output as an explicit variable in a special variant of the demand function.

Similar remarks are relevant to various features of payment conditions, frequently described as 'institutional conditions', affecting the velocity of circulation of money and taken as somehow mechanically determined – such items as whether workers are paid by the day, or week, or month; the use of book credit, and so on. On our approach these, too, are to be regarded as resultants of an economic equilibrating process, not as physical data. Lengthening the pay period, for example, may save bookkeeping and other costs to the employer, who is therefore willing to pay somewhat more than in proportion for a longer than a shorter pay period; on the other hand, it imposes on employees the cost of holding larger cash balances or providing substitutes for cash, and they therefore want to be paid more than in proportion for a longer pay period. Where these will balance depends on how costs vary with length of pay period. The cost to the employee depends in considerable part on the factors entering into his demand curve for money for a fixed pay period. If he would in any event be holding relatively larger average balances, the additional costs imposed by a lengthened pay period tend to be less than if he would be holding relatively small average balances, and so it will take less of an inducement to get him to accept a longer pay period. For given cost savings to the employer, therefore, the pay period can be expected to be longer in the first case than in the second. Surely, the increase in the average cash balance over the past century in this country that has occurred for other reasons has been a factor producing a lengthening of pay periods and not the other way around. Or, again, experience in hyperinflations shows how rapidly payment practices change under the impact of drastic changes in the cost of holding money.

12. The upshot of these considerations is that the demand for money on the part of business enterprises can be regarded as expressed by a function of the same kind as equation 7, with the same variables on the right-hand side. And, like 7, since the analysis is based on informed maximization of returns by enterprises, only 'real' quantities matter, so it must be homogeneous of the first degree in Y and P. In consequence, we can interpret 7 and its variants, equations 11 and 13 as describing the demand for money on the part of a business enterprise as well as on the part of an ultimate wealth-owning unit, provided only that we broaden our interpretation of u.

13. Strictly speaking, the equations 7, 11 and 13 are for an individual wealth-owning unit or business enterprise. If we aggregate 7 for all wealth-owning units and business enterprises in the society, the result, in principle, depends on the distribution of the units by the several variables. This raises no serious problem about P, r_b and r_e, for these can be taken as the same for all, or about u, for this is an unspecified portmanteau variable to be filled in as the occasion demands. We have been interpreting $(1/P)\,(dP/dt)$ as the expected rate of price rise, so there is no reason why this variable should be the same for all, and w and Y clearly differ substantially among units. An approximation is to neglect these difficulties and take equation 7 and the associated 11 and 13 as applying to the aggregate demand for money, with $(1/P)\,(dP/dt)$ interpreted as some kind of an average expected rate of change of prices, w as the ratio of total income from non-human wealth to income from human wealth and Y as aggregate income. This is the procedure that has generally been followed,

and it seems the right one until serious departures between this linear approximation and experience make it necessary to introduce measures of dispersion with respect to one or more of the variables.

14. It is perhaps worth noting explicitly that the model does not use the distinction between 'active balances' and 'idle balances' or the closely allied distinction between 'transaction balances' and 'speculative balances' that is so widely used in the literature. The distinction between money holdings of ultimate wealth-owners and of business enterprises is related to this distinction but only distantly so. Each of these categories of money-holders can be said to demand money partly from 'transaction' motives, partly from 'speculative' or 'asset' motives, but dollars of money are not distinguished according as they are said to be held for one or the other purpose. Rather, each dollar is, as it were, regarded as rendering a variety of services, and the holder of money as altering his money holdings until the value to him of the addition to the total flow of services produced by adding a dollar to his money stock is equal to the reduction in the flow of services produced by subtracting a dollar from each of the other forms in which he holds assets.

15. Nothing has been said above about 'banks' or producers of money. This is because their main role is in connexion with the supply of money rather than the demand for it. Their introduction does, however, blur some of the points in the above analysis: the existence of banks enables productive enterprises to acquire money balances without raising capital from ultimate wealth-owners. Instead of selling claims (bonds or equities) to them, it can sell its claims to banks, getting 'money' in exchange: in the phrase that was once so common in textbooks on money, the bank coins specific liabilities into generally acceptable liabilities. But this possibility does not alter the preceding analysis in any essential way.

16. Suppose the supply of money in nominal units is regarded as fixed or more generally autonomously determined. Equation 13 then defines the conditions under which this nominal stock of money will be the amount demanded. Even under these conditions, equation 13 alone is not sufficient to determine money income. In order to have a complete model for the determination

of money income, it would be necessary to specify the determinants of the structure of interest rates, of real income, and of the path of adjustment in the price level. Even if we suppose interest rates determined independently – by productivity, thrift and the like – and real income as also given by other forces, equation 13 only determines a unique equilibrium level of money income if we mean by this the level at which prices are stable. More generally, it determines a time path of money income for given initial values of money income.

In order to convert equation 13 into a 'complete' model of income determination, therefore, it is necessary to suppose either that the demand for money is highly inelastic with respect to the variables in v or that all these variables are to be taken as rigid and fixed.

17. Even under the most favorable conditions, for example, that the demand for money is quite inelastic with respect to the variables in v, equation 13 gives at most a theory of money income. It then says that changes in money income mirror changes in the nominal quantity of money, but it tells nothing about how much of any change in Y is reflected in real output and how much in prices. To infer this requires bringing in outside information, as, for example, that real output is at its feasible maximum, in which case any increase in money would produce the same or a larger percentage increase in prices; and so on.

18. In light of the preceding exposition, the question arises what it means to say that someone is or is not a 'quantity theorist'. Almost every economist will accept the general lines of the preceding analysis on a purely formal and abstract level, although each would doubtless choose to express it differently in detail. Yet there clearly are deep and fundamental differences about the importance of this analysis for the understanding of short- and long-term movements in general economic activity. This difference of opinion arises with respect to three different issues: (i) the stability and importance of the demand function for money; (ii) the independence of the factors affecting demand and supply; and (iii) the form of the demand function or related functions.

(i) The quantity theorist accepts the empirical hypothesis that the demand for money is highly stable – more stable than functions such as the consumption function that are offered as alternative key relations. This hypothesis needs to be hedged on both sides. On the one side, the quantity theorist need not, and generally does not, mean that the real quantity of money demanded per unit of output, or the velocity of circulation of money, is to be regarded as numerically constant over time; he does not, for example, regard it as a contradiction to the stability of the demand for money that the velocity of circulation of money rises drastically during hyperinflations. For the stability he expects is in the functional relation between the quantity of money demanded and the variables that determine it, and the sharp rise in the velocity of circulation of money during hyperinflations is entirely consistent with a stable functional relation [. . .]. On the other side, the quantity theorist must sharply limit and be prepared to specify explicitly, the variables that it is empirically important to include in the function. For to expand the number of variables regarded as significant is to empty the hypothesis of its empirical content; there is indeed little if any difference between asserting that the demand for money is highly unstable and asserting that it is a perfectly stable function of an indefinitely large number of variables.

The quantity theorist not only regards the demand function for money as stable; he also regards it as playing a vital role in determining variables that he regards as of great importance for the analysis of the economy as a whole, such as the level of money income or of prices. It is this that leads him to put greater emphasis on the demand for money than on, let us say, the demand for pins, even though the latter might be as stable as the former. It is not easy to state this point precisely, and I cannot pretend to have done so. See item (iii) below for an example of an argument against the quantity theorist along these lines.

The reaction against the quantity theory in the 1930s came largely, I believe, under this head. The demand for money, it was asserted, is a will-o'-the-wisp, shifting erratically and unpredictably with every rumor and expectation; one cannot, it was asserted, reliably specify a limited number of variables on which it depends. However, although the reaction came under this head, it was largely rationalized under the two succeeding heads.

(ii) The quantity theorist also holds that there are important factors affecting the supply of money that do not affect the demand for money. Under some circumstances these are technical conditions affecting the supply of specie; under others, political or psychological conditions determining the policies of monetary authorities and the banking system. A stable demand function is useful precisely in order to trace out the effects of changes in supply, which means that it is useful only if supply is affected by at least some factors other than those regarded as affecting demand.

The classical version of the objection under this head to the quantity theory is the so-called real-bills doctrine: that changes in the demand for money call forth corresponding changes in supply and that supply cannot change otherwise, or at least cannot do so under specified institutional arrangements. The forms which this argument takes are legion and are still widespread. Another version is the argument that the quantity theory cannot explain large price rises, because the price rise produced both the increase in demand for nominal money holdings and the increase in supply of money to meet it; that is, implicitly that the same forces affect both the demand for and the supply of money, and in the same way.

(iii) The attack on the quantity theory associated with the Keynesian underemployment analysis is based primarily on an assertion about the form of equation 7 or 11. The demand for money, it is said, is infinitely elastic at a 'small' positive interest rate. At this interest rate, which can be expected to prevail under underemployment conditions, changes in the real supply of money, whether produced by changes in prices or in the nominal stock of money, have no effect on anything. This is the famous 'liquidity trap'. A rather more complex version involves the shape of other functions as well: the magnitudes in equation 7 other than *the* interest rate, it is argued, enter into other relations in the economic system and can be regarded as determined there; the interest rate does not enter into these other functions; it can therefore be regarded as determined by this equation. So the only role of the stock of money and the demand for money is to determine the interest rate. [. . .]

25. One of the chief reproaches directed at economics as an allegedly empirical science is that it can offer so few numerical

'constants', that it has isolated so few fundamental regularities. The field of money is the chief example one can offer in rebuttal. There is perhaps no other empirical relation in economics that has been observed to recur so uniformly under so wide a variety of circumstances as the relation between substantial changes over short periods in the stock of money and in prices; the one is invariably linked with the other and is in the same direction; this uniformity is, I suspect, of the same order as many of the uniformities that form the basis of the physical sciences. And the uniformity is in more than direction. There is an extraordinary empirical stability and regularity to such magnitudes as income velocity that cannot but impress anyone who works extensively with monetary data. This very stability and regularity contributed to the downfall of the quantity theory, for it was overstated and expressed in unduly simple form; the numerical value of the velocity itself, whether income or transactions, was treated as a natural 'constant'. Now this it is not; and its failure to be so, first during and after World War I and then, to a lesser extent, after the crash of 1929, helped greatly to foster the reaction against the quantity theory. The studies [to which this essay is an introduction] are premised on a stability and regularity in monetary relations of a more sophisticated form than a numerically constant velocity. And they make, I believe, an important contribution toward extracting this stability and regularity, toward isolating the numerical 'constants' of monetary behavior. [. . .]

8 M. L. Burstein

The Quantity Theory of Money: A Critique

Excerpt from M. L. Burstein (1963), 'The quantity theory of money', *Money*, Schenkman, ch. 14, pp. 729–36.

The quantity theory of money can be viewed as a set of predictions of how *observed* prices and incomes will react over varying lengths of time to changes in monetary variables; or as a theorem on the comparative statics of certain models. Unqualified earlier formulations of the quantity theory as an empirical law have not held up. Neo-quantity theorists have made more qualified predictions. [. . .] Here too the verdict is negative: quantity theorists offer a trivial theorem in the context of simple models; it is incorrect in more complex models. [. . .]

I

There is perhaps no other empirical relation in economics that has been observed to recur so uniformly under so wide a variety of circumstances as the relation between substantial changes over short periods in the stock of money and in prices; the one is invariably linked with the other and is in the same direction; this uniformity is, I suspect, of the same order as many of the uniformities that form the basis of the physical sciences. And the uniformity is in more than direction. There is an extraordinary empirical stability and regularity to such magnitudes as income velocity that cannot but impress anyone who works extensively with monetary data. This very stability and regularity contributed to the downfall of the quantity theory, for it was overstated and expressed in unduly simple form; the numerical value of velocity itself, whether income or transactions, was treated as a natural 'constant'. Now this it is not; and its failure to be so, first during and after World War I and then, to a lesser extent, after the crash of 1929, helped greatly to foster the reaction against the quantity theory. (1, pp. 20–21.)

Since Professor Friedman is probably the most famous contemporary 'quantity theorist', this excerpt should be a good start.

However, a small cloud the size of a man's hand appears early in the game; nowhere in this essay does Friedman define the quantity theory. 'The quantity theory of money is a term evocative of a general approach rather than a label for a well-defined theory' (1, p. 3).

Let us pursue the method of science: observation made precise through quantification, formation of hypotheses intended to explain the data, test of hypotheses on additional data, reformulation, retesting, etc. Then a simple and natural transition can be made to discussion of whether quantity-theory statics concern *structures* or *reduced forms* of economic models, and whether comparative-statics properties are pertinent for purposes of prediction.

Friedman refers to awesome regularities demanding that close attention be given to monetary phenomena. We proceed to do just that – relying upon the *Chart Book* (2) – but first must make a tentative statement of the *quantity theory of money*: the chapter's themes cannot be developed without using the term.

The statement should be operational and empirically oriented. I consider the quantity theory to predict that changes in the quantity of money – defined as including currency and demand deposits and sometimes time deposits – in period t should be strongly and quite precisely associated with changes in the nominal value of transactions and income streams in period $t + 1$, surely in period $t + 6$, where the unit period is, say, a month or bimonthly. Furthermore, at full employment there should be proportional variation in the money stock and prices.[1] It holds that the single most important policy variable is the money stock or, more precisely, parameters controlling the size of the money stock. A quantity theorist puts great stress on the importance of the authorities having a firm grip on the money supply (even if this is but to facilitate execution of a non-discretionary rule). He might advocate 100 per cent reserve banking and similar reforms. He might or might not stress structural as against reduced-form relations. Still he is likely to claim that the determinants of demand for money balances are relatively few in number and sure in operation.

1. An exception would be made where price experience generates non-unitary elasticities of expectation.

Traditional Doctrine: The Quantity Theory of Money

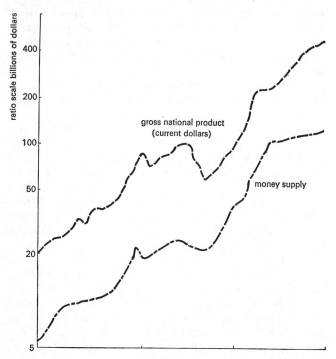

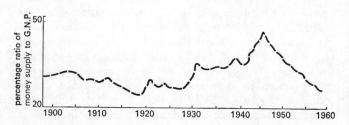

Figure 1 Gross national product and money supply

We now turn to some data. Figure 1 shows strong positive correlation between the money stock and nominal G.N.P. but, as its lower part shows, this correspondence is far from those comprising the 'basis of the physical sciences'. Obviously the relationship between the stock of money and flows highly correlated with G.N.P. is subject to substantial variation in both the short and long run. 'Unduly simple' characterizations of the association of monetary and price (and/or income) series are apt to be crashing failures.

More elaborate formulations can permit better statistical fits, perhaps at the expense of introducing a large number of variables as parameters that are not controllable or even forecastable. These estimating equations might be empirically useless; they might achieve retroactive accuracy, but of what use is it to know that variations in M shortly will lead to well-defined variations in G.N.P. only if innumerable other variables are kept under control or can accurately be predicted? Indeed there is a more important consequence of 'complicated' formulations, at least for

Table 1

U.K. Variables 1954–7 (based on the *Economist*, 1 June 1957, p. 824)[2]

Year	Wage Rate[3]	Prices[4]	Money Supply[5]	Output[6]
1954	236	244	5·72	130
1955	252	256	5·70	137
1956	272	263	5·76	136
1957 (April)	279	278	5·39	
1957 (October)	290	278	5·58 (Sept.)	143

our immediate purposes; they imply that there will *not* be proportional variation in the short run between the stock of money and, say, nominal G.N.P. even when the economy is at

2. International Monetary Fund statistics.
3. Money wages per hour, 1939 = 100.
4. Consumer price index (all retail goods), 1938 = 100.
5. Billions of pounds sterling.
6. 1948 = 100.

full employment; at least not unless an extraordinary concatenation of events occurs.

Figure 1 does not convey the full flavor of short-run fluctuation in ratios linking the money stock with national income, transactions, rates, etc. English and American experience in the 1950s does. Table 1 sketches United Kingdom experience from December 1954 through Fall 1957. The supply of money – including currency and bank deposits – fell slightly while transactions flows (nominally valued) increased substantially. The nominal value of output rose by about 16 per cent, prices by 14·5 per cent and wages by 23 per cent. Monetary velocity substantially increased. Surely the table cannot be explained by a profound regularity linking the money-supply series to any of the others.

The 1955–7 episode in the U.S. is another example:

The wholesale price index rose from an average of 110·7 during 1955 to 118·4 in August 1957. The retail price index from 114·5 to 121. Nominally valued gross national product increased from $397·5 billion in 1955 to $442·5 billion in 1957; its implicit price deflator from 100·7 to 107·3. The daily average of free reserves of member banks was $21 million in 1955 and $320 million in 1957 ($471 million in August 1957).

Money was tight, but, once again, countervailing forces were interposed. At least the authorities could not rely on automatic linkage between money stocks and income flows and price levels. Many other illustrations are available. It is hard to work annual, let alone quarterly, data of this kind to reveal overwhelming regularities. And then the outlandishly large free reserves of the 1930–41 period have mercifully been repressed.

But at least two points should be noted: (a) the theoretical underpinnings of the quantity-theory literature are interesting and informative; (b) enough regularity has been turned up to suggest that impressive 'simple' uniformities would appear if only the parameters of the system (other than the money stock) would stay put and that, if we account for the influence of relatively few other variables, a neo-quantity theory can be formulated, supporting monetary control if not the classical formulation.[7] After

7. An irregular simple empirical relationship between the stock of money and nominal G.N.P., for example, is not necessarily adverse for monetary

all, Professors Friedman, Cagan, Selden *et al.* have obtained high correlations between series of money stocks and of income and output variables when various secular, expectational and cyclical phenomena are accounted for (1, 4).

II

There is another topic under the general heading of *empirical relations*. R. S. Sayers has written:

> ... To label something as 'money', the supply of which is to behave according to rules laid down by legal authority, is to build on shifting sand .... There is no hard and fast line between what is money and what is not money .... When we worry ourselves about changes in the supply of money, our concern is in fact with the shifting liquidity position of the economy .... There is not even finality in the list of financial institutions whose behavior is relevant. New financial institutions arise to exploit new opportunities .... It is idle to say that one can somewhere find an ultimate form of money and rule that off as the grand regulator of the economic situation, a regulator that can be made to behave properly by legislator's orders ....[8]

As a proposition about comparative statics, the quantity theory would be undamaged *a priori* by Professor Sayers' strictures. Even if the relative importance of instruments classified as money were declining over time,[9] no dent would be made in its argument. Consider a system in which (non-banking) traders lacked money illusion. Control of the nominal stock of demand deposits (or of any other nominal stock) suffices to determine the equilibrium price level – and, *if nominal quantities of all other stocks are free*

---

policy if various exogenous and predetermined variables can be controlled or predicted. But a quantity theory of money does *not* emerge. Thus, I might assert with strong confidence that a 31 per cent reduction in the money supply will cause prices to fall 2 per cent over the next six months. To me, this is not a quantity-theory assertion.

8. R. S. Sayers (3, pp. 5–6). He goes on to say (footnote 1, pp. 6–7) that proposals such as 100 per cent reserve banking designed to 'eliminate private creation or destruction of money and discretionary control by central-bank authority' – the words are Friedman's – are based on 'the supposed possibility of identifying once and for all something called "money" ... I find all such proposals tempting, but they are based on a complete misconception of the origin of money.'

9. Our charts do not encourage this conclusion.

to vary, the equilibrium price level will vary proportionately with the nominal value of the 'controlled' stock. (Compare Clower and Burstein [see part three of this volume].)[10]

The Sayers argument does imply that, at the least, transitional interest-rate changes can break up the proportionality of changes in the money supply and the price level (or nominal national income) in the short run. But this need not undermine the neo-quantity theorists. Surely one will want to know about mutual savings banks, building and loan associations, insurance companies, trade-credit expansion possibilities, etc. These can determine how much pressure must be put on the commercial banks for a given end result. But the crucial concern of the neo-quantity theorists is with equation **1**:

$$y_{i(t+1)} = f^i(M_t, z_t, u_{t+1}), \qquad\qquad \mathbf{1}$$

where $y_{i(t+1)}$ is the observed value of the ith endogenous variable (say the price level) next period and where u_{t+1} is a disturbance term. M could even be defined as the supply of currency. The question is whether $y_{i(t+1)}$ can accurately be predicted from M_t or whether enough evidence has accumulated to justify the assumption that manipulation of this period's stock of currency *somehow* leads to well-defined changes in y_i. The structure through which such changes occur might be unspecified. Still, if the monetary authorities know z_t, and if the expectation of u_{t+1} is small, all will be well for the neo-quantity theorist.

Perhaps this is a roundabout way of putting the following proposition: the importance of growth of non-banking financial institutions and other sources of liquid debt instruments for effectiveness of conventional monetary policy (if manipulation of the currency supply can be conventional) is not in effects of such institutions on the level of velocity or its secular trend or cyclical movement but rather on its *predictability*. If new sources of instability are not unearthed, creation and destruction of money substitutes is not a cause for concern for neo-quantity theorists.

10. This conclusion can be intuited: equilibrium values will always be in real (as against nominal) terms. Beginning with a set of equilibrium values change the policy-determined numerator. If the other numerators and the price level change in the same proportion, the initial real state can be restored. 'The other numerators' are readily enough adjusted: more bonds are issued, etc. The italicized words in the text are crucial.

And one suspects that the professional managers of the institutions are more likely to add to than detract from predictability of financial variables.

III

We have done no more than explain why the inability of what had been known as the quantity theory of money to explain data does not *per se* undermine the neo-quantity theorists. We do not intend to concede them the field. Not at all. Indeed they are on uncertain ground. Since the neo-quantity theorists do not specify a model or even an elaborated mechanism of adjustment, it is impossible to grant them identification clearance. Furthermore, their prediction has been retroactive. Their regression analysis suggests that lags are important and that the z-vector contains variables not easily ascertained, let alone controlled, by the officials. They themselves believe that discretionary monetary control is *destabilizing*. They call for automatic rules, but are not altogether clear as to why the rules should overcome the lags. They are unclear whether interest rates are the engine of monetary policy but do not rely on real-balance effects (and in fact cannot in a credit-money world). Thus they have not offered a precise alternative *modus operandi*. In many ways the neo-quantity theory is more a mystique than a theory – at least when it ventures outside the stout bastion of logical positivism. [. . .]

References

1. M. FRIEDMAN, 'The quantity theory of money: a restatement', *Studies in the Quantity Theory of Money*, Chicago University Press, 1956, pp. 3–21.
2. CHART BOOK (Washington), U.S. Govt Printing Office, 1961.
3. R. S. SAYERS, *Central Banking after Bagehot*, Clarendon Press, 1957.
4. M. FRIEDMAN, 'The demand for money: some theoretical and empirical results', *Journal of Political Economy*, vol. 67, 1959, pp. 327–51.

Part Three Contemporary Theory: Neo-Walrasian Equilibrium Analysis

Monetary theory as an intellectual discipline appeared to be dying of inanition when Don Patinkin infused new life into the subject in a series of analytical transfusions between 1948 and 1956. In retrospect, what then appeared to be a major reorientation of accepted theory was more in the nature of a final consolidation of classical and neo-classical ideas. Patinkin's conceptual universe now appears to be just a more precise and elaborate portrait of the barter world of Mill, Walras and Marshall, its only novel feature being that 'money' appears among the set of commodities bartered. The significance of Patinkin's work thus lies not so much in what he says about monetary theory as in what he unintentionally reveals about the analytical and empirical weaknesses of established price theory.

9 D. Patinkin

Money and Prices

Excerpt from D. Patinkin (1965), *Money, Interest and Prices*, Harper & Row, 2nd edn, ch. 3, pp. 34–59.

I The Problem Defined: Walras' Law

[. . .] to explain the determination of equilibrium prices in the market [. . .] we take as our independent variables [. . .] the individuals' initial endowments, their tastes and the structure of the market. We shall be interested in presenting first a static analysis of our problem (the nature of the equilibrium position), then a dynamic analysis (the nature of the market forces which bring the economy to equilibrium from an initial position of disequilibrium), and finally a comparative-static analysis (a comparison of equilibrium positions before and after a specified change in one or more of the independent variables). [. . .]

In general, what is an equilibrium set of prices for one array of initial endowments will not be an equilibrium set for another. For assume that we begin with a market in equilibrium at a certain set of prices, and that there occurs an arbitrary change in initial endowments, either in their distribution among individuals in the economy and/or in the sum total of initial endowments of one or more goods. We know that under these circumstances there will be changes in the amounts of excess demands. At the original set of prices, there will now exist positive or negative amounts of excess demands in at least some of the markets. Hence this original set is no longer an equilibrium one. Thus the term 'equilibrium prices' must always be expressly or tacitly qualified by the phrase 'at a given array of initial endowments'. The same qualification must be made, *mutatis mutandis*, for the other independent variables of the analysis.

There is one fundamental property of equilibrium prices in our economy which must be noted at the outset. Assume that at a certain set of prices each of the commodity markets is in equilibrium. It follows that the money market must also be in equilibrium. For the amount of excess demand for money equals the aggregate value of the amounts of excess supplies of commodities. In equilibrium, the amount of excess supply in each commodity market is, by definition, zero. Hence the amount of excess demand for money must also be zero. Thus, in order to determine whether a certain set of prices is an equilibrium set for our economy, it is not necessary to examine the money market; instead, it suffices to show that this set of prices establishes equilibrium in each of the commodity markets alone. This relationship, which is a particular form of what is known as Walras' law, is basic to the following analysis.[1]

It should be emphasized that there is no implication here that the equilibrating process in the money market is in any sense less significant than that in any other market. We could just as well have arbitrarily selected any one market and stated that equilibrium in all the other markets implies equilibrium in the chosen one too. This is the general form of Walras' law, which follows from the general form of the budget restraint in our economy. If we have chosen to work with the particular form of this law set out in the preceding paragraph, it is only out of considerations of symmetry and simplicity.

It should also be emphasized that though they are logically connected in our economy, Walras' law and the budget restraint are conceptually distinct relations. To anticipate the terminology of the next section, the former deals with excess-demand *equations*, the latter with excess-demand *functions*. Indeed, we can conceive of an economy in which the existence of the restraint does *not* imply the existence of the law. This special case also makes clear the impropriety of referring to Walras' law as an 'identity' which must always be true.

II The Equality of the Number of Equations and Variables

Let us now examine the static meaning of the equilibrium set of prices. Define first the market excess-demand equation for a given good. This is a restriction which states that prices are such that the amount of market excess demand – that is, the value of the

1. See reference (1). This law was so named by O. Lange (2).

market excess-demand function for the good in question – is zero. By definition, this equation is satisfied if and only if the market for the good is in equilibrium.

Assume now that there are n goods in the economy: $n-1$ commodities and paper money. As will be recalled, this money serves as the medium of exchange and store of value but not as the unit of account. To these n goods correspond, respectively, n market excess-demand equations. Actually, however, only $n-1$ (at most) of these equations are independent. That is, only $n-1$ of these equations place independent restrictions on the unknown equilibrium prices. For any set of prices which satisfies $n-1$ market excess-demand equations must also necessarily satisfy the nth. This, of course, is an alternative statement of Walras' law.

Thus the equilibrium set of money prices can be regarded as the solution to a set of $n-1$ independent, simultaneous equations in these $n-1$ unknown prices. Now, equality between the number of unknowns and the number of independent equations is neither a necessary nor a sufficient condition for the existence of a solution. Nor does it insure that solutions, if they do exist, will be only finite in number. For our purposes, however, these highly complicated issues can be ignored. Instead, we shall accept such equality as justifying the reasonableness of the assumption that one and the same set of money prices can simultaneously create equilibrium in each and every market. We shall also assume that only one such set exists.

Quite deliberately, we have omitted all discussion of the choice of the dependent equation to be 'eliminated'. Posing the question in this form might lead to misconceptions. It might be taken to imply that less is known about economic behavior in the 'eliminated' market than in others or that the 'eliminated' market is in some sense less significant. It might be taken to imply that there is a substantive choice involved and that different decisions as to which equation to 'eliminate' will produce different results. Actually, of course, none of these statements is true. As can readily be deduced from the general form of the budget restraint, the properties of the 'eliminated' excess-demand equation are completely specified by those of the other $n-1$ equations. The corresponding general form of Walras' law then brings out the complete neutrality of the 'elimination' process. It should also make clear that no matter what equation is eliminated, the solution for the equilibrium set of prices obtained from the remaining equations is always the same.

In order to avoid any such possible misconceptions, it is advisable not to 'eliminate' explicitly any equation at all. Instead, the system is best considered as having n equations, equal in number to the n goods in the economy. But the excess-demand equation for money should be written in the form dictated by the budget restraint. This makes clear the nature of the equational dependence described by Walras' law.

The discussion has until now been concerned with the $n-1$ money prices. A unique solution for these implies, of course, a unique solution for the $n-2$ relative prices. On the other hand, it does not imply a unique solution for the n accounting prices. For if one set of accounting prices yields (after dividing through by the accounting price of money) a given set of money prices, any multiple of that set will also yield this given set. Thus there is an infinite number of sets of accounting prices corresponding to the same set of money prices. We might also explain this indeterminacy of equilibrium accounting prices by noting that there are n such prices and only $n-1$ independent excess-demand equations. An economic interpretation of this indeterminacy is presented in what immediately follows.[2]

III The Method of Successive Approximation: The Determinacy of Relative and Money Prices; the Indeterminacy of Accounting prices

Who solves the equations?

The fact that the number of independent excess-demand equations is equal to the number of unknown money prices and that the system can be formally solved might some day interest a central planning bureau, duly equipped with electronic computers and charged with setting equilibrium prices by decree. But what

2. Note that this proves the indeterminacy of accounting prices *without* resorting to the mere counting of equations and unknowns.

is the relevance of this fact for a free market functioning under conditions of perfect competition?

It was concern with this question which led Walras to formulate his celebrated theory of *tâtonnement*. This was a crucial element in his vision of the economy as reflecting the operations of a set of simultaneous equations. In simplest terms, this theory states that the free market itself acts like a vast computer. For start with any arbitrary set of prices – Walras' '*prix criés au hasard*'. In general, it will not be an equilibrium one. That is, at this set of prices there will be some markets with positive amounts of excess demand and others with negative amounts. Prices will then rise in the former markets and fall in the latter, bringing us to a new set of prices. In general, this set, too, will not be an equilibrium one. Once again prices will change in accordance with the state of excess demand in the various markets, a third set of prices will thereby be reached, and so the process will go on. It is by this continuous groping – *tâtonnement* – that the economy ultimately finds its way to the equilibrium position.

The principle by which the market automatically generates these successive approximations is admittedly a primitive one. Actual computers operate according to much more efficient principles. But what our imaginary computer lacks in the elegance of its principle it makes up by its size. Indeed, this size enables it to deal with systems of equations far beyond the practical capacity of any existing computer. Thus, not only is there no need for a conscious mind to solve our excess-demand equations, but it is also doubtful if any mind – human or electronic – could today be depended upon for such a solution.

So far we have followed Walras in failing to deal adequately with one fundamental issue. It is one thing to say that the process of *tâtonnement* prevents the market from remaining at a non-equilibrium set of prices and even exerts some sort of pressure in the direction of equilibrium. It is quite another to say that this process must ultimately bring the market to the equilibrium prices themselves. In other words, Walras' theory of *tâtonnement* depends for its ultimate and rigorous validation on the modern economic theory of dynamics. Conversely, the significance of this latter theory can best be appreciated within the framework provided by Walras. From this viewpoint, a stable system is one in which the process of *tâtonnement* will succeed in establishing equilibrium prices; an unstable system is one in which it will not.[3]

This whole process of successive approximation is assumed to take place during the marketing period, Monday afternoon. To give it concrete embodiment, we might think of a central registry where all offers to buy and sell at the proclaimed prices are recorded. The registry is presided over by a chairman whose function is to raise the price of any commodity for which the registry shows an excess of buyers and to lower the price of any commodity for which it shows an excess of sellers. As indicated above, none of the offers are binding unless the proclaimed set of prices at which they were made turns out to be the equilibrium set. If it does not, individuals are free to recontract at the new set of prices proclaimed accordingly by the chairman. This Edgeworthian assumption (4) serves its usual purpose of precluding the completion of any prior purchases which might otherwise affect the final equilibrium position itself. In other words, this assumption assures that no matter which of the infinite number of paths open to it a convergent sequence of approximations takes, it must always reach the same equilibrium set of prices.

Let us use this assumption of recontract to show how the corresponding process of *tâtonnement* can be used to explain two main results: the determinacy of equilibrium money prices and the indeterminacy of equilibrium accounting prices.[4]

Consider an economy during the marketing period. Assume first that the process of *tâtonnement* is at a stage where the absolute level of the presently proclaimed prices is the same as that in the ultimate equilibrium position but that the ratios between these proclaimed money prices differ from the corresponding equilibrium ratios. Then there are amounts of excess

3. The implicit reference here is, of course, to the dynamic theory first presented by Samuelson and subsequently developed by Arrow, Block, Hurwicz and others.

Some time after the above was written, I discovered that R. M. Goodwin had presented the same concept of dynamic analysis (3), but he misinterprets Walras and fails to see that this is precisely the role that Walras assigned to his *tâtonnement*.

4. The approach of the following three paragraphs is adapted from that of Wicksell, *Interest and Prices* (15, pp. 23–4, 39–40).

demand for those commodities whose relative prices are respectively lower than the corresponding equilibrium prices and amounts of excess supply for those commodities whose relative prices are respectively higher. Accordingly, in the next round of approximations, prices of the former goods will be raised and prices of the latter lowered. In brief, the existence of any discrepancy between the proclaimed relative prices and the equilibrium ones automatically generates market forces which themselves tend to eliminate the initial discrepancy. Clearly, these same corrective forces are also automatically called into being by

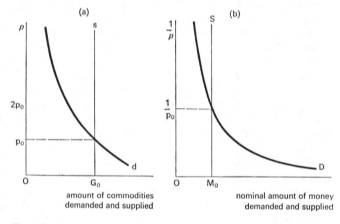

Figure 1

any accidental departure from equilibrium values, should they once be reached.

Assume now that the process is at a stage where relative prices are the same as in the ultimate equilibrium position, but the absolute level of money prices is, say, lower. This implies that the real value of money balances is higher than in the equilibrium position. Correspondingly, there exist amounts of excess demand in the various markets exerting corrective pressures on the prices. In this case the stability of the dynamic process need not be assumed, but can be readily established by graphical analysis. For since relative prices are assumed constant during the *tâtonnement*, all commodities can be considered as a single composite good with the price p. Assume (as is reasonable) that this good is not an inferior one. Then the positive real-balance effect generated by a decrease in p causes the amount demanded to increase. This is represented by the negatively sloped demand curve d in Figure 1(a). On the other hand, the supply of commodities in our exchange economy is fixed: hence this is represented by the vertical line s. It is clear from Figure 1(a) that at any point below (above) p_0 there is an excess demand (supply) driving the price level upwards (downwards) again. Hence no matter what the initial level of p, the automatic functioning of the market will bring it to the equilibrium level p_0. Under the stated assumptions, the system is stable in the large as well as in the small.

By Walras' law, this conclusion can alternatively (and equivalently) be demonstrated in terms of the demand (D) and supply (S) for nominal money holdings. This is done in Figure 1(b). The demand curve for these holdings is generally negatively sloped. Furthermore, it can be shown that even in the special case where this demand curve does have a positive slope in some regions, these regions must (if commodities are not inferior) lie leftwards of M_0. Hence we see from Figure 1(b) that at any point above (below) $1/p_0$ there exists an excess supply (demand) for money driving the reciprocal of the absolute price level downwards (upwards) again.[5]

Let us now return to our process of *tâtonnement* and assume that it has reached equilibrium but that the chairman accidentally continues to 'cry out' prices. In particular, assume that he proclaims a new set of accounting prices, each of which exceeds the corresponding price of the equilibrium set by a constant percentage. This increase changes neither relative prices, nor real incomes, nor the real value of initial money balances. Hence none of the amounts of excess demand for commodities are thereby

5. Note that the assumption of equiproportionate price movements effectively reduces the stability problem to the relatively simple one of a two-good economy.

Note also that the supply curve in Figure 1(a) would remain a vertical line even if we were to drop the assumption of an exchange economy and assume that supply depends only upon relative prices. Nor would the argument be affected if we assumed supply to depend also on real balances – provided it was a decreasing function of such balances, so that the supply curve in Figure 1(b) would have a positive slope.

affected. Therefore, since the commodity markets were in equilibrium before this unnecessary *tâtonnement*, they must remain so afterwards too. By Walras' law, the equilibrium of the money market must, therefore, also remain undisturbed. Thus the accidental proportionate departure of accounting prices from an initial equilibrium position creates no amounts of excess demand for any good – and hence generates no market forces anywhere in the economy – which might operate to force these prices back to their original levels. Therefore, if one set of accounting prices is an equilibrium set, every multiple of that set must also be one. Accounting prices are indeterminate.

Actually, the existence of this indeterminacy is almost self-evident. Accounting prices are not even observable market phenomena. Hence it is certainly not surprising that their equilibrium values cannot be determined by market forces. Instead, these forces must be supplemented by an external decree arbitrarily fixing the accounting price of one – and only one – of the goods in the economy. If equilibrium money prices are already determined, this suffices to determine the equilibrium accounting prices of all other goods. Thus, for example, if we know the pound prices of goods and are told that the accounting price of a paper pound is arbitrarily set at 20/21 guineas, we can immediately determine the corresponding guinea prices of all other goods by simply multiplying their pound prices by 20/21. Similarly, if the accounting price of the pound were to be arbitrarily doubled and set instead at 40/21 guineas, this would immediately fix the guinea prices of all other goods at levels which were also double those of the original case. Clearly, the money and relative prices of these two cases are, respectively, identical. Equally clearly, in the absence of such an arbitrary specification, equilibrium guinea prices cannot possibly be determined.

Thus equilibrium money prices and equilibrium accounting prices are determined by two distinct processes: the former by internal market forces, the latter by the arbitrary decree of a *deus ex machina*. No such distinction exists between money prices and relative prices. Both of these are simultaneously determined by market forces alone. Only conceptually can we decompose these forces into two components, one which operates through the real-balance effect and thereby determines the absolute level of money

131

prices, and one which operates through the substitution effects and thereby determines the ratios of these prices.

IV The Effects of an Increase in the Quantity of Money Analysed in the Commodity Markets

Let us now consider an economy in equilibrium and examine the effect of injecting into it an additional quantity of money. We continue with the assumption that to every set of given conditions there corresponds one and only one equilibrium position and that the process of successive approximation described in Section III always succeeds in reaching this position.

Assume that we stand at the close of the Monday marketing period with the set of equilibrium prices having just been reached. Let there now be some external force which, say, suddenly doubles the initial money holdings of each individual of the economy. The immediate implication of this increase is that the marketing period must be reopened and the *tâtonnement* recommenced, for what constituted the equilibrium set of prices before the increase cannot constitute one afterwards. In particular, at these prices real balances are now higher than in the original equilibrium position, whereas relative prices and nonmonetary wealth are the same. Hence at these prices a universal state of excess demand now replaces the original state of equilibrium.

In accordance with our accepted dynamic principle, these pressures of excess demand initiate a series of successive approximations which push proclaimed money prices upwards. Assume first, for simplicity, that these prices rise during the *tâtonnement* in an equiproportionate manner. Use can then be made of Figure 1(a) to represent the effect of the doubling of the quantity of money on the demand for commodities by an upward shift in curve d which brings it to twice its original height at each and every quantity. On the other hand, the monetary increase does not affect the supply curve s. Hence the reopened *tâtonnement* will bring the price level to the new intersection point at $2p_0$.

Even if we drop the assumption about the nature of price movements during the *tâtonnement*, it can readily be seen that the equilibrium set of prices corresponding to the doubled quantity of money is one in which each and every price is doubled. For relative prices and real wealth (inclusive of initial money holdings) corresponding to this new set are the same as they were in the original equilibrium position; hence the amounts of market excess demand for each commodity and for real money holdings must respectively also be the same as in this position, that is, zero. Hence, if the system is stable, and if to every set of conditions there corresponds a unique equilibrium, the economy must reach the new equilibrium position just described.[6]

The validity of this conclusion clearly depends on the assumption that the individuals' initial money holdings are all increased in the same proportion, for consider a doubling of the total quantity of money in the economy which does not take place in this way. In such a case the economy need not be restored to equilibrium by a doubling of all prices. For the real value of the increased money holdings of *each* individual (and hence his real wealth) will then not be the same as in the original equilibrium position. Hence the amounts of market excess demands will also not be the same. In general, the new equilibrium position in this case will involve higher relative prices for those goods favored by individuals whose money holdings have more than doubled and lower relative prices for those goods favored by individuals whose holdings have less than doubled. This fact was duly emphasized by the classical and neo-classical advocates of the quantity theory of money.

On the other hand, the preceding argument does not presume any restriction on the nature of the dependence of the commodity excess demand on real wealth, inclusive of real balances. As a corollary, neither does it presume that all individuals in the economy must react in the same way to changes in this wealth. For since real balances in the two equilibrium positions are identically the same, the question of what would happen to excess demands if these balances were changed can have no relevance

6. Note that the assumption that there exists an original equilibrium set of prices implies that there also exists a new one; no separate existence assumption on this score is required. Note also that even if we permit several solutions, one of them must be a multiple of the original set. But in this case an increase in the quantity of money need not increase prices proportionately; for prices may move to a new equilibrium set which is *not* this multiple.

for the comparative-static analysis. But it is very much relevant to the dynamic analysis, for the path followed by the economy during the period of dynamic adjustment is clearly dependent upon the way in which individuals react to the temporarily increased real balances which mark this period. These observations hold even if we assume that some of the commodities are inferior. As just explained, this cannot affect the nature of the new equilibrium position itself, but it can and does affect the dynamic process by which this position is reached and in some cases might even prevent it being reached at all.

One further point might be noted. It is frequently said that a change in the quantity of money is equivalent to a change in the monetary unit. There is much truth in this statement, but it is also subject to two fundamental reservations. Firstly, in the case of a change of the monetary unit everyone is aware that the change in the quantity of money has taken place in an equiproportionate way for all individuals. Hence – generalizing from their own behavior – they expect everyone's demand prices to change in the same proportion. Secondly, when monetary authorities announce such a change, they also effectively announce the new set of equilibrium prices which corresponds to it: they effectively inform the public by how many places to move over the decimal point in the price quotations. Thus there is actually someone 'solving the equations'. For both these reasons there is no need for the new equilibrium prices in such cases to be determined by the workings of the dynamic market forces described above.

V The Effects of an Increase in the Quantity of Money Analysed in the Money Market

Let us now approach the problem from the viewpoint of the money market. Clearly, we must reach the same conclusions as in the preceding analysis, where the approach is from that of the commodity markets. Nevertheless, it is interesting to show explicitly the obverse relationship that exists between these two approaches.

Assume once again for simplicity that prices change during the *tâtonnement* in an equiproportionate manner. Then the demand and supply for nominal money holdings corresponding to the aggregate initial endowment of money M_0 (distributed in a given way among the individuals of the economy) can be represented respectively by the curves D and S of Figure 1(b), reproduced here in Figure 2.

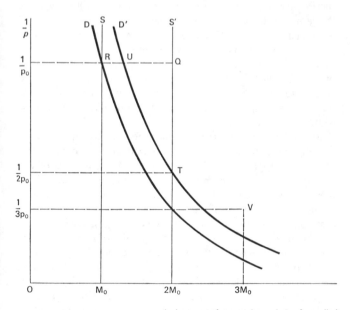

nominal amount of money demanded and supplied

Figure 2

Assume now that the initial money endowments are all doubled, so that the total quantity of money in the economy rises to $2M_0$. This clearly causes a rightward shift of the supply curve to S' in Figure 2. Consider now the demand curve. Not all of the increased endowment is expended in the commodity markets. That is, there is also a real-balance effect in the money market. This is reflected diagrammatically as a rightward shift from D to D': at the same level of absolute prices, individuals – because of

135

their increased wealth – feel themselves able to indulge in a higher level of liquidity.

We now note that the form of D, together with the assumption that there is no money illusion, completely specify the form of D'. For if according to curve D a certain amount of money is demanded at a given price level, then at twice that level – and twice the initial endowment of money – the curve D' will show twice that amount demanded. In particular, since point R in Figure 2 lies on curve D, point T must lie on curve D'. But point T must obviously also lie on S'. Hence the form of D' is necessarily such that it intersects S' at the point T, corresponding to a price level of $2p_0$. Similarly, if the initial endowment of money were increased to $3M_0$, the new demand curve (not drawn in Figure 2) must intersect the new supply curve at the point V, corresponding to the price level $3p_0$.

It remains to describe the dynamic process by which the market actually moves from R to T. It is here that we can see the advantage of the approach of the preceding section over that of this one. For the essential nature of the market forces which activate this process are neither directly nor concretely pictured in Figure 2. Instead, we must resort to the reflection which this diagram casts on the state of demand in the commodity markets. Thus consider the price level p_0. After the quantity of money has been doubled, there exists at this price an amount of excess supply equal to UQ. But an excess supply of money means an excess demand for commodities. Therefore, at this price level pressures exist in the commodity markets to drive p up and hence $1/p$ down. Figure 2 can thus be used only indirectly to explain the *tâtonnement* by which the point T is finally reached. Nevertheless, we do in this way ultimately reaffirm the conclusion of the preceding section: that an increase in the quantity of money causes a proportionate increase in equilibrium money prices.

VI Demand Curves and Market-Equilibrium Curves

Let us now consider the points R, T and V in Figure 2 – and all other possible equilibrium points that can be generated by changing the quantity of money. The locus of these points is traced out in Figure 3. It is obvious that the curve which emerges in this diagram is a rectangular hyperbola. It is equally obvious that it is *not* a demand curve. Indeed, by construction it is the locus of intersection points of demand curves and their corresponding supply curves.

To be more precise, behind Figure 3 there is a conceptual

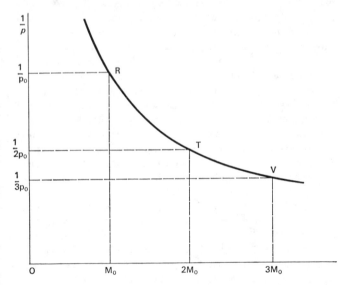

nominal quantity of money in the economy

Figure 3

market-experiment in which we take an economy in equilibrium, introduce into it a disturbance in the form of an equiproportionate change in initial money holdings, and then let this disturbance work itself out in all its manifestations until the economy returns again to an equilibrium position. The results of this experiment give us one point in Figure 3 – a point which associates a quantity of money in the economy with its corresponding equilibrium level of money prices. By continuing to change the quantity of money in this way we generate additional points. In accordance with the direct proportionate relationship that has been shown to hold

137

between this quantity and the equilibrium price level, these points must trace out a rectangular hyperbola.

A curve generated in this way from market-experiments will be denoted henceforth by the term 'market-equilibrium curve'. It must be sharply distinguished conceptually from a demand curve – which, by definition, is generated by individual-experiments. In particular, it cannot be overemphasized that the market-equilibrium curve of Figure 3 will have the form of a rectangular hyperbola regardless of the form of the demand curves of Figure 2. This is evident from the graphical argument of the preceding section. In terms of our present terminology we can explain this independence by noting that these demand curves describe the outcome of an individual-experiment which is not at all relevant to the market-experiment under consideration. For at the close of this market-experiment, the individual finds himself confronted with an equiproportionate change in prices *and* in his initial money holdings; whereas any *given* demand curve of Figure 2 describes the results of an individual-experiment in which prices are changed, but the individual's initial money holdings are kept constant.

This independence obviously disappears as soon as we consider a market-experiment and a *relevant* individual-experiment. Thus the market-equilibrium curve of Figure 3 implies that in an individual-experiment in which the individual is confronted with an equiproportionate change in prices and initial money holdings, he increases the amount of money demanded proportionately.

VII Long-run and Short-run Equilibria

The discussion until now has been tacitly restricted to short-run equilibrium analysis; it has examined the forces that bring the economy to the equilibrium position that corresponds to the initial distribution of money endowments. But this equilibrium position will not generally be a long-run one in the sense that (other things equal) it will continue to prevail week after week. It is to this question that we now turn.[7]

7. On this distinction between short and long run, see (5, pp. 170–71). It is, however, not appropriate to describe this distinction as one between

The nature of the problem is most conveniently illustrated by Figure 4. For simplicity, assume that the economy consists of only two individuals, A and B, and that each has exactly the same Engel curve for real balances. Assume further that the equilibrium price level determined at the end of Week I is p_1, and that when evaluated at this price level the initial real balances of A and B are Oq and Or, respectively. Thus A has increased his cash balances over the week by an amount measured by PQ = QV, while B has drawn his down by SR = RX. By the assumption that p_1 is the equilibrium price, PQ = SR; that is, A's excess demand for money *equals* B's excess supply.

Assume now that our individuals start Week II with the money balances carried over from the end of Week I; but with a new commodity endowment exactly equal to that received the preceding Monday. Two related things now happen: Firstly, though the real incomes of the individuals in Week II are, by assumption, the same as in Week I, their initial value of real balances (evaluated at p_1) are different. Hence, the amounts they demand of commodities and real balances in Week II will also differ. In particular, A's initial balances are now Ou instead of Oq; correspondingly, the amount of balances he wishes to hold are uU instead of qQ. Similarly, B's initial balances are Ow instead of Or, and his amount demanded wW instead of rR. In terms of Figure 1, shifts in the demand curves have taken place.

'flow equilibrium' and 'stock equilibrium', for in the present context the variables of both the short- and long-run analyses have the dimensions of a stock.

I might also note that the distinction here between short- and long-run equilibrium is related to Hicks' distinction between 'temporary equilibrium' and 'equilibrium over time' (14, p. 132). The latter, however, is defined by Hicks primarily in terms of constancy of prices, whereas (following Bushaw and Clower) we shall be interested in constancy of quantities as well.

The absence of any long-run analysis in the first edition of this book has been justly criticized by G. C. Archibald and R. G. Lipsey (6). Contrary to their implications, however, it will be seen that the filling of this lacuna does not require any fundamental changes in the analytical framework developed above.

The following is based on the Archibald–Lipsey treatment. We shall, however, present the argument in terms of Engel curves – whereas they have done so in terms of indifference-curve analysis. The Engel-curve approach is simpler and also lends itself more readily to a discussion of the determination and stability of the long-run equilibrium position.

Secondly, the price level p_1 will generally no longer be an equilibrium one.[8] For it is clear from Figure 4 that A's excess demand (UV) exceeds B's excess supply (WX). Hence there exists an excess supply in the commodity markets pushing prices down

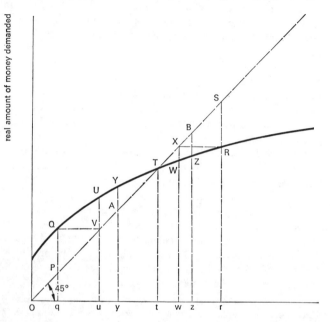

initial value of real balances

Figure 4

there. As the price level falls, the initial balances of both A and B increase in value. This will continue until the resulting real-balance effect will once again equate A's excess demand with B's excess supply. This is portrayed in Figure 4 as occurring when A and B's initial real balances are Oy and Oz, respectively. The equilibrium nature of this position is reflected in the fact that AY = BZ.

8. In principle, it is possible for the equilibrium level to remain the same. As can be seen from Figure 4, this would be the case if the Engel curve were linear. (Cf. 6, p. 6, footnote 1.)

Obviously, this process will not stop at this point. Week III will find the individuals once again starting with different initial balances than they did in Week II, and this in turn will generally cause the equilibrium price level of Week III to differ from that of Week II. Let us assume that this process continues: that is, every week the individual starts anew with exactly the same commodity endowment, and with the cash balances carried over from the end of the preceding week. Let us also assume that the economy converges in this way to point T. At this point long-run equilibrium will have been reached; for an individual with the initial cash balances Ot will neither add to nor subtract from them over the week. Hence he will start every week with exactly the same cash balances as the preceding one; hence his amounts demanded will remain the same; and hence the equilibrium price level will remain the same.[9]

Note that the process of reaching long-run equilibrium is marked not only by changes in the price level, but also (and even more fundamentally) by a redistribution of money balances between A and B. More generally, the movement toward long-run equilibrium generates a unique distribution of initial balances among the individuals in the economy. In other words, the initial balances of the individuals in their position of long-run equilibrium are not among the given conditions of the analysis (as is the case with the corresponding balances of the short run), but among the dependent variables determined by the analysis itself.

Let us now take a step backwards and construct demand curves within a long-run equilibrium framework. We shall say that an individual is in long-run equilibrium if he is neither adding to nor subtracting from his initial cash balances under the given endowment and price-level conditions with which he is confronted. That is, the individual is at T in Figure 5. Let us now take this individual and conduct the following individual-experiment with him: We lower the price level, wait for him to return once again to a position of long-run equilibrium, and then compare the

9. Clearly, the system need not necessarily converge to T. The determination of the conditions under which such convergence will take place (i.e. under which the system is stable) involves the solution of a system of non-linear difference equations – something which cannot be attempted here.

amount of money demanded in this new position with that in his original one.

The results of such an experiment can be traced out in Figure 5. As a result of the price decrease with which he is confronted, the real value of the individual's initial real balances increases from Ot to Oa.

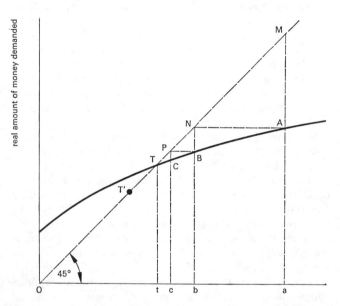

Figure 5

At this point the individual is drawing down his real balances by AM = AN; so that he starts the following week with balances of Ob. Here the individual continues to draw down his balances – this time by BN = BP. This process will continue until the individual returns once again to the same level of real balances – Ot – from which he started. Thus we see from Figure 5 that the long-run demand for real cash balances is a constant, independent of the price level.

There is a straightforward interpretation of this result. What

Figure 5 tells us is that the initial decline in the price level effectively presents the individual with a windfall gain which increases his wealth, and that within our simple model the individual will plan to make use of this gain entirely for the purpose of purchasing additional commodities in the subsequent weeks. This means that when the individual enters the 'last' week (i.e. the one in which he re-establishes his state of long-run equilibrium), he does so with initial *real* cash balances equal to those of the original week of long-run equilibrium. That is, his initial *nominal* balances of this 'last' week have been reduced (as compared with the original equilibrium position) in the same proportion as the price level. Thus, demand remains invariant under a change in the price level; which means that the demand for *nominal* balances has the form of a rectangular hyperbola.[10]

Let us now conduct an alternative long-run conceptual individual-experiment. Consider an individual whose long-run equilibrium demand curve for nominal money balances is represented by the rectangular hyperbola D in Figure 6 (for the moment ignore the vertical lines at M_0 and $2M_0$). Assume that the individual is at point A on this curve and let us make a once-and-for-all increase in his initial money holdings – while keeping the price level constant. From the argument just presented, it is clear that the individual will choose to use up this windfall gain entirely in the acquisition of commodities during the ensuing weeks; so that in the long run he will return to nominal money holdings of M_0. This means that the increase in the quantity of money will not cause any shift in the long-run demand curve depicted in Figure 6. This will obviously also be true if the curve D were to represent the long-run demand curve of the economy as a whole.

Let us now turn from individual experiments to market experiments. Consider an economy whose demand and supply curves for money are represented by D and S, respectively, in

10. Note also the identity with the short-run individual-experiment, in which the individual is confronted with a change in the price level only – but in which the resulting real-balance effect is used even in the short run entirely to increase the demand for commodities.

The quotation marks around 'last' in this paragraph reflect the fact that – as can be seen from Figure 5 – the individual will converge to his new position of long-run equilibrium only after an infinite number of weeks.

Figure 6. Assume that the economy is in the initial position of long-run equilibrium represented by point A. Let the quantity of money in the economy now double. As we have just seen, this does not cause any shift in the demand curve D. On the other hand, it causes the supply curve to shift from S to S' – thus creating an excess supply of money equal to AB. Just as in our

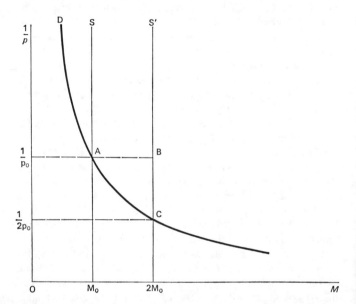

Figure 6

analysis of the short-run equilibrium (above, Figure 2), this means that there is an excess demand for commodities – generated by the positive real-balance effect – driving prices upwards. This process will continue until the economy reaches the new position of long-run equilibrium C with a price level twice as high as the original one. Thus in the long run, as in the short run, a mere comparison of the two equilibrium positions will not reveal any real-balance effect.[11] On the other hand, the stability of the

11. But to infer from this that for 'comparative statics the real-balance effect is irrelevant' (6, p. 9) is like inferring from the equality of the equilib-

equilibrium position in both 'runs' is vitally dependent on the real-balance effect generated by any chance departure of the price level from it. Thus when we come to evaluate the significance of the real-balance effect for economic theory, the really important distinction that we must make is not between short run and long run, but between being concerned with the stability of an equilibrium position – with the possibility of its being reached by the automatic workings of a market economy – and not being concerned.[12]

There is, however, one noteworthy difference between the short- and long-run analyses: namely, that the doubling of the price level in Figure 6 is independent of the way the new quantity of money is injected into the economy (6, pp. 8–9).[13] In technical terms, since each individual's long-run curve remains invariant under an increase in the quantity of money, so must the aggregate of these curves, irrespective of the way this increase is distributed among the individuals of the economy.

It might also be noted – though this is really inherent in all of the above – that if the quantity of money is doubled when the economy is *not* in long-run equilibrium, then the subsequent long-run equilibrium position will *not* be marked by a price level

---

rium marginal rates of transformation in the increasing-cost case of international trade that the law of comparative advantage is then irrelevant for comparative-statics analysis (cf. also 7).

12. As Baumol has already indicated, Archibald and Lipsey's discussion of the real-balance effect is misleading because of its failure to see the dynamic stability context in which the role of this effect has been presented (8).

13. Another difference between the short-run analysis of Figure 2 and the long-run one of Figure 6 is that the two equilibrium positions (A and C) of the latter correspond to two different weeks, whereas the two positions of the former (R and T) correspond to two alternative positions of the same week, one with the initial quantity of money M_0, and one, $2M_0$. This is related to the discussion in the next paragraph of the text.

It might, however, be argued that Figure 2 corresponds more closely to the true sense of the traditional quantity theory in showing that the changed quantity of money makes the price level different *from what it otherwise would have been*. For such a note in the writings of Ricardo, see J. Viner (9, pp. 126–7, 176–7).

Views similar to the following have already been expressed by R. J. Ball and R. Bodkin (10) and Hahn (7, p. 38).

double that of the time of injection. For, as shown at the beginning of this section, the original short-run equilibrium price level would have changed over time even if no change in the quantity of money had taken place. Thus the effect of doubling the quantity of money can be measured only by comparing the actual price level in the long-run equilibrium position with the level which would have prevailed had the quantity of money remained constant. More generally, any change in price level between two periods must be decomposed into that part which would in any event have taken place in the course of the long-run equilibrating process and that part which takes place as a result of a change in one or more of the exogenous variables.

In order not to leave a misleading impression, we must conclude this long-run analysis (and particularly the discussion of the rectangular-hyperbola demand curve of Figure 6) by reminding the reader that it is actually restricted to a very special and somewhat incongruous case. For though attempting to deal with long-run problems, the analysis has continued to be based on a model of one-week-horizon men whose real income (and wealth) is constant over time and who can hold their excess of income over consumption (i.e. their savings) only in the form of the sterile assets, money. As soon, however, as we extend the argument to the standard case in which savings can also be held in the form of an interest-yielding asset (say, the bond), the foregoing results will generally no longer obtain. In particular, it can then be shown that under fairly reasonable assumptions about consumers' behavior there does not exist a stable long-run equilibrium for the individual in the sense defined at the beginning of this section. Instead, the individual will make use of his interest earnings on savings to generate continuous growth in his levels of wealth, income and consumption. Correspondingly, he will generally not consume all of the windfall gain represented by the real-balance effect, but will devote part of it to increase his savings and thereby generate a permanent upward shift in the planned growth-path of his wealth holdings – including wealth in the form of money.[14]

14. See the paper by Nissan Liviatan, 'On the long-run theory of consumption and real balances' (11). This also shows that the contrary implication of R. W. Clower and M. L. Burstein (12) is a consequence of their special assumptions.

Thus the demand for money in this case will not be independent of the price level.

In a similar way, the concept of long-run equilibrium loses its meaning in a production economy with investment – and even in the simplest of Keynesian models.[15] What becomes relevant instead is the equilibrium expansion-path of the system. And the nature of this path (particularly the price-level developments which characterize it) will generally be influenced by the real-balance effect. Similarly, the distribution effect of the increased quantity of money need no longer be neutral, but may influence the rate of capital accumulation and hence the rate of growth. This is the process of 'forced savings' which constitutes an important element of certain theories of economic development (13).

References

1. L. WALRAS, *Elements of Pure Economics*, W. Jaffé (ed.), 1954, pp. 162, 241, 281–2.
2. O. LANGE, 'Say's law: a restatement and criticism', *Studies in Mathematical Economics and Econometrics*, University of Chicago Press, 1942, p. 50.
3. R. M. GOODWIN, 'Iteration, automatic computers and economic dynamics', *Metroeconomica*, vol. 3, 1951, pp. 1–7.
4. N. KALDOR, 'A classifactory note on the determinateness of equilibrium', *Review of Economic Studies*, vol. 1, 1933, pp. 126–9.
5. D. W. BUSHAW and R. W. CLOWER, *Introduction to Mathematical Economics*, Irwin, 1957.
6. G. C. ARCHIBALD and R. G. LIPSEY, 'Monetary and value theory: a critique of Lange and Patinkin', *Review of Economic Studies*, vol. 26, 1958, pp. 2–9.
7. F. H. HAHN, 'The Patinkin controversy', *Review of Economic Studies*, vol. 28, October 1960, pp. 40–41, 42 footnote 2.
8. W. J. BAUMOL, 'Monetary and value theory: comments', *Review of Economic Studies*, vol. 28, 1960, p. 30.
9. J. VINER, *Studies in the Theory of International Trade*, Allen & Unwin, 1937.
10. R. J. BALL and R. BODKIN, 'The real-balance effect and orthodox demand theory: a critique of Archibald and Lipsey', *Review of Economic Studies*, vol. 28, 1960, pp. 46–7.
11. N. LIVIATAN, 'On the long-run theory of consumption and real balances', *Oxford Economic Papers*, vol. 17, 1965, pp. 205–18.
12. R. W. CLOWER and M. L. BURSTEIN, 'On the invariance of demand for cash and other assets', *Review of Economic Studies*, vol. 28, 1960, pp. 32–6.

15. This has been emphasized by Ball and Bodkin (10, p. 48).

13. J. A. SCHUMPETER, 'Money and the social product', translated in *International Economic Papers*, 1956, no. 6, pp. 191–2, 204–6; also in *Theory of Economic Development*, Harvard University Press, 1934, ch. 3, pp. 95–127.
14. J. R. HICKS, *Value and Capital*, Clarendon Press, 1939.
15. K. WICKSELL, *Interest and Prices*, Macmillan, 1936.

10 G. C. Archibald and R. G. Lipsey

Value and Monetary Theory: Temporary *versus*
Full Equilibrium

G. C. Archibald and R. G. Lipsey (1958), 'Monetary and value theory: a
critique of Lange and Patinkin',[1] *Review of Economic Studies*, vol. 26,
pp. 1–22.

A change in the price level which causes a departure of desired
from actual real balances may lead to a change in individuals'
spending. The object of this paper is to inquire into the operation
and significance of this real-balance effect in classical value and
monetary theory, about which there has for some time been
controversy. Lange argued that the classical dichotomy between
the real and monetary sectors of the economy is invalid, and that
an integration of value and monetary theory is required. Patinkin
has attempted this integration in his book *Money, Interest and
Prices* (1), arguing that the real-balance effect provides the necessary link between the two parts of the system. In this paper we
[. . .] inquire into the operation of the real-balance effect in a
classical exchange model. This is necessary because Patinkin's
analysis is incomplete and leaves many important points obscure.
We find that, while the price level is of course determined by the
desire to hold balances together with the stock of money, the role
of the real-balance effect is *only* to provide an explanation of how
the system behaves in disequilibrium. Thus the real-balance effect
is irrelevant to those famous propositions of the quantity theory
which are the result of comparative-static analysis. [. . .]

1. Our interest in the matters discussed in this paper was aroused by the
discussion in Professor Robbins' seminar at the London School of Economics of Professor Patinkin's book *Money, Interest and Prices* (1). We are
indebted to all members of the seminar for the stimulus afforded by these
discussions, and for their comments on an earlier paper by R. G. Lipsey.
For their criticisms of an earlier draft of the present paper we are particularly indebted to Professor A. Harberger and Professor Harry Johnson,
Messrs P. Kenen and K. Klappholz, Dr E. J. Mishan, Mr M. H. Peston,
Dr A. W. Phillips and Mr R. Turvey. We also benefited from earlier discussions with Professor Philip Bell and Mr Lucian Foldes.

We start by considering the exchange model of the first part of Patinkin's book. In this model, in which time is divided into discrete contracting periods called weeks, it is important to distinguish between equilibrium at a point of time and equilibrium over time. As Hicks has put it, a stationary economy '. . . is in full equilibrium, not merely when demands equal supplies at the currently established prices, but also when the same prices continue to rule at all dates . . .' (2). Patinkin apparently overlooks this distinction; his analysis never goes beyond the conditions for equilibrium in one week. It is, as we shall see in 7 below, for this reason that he is forced to make some unusual assumptions to obtain the classical results. Our investigation of the properties of the model in full, as well as in weekly, equilibrium is necessary in order to understand how Patinkin arrives at his results, how the classical results may in fact be obtained directly from the comparative-static analysis of the model in full equilibrium, and what role is played by the real-balance effect in the many cases that may be studied.

The individual is assumed to have a given real income paid in goods,[2] and a given initial stock of money. We assume for the moment that relative prices do not vary so that goods may be treated as a single composite, G, with a single price, p. The individual's stock of money divided by p is his real balance H. We assume an indifference system between *holding* real balances for the week and *consuming* goods. The demand for balances is assumed to be purely a transactions demand.[3] The market opens

2. Each individual is assumed throughout the analysis to receive the same bundle of goods at the beginning of each week. The total income of the community is consumed each week, i.e. no stocks of goods are carried forward from week to week.

3. It is always necessary, but not always easy, to provide a motive for the stock demand for money without which its marginal utility and hence its price would be zero. Patinkin endeavours to solve this problem by constructing an elaborate system of random payments in which a balance is required to provide security against the risk of default caused by the lack of synchronization between payments and receipts. There are some awkward problems involved: it is difficult to make the transition from a demand for security in Patinkin's model, in which the security provided by balances of given size depends non-linearly upon the volume of the individual's transactions, to a unique relationship between total resources and desired balances. These problems were the subject of a paper circulated to the

every Monday, and a process of *tâtonnement* and recontract continues until equilibrium prices are reached. The market then closes, all contracts become binding, and trade takes place. The *tâtonnement*, in which equilibrium prices are found, is quite distinct from the actual trading, which takes place afterwards. The conditions for *weekly* equilibrium are, for the individual, that he has achieved the preferred division of his total resources between consumption and holding balances for the week, and, for the market, that supplies of and demands for goods are equal. It is consistent with these conditions, however, that the individual shall have added to or subtracted from his balances. If this is the case, he will begin the following week with a different total of resources, and his behaviour will be different. *Full* equilibrium obtains when market prices are unchanged from week to week. This requires that each individual's behaviour be unchanged from week to week, that is, that his consumption be constant. Since in this model an individual must divide the whole of his resources between consumption and balances it follows that, when his consumption is constant, so also are his balances (i.e. he consumes a bundle of goods equal in value to the bundle with which he was endowed at the beginning of the week). Thus the full equilibrium level of consumption is necessarily equal to total income, and independent of the desire to hold balances, the stock of money and the equilibrium level of prices.

In order to understand how this model works, it is necessary to analyse:

1. the individual's weekly equilibrium;
2. how he reaches full equilibrium;
3. how this full equilibrium is altered by a changed desire for balances;

---

members of Professor Robbins' seminar by G. C. Archibald in January 1957. In the present paper we merely assume that the individual's tastes are such that the allocation of his total resources between consumption and balances depends uniquely on the amount of his total resources. This means that the demand for balances depends on income *and* existing balances. It is one of the purposes of this section to show that a model based on this assumption produces, in full equilibrium, results identical with those which follow from the more usual assumption that the demand for balances is a function of income only.

4. how it is altered by a change in the price level;
5. how the market reaches full equilibrium;
6. how full equilibrium in the market is altered by a change in the money stock;
7. how weekly market equilibrium is altered by a change in the money stock which takes place when full equilibrium does not obtain;
8. the effects on the market of a non-proportional change in individuals' stocks of money;
9. the bearing of the above on the demand for money; and
10. the part played in the above by the real-balance effect.

Since Patinkin neglects the conditions for full equilibrium, his analysis is devoted mainly to 1, 7, 8 and 9.

1. The individual's behaviour in this model may now be analysed with the aid of Patinkin's diagram. In Figure 1, units of the composite good are measured along the G-axis and of *real* balances along the H-axis. The budget lines relating real goods to

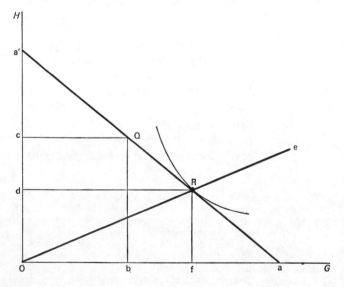

Figure 1

real balances must have an invariant slope of 135°; in Patinkin's words, 'The unitary negative slope of this line reflects the fact that, by definition, one unit of liquid command over commodities-in-general (real balances) can always be exchanged for one unit of actual commodities-in-general' (1, p. 69). At the beginning of any week the individual's total resources consist of his income for that week *plus* his stock of real balances (money balances held over from the previous week divided by the price level which, for the moment, we assume to remain constant). If this total equals Oa in goods, it is necessarily also Oa' in balances, where Oa = Oa', and the budget line is aa'. The individual is in equilibrium for the week when he is at a point of tangency between his budget line and an indifference curve. The locus of such points of tangency defines an expansion path Oe.

2. We now come to the essential part of the argument that Patinkin overlooked. Intersection of the budget line and the expansion path only provides an equilibrium for the week in question. Suppose that the individual, in the diagram just considered, starts the week in the position Q. This means that he has received income equal to Ob, and has retained balances equal to Oc (= ba). To attain his preferred position, R, he spends cd (= bf of goods) from his balances, in addition to spending his whole income. Thus his balances carried over to next week will be only Od. Hence, even if he receives the same income next week, he starts the period with a different (smaller) total of resources. The budget line the following Monday will be closer to the origin by the distance bf = cd, and the individual's market behaviour will therefore be changed. Full (stock) equilibrium, which is only attained when his behaviour is repeated each week, requires that the division of his resources between goods and balances with which he starts the week is the preferred division for that total of resources. We now amend Patinkin's diagram to make explicit the distinction between expenditure out of income and expenditure out of balances. Consider Figure 2. The individual has a constant real income OY. Erect a perpendicular YY' which intersects the expansion path Oe at i. If his initial real balances are Ya, his budget line is aa', his initial position S_1, at the intersection of aa' with YY', and his preferred position P_1. In the first week he therefore consumes Og goods, running down his balances

by Yg.[4] It follows that next period his budget line will be jj′ (ja = Yg), and his initial position S_2. The preferred position is now P_2, obtained by spending $S_3 P_2$ from balances; and the starting point for the next period is in turn S_3. It is clear that this process continues, with ever smaller adjustments, as the individual approaches ever closer to i (which cannot be attained in a

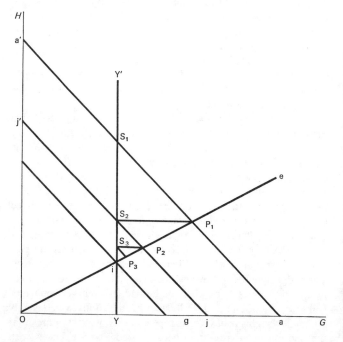

Figure 2

finite number of periods). Only when the individual is at i is he in full stock equilibrium; that is to say, at i he spends the whole of his income OY, while maintaining his stock of balances unchanged. (This analysis can obviously be repeated for the case in which the individual starts with too low a level of real balances.)

4. The perpendicular from P_1 to g has been omitted from the figure.

154

3. Suppose that a change in tastes were to alter the expansion path in Figure 3 from Oe to Oe′, indicating an increase in the desire to hold balances. The position of stock equilibrium is given by the intersection of YY′ with the new expansion path at k. The equilibrium level of real balances is increased by ik; the equilibrium level of consumption is unchanged at OY, i.e. is independent of the desired level of balances, although, in the weeks in which balances are being built up, consumption is less than income.

4. Suppose that the individual is in a position of full equilibrium, i in Figure 2, where with income OY his balances are

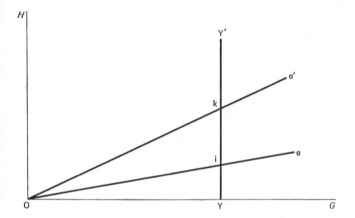

Figure 3

constant at Yi. Now, if the price level changes, his stock of real balances (nominal money balances divided by the price level) changes in proportion. A change in the price level therefore has the effect of moving his budget line.[5] If the price level is halved, his real balances are doubled, and the budget line moves to jj′ (Yi = iS₂). His preferred position the following week is P₂, and, if the price level remains constant at the new level, he will return

5. It will be noticed that, if real income is constant, the budget line can move only if real balances change, while real balances change either if consumption is not equal to income or if the price level changes.

to i, by weekly steps, in the fashion already analysed. Thus the full-equilibrium levels of consumption and real balances are independent of the price level.

5. For the market to be in weekly equilibrium, it is necessary that the demand for and supply of each good be equal. Individuals may, however, consume more or less than their income by

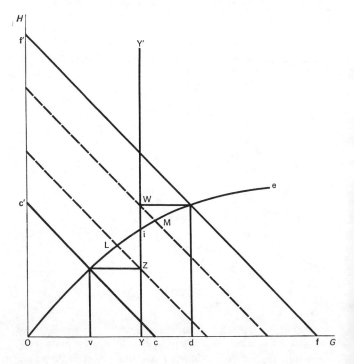

Figure 4

running down or adding to their balances. The equality of demand for and supply of goods implies that, if any individuals are running down balances, others are increasing theirs by exactly the same amount. Thus if all individuals are not in stock equilibrium, balances change hands each period. *Full stock equilibrium thus requires a unique distribution of balances* among the individuals in the market. Except in a special case, the process of redistributing balances by trade will cause the price level to vary from week to week.[6] Apart from this special case, a constant price level requires full equilibrium for each consumer.

Let us take a simple example, illustrated in Figure 4, in which there are only two individuals with identical incomes of OY, identical non-linear expansion paths Oe, but different initial balances. Individual I has balances Yc and budget line cc′; individual II has balances Yf and budget line ff′. I now wishes to add Yv to his balances, and is therefore an excess supplier of goods by the same amount. II wishes to spend Yd out of his balances, and is therefore an excess demander of goods by the same amount. Equilibrium in the market this week requires that Yv = Yd. Assume that this is the case, and that the *tâtonnement* is therefore concluded and trade takes place. Next week I's budget line, which has moved out by Yv = Yd, passes through Z; and II's, which has moved in by Yd = Yv, passes through W. I wishes to move to L, and II to M. Given the shape of Oe, the horizontal distance of L from YY′ exceeds that of M from YY′. Hence I's excess supply of goods exceeds II's excess demand, and trade cannot take place at last week's price level. Prices are therefore bid down. This, however, increases the real balances of both individuals, and therefore moves both budget lines to the right. As the budget lines move to the right, I's excess supply of goods diminishes, and II's excess demand increases. When the two have been brought into equality the *tâtonnement* ends, and the market is in equilibrium this week. The process of adjustment is therefore as follows[7]: trade each week moves the two budget lines closer together; the price reduction required to equilibrate the market the following week moves them both to the right; the week's trade then again brings them closer together. Ultimately the two budget lines coincide, passing through i, the position of

6. If all individuals have identical linear-expansion paths, then balances can be redistributed until full stock equilibrium is reached without variation in the price level.

7. We cannot assume that relative prices are constant in this process. We are therefore involved in an index number problem in measuring G and H. The argument of the text, however, does not depend on the assumption of constant relative prices, although, strictly speaking, the graphical illustration does.

full equilibrium for each individual. Only then will the price level cease to vary. (This analysis can obviously be repeated for the case in which the price level increases from week to week.)

6. Now suppose that each individual in the market is in a position of full equilibrium, such as point i in Figure 2, when the stock of money is doubled. In order to avoid distribution effects we shall assume for the present that each individual simply wakes up on Monday morning to find his nominal money balances doubled. At the prevailing price level each individual's budget line therefore moves out, e.g. to jj′ in Figure 2. Now *each* individual wishes to spend out of balances. When the market opens there is therefore an excess demand for goods (equal to S_3P_2 for the individual in Figure 2). This excess demand causes a rise in the price level, which continues, through the process of *tâtonnement*, until supply and demand for goods are restored to equality. The rising price level *during* the *tâtonnement* reduces each individual's real balances, and therefore moves his budget line inwards *without trade taking place*. The *tâtonnement* must continue, with the price level rising, until the excess demand for goods has been removed. This requires that individuals cease to attempt to alter their balances. This in turn requires that the price level rise until balances are restored to their original real worth, i.e., that the price level is doubled. In terms of Figure 2, the individual endeavouring to spend S_3P_2 of his newly increased balances finds that the efforts of others to do likewise are increasing the price level. The increase moves his budget line closer to the origin, and continues until the budget line is restored to its original position. Thus a doubling of each individual's stock of cash leads to a doubling of the price level on the first occasion that the market opens. When the whole market starts from full equilibrium, full equilibrium is restored by the *tâtonnement alone*, there being no actual expenditure out of balances and no week-by-week adjustment.

7. In 6 we saw that a change in the stock of money leads to a proportionate change in the full equilibrium price level. Patinkin, however, does not analyse the model in full equilibrium: he considers a change in the stock of money which takes place during a process of adjustment such as that analysed in 5 above. We may now see how he obtains his results. Suppose that the *tâtonnement*

has just ended, *but that no goods have yet changed hands*. The price level is therefore such as would clear the market this week, i.e. the excess supply of goods offered by some individuals is equal to the excess demanded by the others (the price level is not, however, one which will necessarily be repeated the following week, nor the same as that which prevailed in the preceding week). Now we follow Patinkin in doubling the stock of money by doubling the balances of each individual. We cancel all the contracts of the previous *tâtonnement* and start a new *tâtonnement*. Those individuals who had contracted to reduce their balances will now wish to make a larger reduction, and will therefore increase their excess demand for goods; those who had contracted to add to their balances will now wish to make a smaller addition, and will therefore decrease their excess supply of goods. Thus the price level must rise, and must continue to rise until excess supplies and demands for goods are again equal. This requires that the budget lines be restored to the position they occupied at the close of the previous *tâtonnement*, i.e. that the price level be doubled. The price level that is doubled is not, however, that of the previous week; it is the price level at which trade *would* have taken place this week had the stock of money not doubled. If, in the absence of a change in the stock of money, this week's price level would not have been equal to last week's, a doubling of the stock of money which doubles this week's price level does not cause it to be double last week's. Thus Patinkin obtains conclusions which appear to agree with those of the quantity theory only by comparing prices at which trade takes place (after the second of the week's two *tâtonnements*) with prices at which it would have taken place (after the first) (1, ch. 3, section 4). To obtain the result that doubling the quantity of money doubles actual market prices, we must compare positions of full equilibrium as in 6.

8. The analysis has so far been conducted on Patinkin's assumption that, when the stock of money is increased, there are no distribution effects. Patinkin argues that the absence of distribution effects is a necessary condition for the result that doubling the money stock doubles the price level (1, p. 41). If the doubling is conducted in the fashion analysed in 7 above, this is true. In the usual case, in which positions of full equilibrium are compared, it is not true. Let us now consider the consequences of an

increase in the stock of money which is not distributed in such a fashion as to cause an equiproportionate increase in the money balances of all individuals. Since each individual's final equilibrium is fully defined by his expansion path and his real income, any given increase in the stock of money has the same effect on the position of final equilibrium as that of any other equal increase however it may be initially distributed. In the case of a non-proportionate distribution the equilibrium cannot, of course, be reached *merely* by a change in the price level, but will require a redistribution of balances by the process of adjustment through trade already analysed. The path of adjustment, but not, of course, the final equilibrium, depends on the actual distribution of the increase in the money stock. We must notice that the conclusions obtained in 7, that a doubling of the money stock causes the price level at which trade next takes place to be double what it otherwise would have been, depends on the absence of distribution effects. The conclusion that doubling the stock of money doubles the full equilibrium price level does not depend on this assumption.

9. The equilibrium level of real balances is uniquely determined by tastes and incomes, and invariant to the money stock. Hence the total market demand for nominal money with respect to the reciprocal of the price level is the rectangular hyperbola of the classical writers. Consider, however, the case of an individual who is in full equilibrium when the price level is halved. Since, by assumption, he does not spend the whole increase in his real balances in the first week, his nominal balances are not at once halved. Hence his immediate demand curve for money is of less than unit elasticity. Each week, however, he reduces his balances until, when full equilibrium is restored, his nominal balances are half their original amount. The inelastic individual demand curve discussed by Patinkin (1, ch. 3, sections 5 and 6) therefore belongs solely to weeks in which full equilibrium has not been attained. The individual's curve relating the full equilibrium demand for money to the price level is, of course, always, like the market curve, a rectangular hyperbola.

10. Patinkin defines the real-balance effect as '. . . the influence on demand of a change in real balances, other things being held constant' (1, p. 21). Since in full equilibrium, consumption is equal

to income, a change in real balances can only change real consumption during a process of adjustment. Thus the real-balance effect is a transitory phenomenon, which is operative only in some disequilibrium situations.[8] Its role is to provide a possible *dynamic* explanation of how the economy moves from one position of static equilibrium to another. Thus, if we are interested in those well-known propositions of the quantity theory which are propositions in comparative statics, the real-balance effect is irrelevant.[9]

References

1. D. PATINKIN, *Money, Interest and Prices: An Integration of Monetary Theory*, Row Peterson, 1956.
2. J. R. HICKS, *Value and Capital*, 2nd edn, Clarendon Press, 1946.

8. If the individual is not in full equilibrium, he changes his consumption from week to week as his balances change. Similarly if the market is not in full equilibrium, balances and expenditure change from week to week. If, however, real balances are changed by a change in the money stock without distribution effects when the market is in full equilibrium, equilibrium is restored by the *tâtonnement alone*. Thus correction of a disequilibrium in balances only requires a change in individuals' real consumption when it is necessary to redistribute balances among the individuals in the market. When the disequilibrium can be corrected by a change in the price level alone, then no one in fact alters consumption.

9. Thus we cannot accept Patinkin's claim that the real-balance effect ' . . . is the *sine qua non* of monetary theory' (1, p. 22).

11 R. W. Clower and M. L. Burstein

The Classical Invariance Principle

R. W. Clower and M. L. Burstein (1960), 'On the invariance of demand for cash and other assets', *Review of Economic Studies*, vol. 28, pp. 32–6.

If the stock of cash held currently by an individual trader is defined to be the sum of his net receipts in previous periods plus some arbitrary initial balance, and if fiat money is the only asset that traders can carry over from one market period to another, then as Messrs Archibald and Lipsey have recently demonstrated (1, p. 3ff.), the trader's *equilibrium* demand for real cash balances is independent of the general price level and of initial balances and is governed instead by tastes and real income.[1] It is not clear, however, whether this result is valid in a model where money balances may be used to purchase and hold income-earning assets. If an individual can buy and sell bonds, for example, he can presumably effect a *permanent* change in his real income by substituting bonds for cash in his asset portfolio. Under these circumstances, real income is a variable rather than a parameter and the invariance of equilibrium real balances against a change in nominal money stocks or in the general price level would seem to be endangered.

Archibald and Lipsey also show that, for an economy in which money is the only asset, equilibrium relative prices are invariant with respect to changes in the aggregate quantity of money, regardless of the way in which such a change affects the distribution of money stocks among individual traders (1, pp. 8–9). But the validity of this result also seems to be questionable in an economy where windfall variations in money stocks are capable of leading to permanent changes in the distribution of real income.

On closer analysis, however, it turns out that neither of these

1. Priority for this result appears to belong to C. E. V. Leser (2, pp. 133–4). Mitchell Harwitz called our attention to Leser's demonstration.

doubts is justified. Provided we adhere to the standard assumption of the uniqueness of equilibrium states, (1, p. 18, footnote 2) invariance propositions similar to those enunciated by Archibald and Lipsey continue to hold not only for a bond-and-money economy but also for more general systems. The purpose of the present paper is to elaborate upon this theme and to indicate some of its more immediate implications.

I

Dealing first with notational and terminological preliminaries, suppose that in any given market period (say period t) the typical trader (call him trader 'j') receives '. . . like manna from heaven . . .' quantities $s_j \equiv (s_{1j}, \ldots, s_{nj})$ of n non-durable commodities which may either be consumed directly or traded during the period at market prices $p(t) \equiv [p_1(t), \ldots, p_n(t)]$ so as to achieve at the close of the period a desired consumption pattern represented by $d_j(t) \equiv [d_{1j}(t), \ldots, d_{nj}(t)]$. Suppose further that the trader holds a quantity $S_{Mj}(t)$ of money and a quantity $S_{Bj}(t)$ of bonds at the outset of period t, but assume that these quantities may be increased or decreased through market trading so as to achieve at the end of the period a desired asset portfolio represented by the variables $D_{Mj}(t)$ and $D_{Bj}(t)$[2]. By hypothesis, bonds are perfectly standardized perpetuities which, in each market period, pay one unit of money to their holder and entail payment of one unit of money by their issuer. The market rate of interest, $r(t)$ is therefore equal to the reciprocal of the price of bonds, and the money value of the trader's bond income in period t is numerically equal to his bond holdings, $S_{Bj}(t)$.

II

Turning now to behavior postulates, we follow Patinkin (3, p. 53) and suppose that the demand for each commodity and the real demand for bonds (equivalently, bond income) and for cash balances is in every case a function of real income, relative commodity prices, the rate of interest, real-bond income and real-

2. No explicit constraint is imposed on the quantity of bonds issued by a trader in any single period, but the existence of some kind of limit is implicit throughout the subsequent discussion. On this and related matters see Patinkin (3, p. 53); Archibald and Lipsey (1, p. 2, footnote 3).

money balances. The behavior of the jth trader is thus described, in part, by the relations

$$d_{ij}(t) = d_{ij}\left[s_j, \frac{p(t)}{P(t)}, r(t), \frac{S_{Bj}(t)}{P(t)}, \frac{S_{Mj}(t)}{P(t)}\right] (i = 1, \ldots, n) \quad \mathbf{1}$$

$$\frac{D_{Bj}(t)}{P(t)} = D_{Bj}\left[s_j, \frac{p(t)}{P(t)}, r(t), \frac{S_{Bj}(t)}{P(t)}, \frac{S_{Mj}(t)}{P(t)}\right] \qquad \mathbf{2}$$

$$\frac{D_{Mj}(t)}{P(t)} = D_{Mj}\left[s_j, \frac{p(t)}{P(t)}, r(t), \frac{S_{Bj}(t)}{P(t)}, \frac{S_{Mj}(t)}{P(t)}\right] \qquad \mathbf{3}$$

where $P(t) \equiv \sum w_i p_i(t)$ represents 'the general price level' in market period t and $j = 1, \ldots, m$.[3]

Following Archibald and Lipsey (2, pp. 2ff.), however, we suppose that the behavior of the stock quantities $S_{Bj}(t)$ and $S_{Mj}(t)$, respectively, is described by the relations[4]

$$S_{Bj}(t) = S_{Bj}(t_0) + \sum_{\theta = t_0}^{t-1} [D_{Bj}(\theta) - S_{Bj}(\theta)] \qquad \mathbf{4}$$

and $\qquad S_{Mj}(t) = S_{Mj}(t_0) + \sum_{\theta = t_0}^{t-1} [D_{Mj}(\theta) - S_{Mj}(\theta)].$[5] $\quad \mathbf{5}$

3. All trading is assumed to be constrained by Walras' principle (i.e. expenditure 'sinks' are exactly matched by income 'sources', and vice versa); hence the condition

$$D_{Mj}(t) \equiv S_{Mj}(t) + \frac{S_{Bj}(t) - D_{Bj}(t)}{r(t)} + S_{Bj}(t) - \sum_i p_i(t)[d_{ij}(t) - s_{ij}]$$

is tacitly embedded in the set of equations **1** to **3**. Cf. Footnote 5, below; also Patinkin (3, pp. 292 ff.).

4. This asserts that an individual trader is always in a position to acquire any desired quantity of an asset during a single market period. This seems reasonable for a fictional system in which prices are established by *tâtonnement*, despite its artificiality as applied to any concrete market situation. Patinkin says nothing on this subject, perhaps because to say anything at all about the determination of current asset balances is to say more than can easily be granted on casual empirical grounds. For this reason, Patinkin's model of a 'bond-and-money' economy is more flexible (less restrictive in its assumptions) than ours or, for that matter, the model described by Archibald and Lipsey.

5. Alternatively, equation **5** might be written (cf. footnote 3, above)

$$S_{Mj}(t) = S_{Mj}(t_0) + \sum_{\theta=t_0}^{t-1}\left\{\frac{S_{Bj}(\theta) - D_{Bj}(\theta)}{r(t)} + S_{Bj}(\theta) - \sum p_i(\theta)[d_{ij}(\theta) - s_{ij}]\right\}.$$

Then for any given set of values of the parameters s_j, $p(t)/P(t)$ and $r(t)$, and for arbitrary values of the 'initial asset' quantities $S_{Bj}(t_0)$ and $S_{Mj}(t_0)$, the recursive system **1** to **5** provides a total of $n + 4$ equations for any fixed value of j to determine the values of the $n + 4$ unknowns $d_j(t)$, $D_{Bj}(t)$, $D_{Mj}(t)$, $S_{Bj}(t)$ and $S_{Mj}(t)$ for all values of $t \geq t_0$. In particular, requiring that $\Delta S_{Bj}(t) = \Delta S_{Mj}(t) = 0$ and recalling the uniqueness assumption introduced earlier, equations **1** to **5** yield a determinate statical model comprising $n + 4$ equations to determine the *equilibrium values* $\bar{d}_j$, $\bar{D}_{Bj}$, $\bar{D}_{Mj}$, $\bar{S}_{Bj}$, $\bar{S}_{Mj}$ of the $n + 4$ variables over which the individual trader exercises direct control. Solving to obtain the usual reduced form equations, therefore, we may write the identities

$$\left.\begin{aligned} d_{ij} &\equiv f_{ij}\left[s_j, \frac{p(t)}{P(t)}, r(t)\right] \ (i = 1, \ldots, n) \\[1em] \frac{\bar{D}_{Bj}(t)}{P(t)} &\equiv f_{Bj}\left[s_j, \frac{p(t)}{P(t)}, r(t)\right] \\[1em] \frac{\bar{D}_{Mj}(t)}{P(t)} &\equiv f_{Mj}\left[s_j, \frac{p(t)}{P(t)}, r(t)\right] \\[1em] \frac{\bar{S}_{kj}(t)}{P(t)} &\equiv f_{kj}\left[s_j, \frac{p(t)}{P(t)}, r(t)\right] \ (k = M, B) \end{aligned}\right\} \quad \textbf{S1}$$

The equilibrium values defined by **S1** are obviously independent of 'initial assets'.[6] More precisely, since the quantities $S_{Bj}(t_0)$ and $S_{Mj}(t_0)$ enter the dynamical system **1** to **5** as arbitrary constants (initial conditions) rather than 'structural' parameters, they do not appear in the equations defining a stationary solution

---

6. Following a suggestion by Mr Hahn, 'rational behavior' on the part of an individual trader would seem to require that manna income and real income from bonds be treated as perfect substitutes. If this suggestion is carried through (i.e. if the typical trader is assumed not to discriminate among different values of S_{Bj}/P and $\sum_i p_i s_{ij}/P$ so long as the numerical sum of the two items is the same), then it can be shown that the appropriately modified version of **S1** – i.e. a system of equilibrium identities in which the bond variables S_{Bj} and D_{Bj} in **S1** are replaced by the 'composite' income variables $S_{yj} \equiv S_{Bj} + \sum_i p_i s_{ij}$ and $D_y \equiv D_{Bj} + \sum_i p_i s_{ij}$ – is independent of the manna variables s_{ij} as well as the initial asset variables $S_{Bj}(t_0)$. The explicit appearances of the variables s_j in the system **S1** appear to entail the existence of 'manna illusion' on the part of the individual trader; but this is merely a possible, it is *not* a necessary consequence of our model.

of the system. Moreover, since the system S1 is homogeneous of order zero in the quantities $p_i(t)$, $\bar{D}_{kj}$ and $\bar{S}_{kj}$, the uniqueness assumption implies that the real demand for money and for bond income is independent of the general price level.

The same conclusions may be reached by an alternative route, arguing directly from the properties of the system 1 to 5. Starting from any initial equilibrium state, represented by a set of values of the 'real' variables d_{ij}, $\bar{D}_{kj}/P(t)$, $\bar{S}_{kj}/P(t)$, a once-over change in nominal asset balances or in the general price level involves a momentary relaxation of the dynamical assumptions underlying the system. If the initial 'real' equilibrium state is stable, however, the system must ultimately tend to return to its initial 'real' position. In this sense, equilibrium real balances are invariant against changes in nominal asset stocks. Notice, however, that it is meaningless to talk about the comparative-statics effects of a change in initial asset balances in any *statical* system obtained from 1 to 5; for the only asset quantities that can appear in such a system are $\bar{D}_{kj}$ and $\bar{S}_{kj}$, and these are dependent variables rather than (arbitrary) parameters.[7]

III

Extending the preceding analysis to deal with the determination of commodity prices and the rate of interest, we begin by assuming that the values of the variables $p_i(t)$ and $r(t)$ are chosen via some kind of *tâtonnement* process so as to ensure the simultaneous satisfaction of the set of $n + 1$ 'market clearance' conditions

$$\sum_{i=1}^{m} [d_{ij}(t) - s_{ij}] = 0 \quad (i = 1, \ldots, n) \qquad 6$$

$$\sum_{j=1}^{m} [D_{Bj}(t) - S_{Bj}(t)] = 0, \qquad 7$$

and simply add to these requirements the relations 1 to 5 as set forth in II, above. The resulting system, *which we will call* S2, contains a total of $m(n + 4)$ relations describing *individual*

7. The preceding results can be broadened to apply to a more general 'individual experiment' in which individual traders buy and sell physical assets as well as securities and money, and in which the 'manna' quantities s_j are themselves functions of relative prices and other 'real' variables.

behavior of which only $m(n + 4) - 2$ can be specified independently from a *market* point of view. More particularly, since the total quantity of bonds held by 'creditors' at the beginning of any period is necessarily equal to the total quantity of bonds issued and sold by 'debtors' up to the beginning of the same period, the set of equations 4 must satisfy the linear relation

$$\sum_{j=1}^{m} S_{Bj} \equiv 0. \qquad\qquad 8$$

Similarly, since the aggregate of individual holdings of money balances in any period must equal the total stock of money in the economy, the set of equations 5 must satisfy the linear relation

$$\sum_{j=1}^{m} S_{Mj} \equiv S_M \equiv \text{constant.}^{8} \qquad\qquad 9$$

Taking equation 8 and equation 9 into account along with equations 1 to 7, the recursive system S2 is determinate in the usual sense; i.e. it contains a total of $m(n + 4) + n + 1$ independent equations to determine the values of the $m(n + 4) + n + 1$ variables $d_1, \ldots, d_m, D_{B1}, \ldots, D_{Bm}, D_{M1}, \ldots, D_{Mm}, S_{B1}, \ldots, S_{Bm}, S_{M1}, \ldots, S_{Mm}, p$ and r.

Now suppose that the system S2 has a stable 'steady state' solution, $\bar{p}_i, \bar{r}, \bar{d}_{ij}, \bar{D}_{Bj}, \bar{D}_{Mj}, \bar{S}_{Bj}, \bar{S}_{Mj}$ corresponding to any given set of values s_j^0, S_0^M of the parameters s_j and S_M. Then by direct inspection it can be seen that the set of values $\lambda \bar{p}_i, \bar{r}, \bar{d}_{ij}, \lambda \bar{D}_{Bj}, \lambda \bar{D}_{Mj}, \lambda \bar{S}_{Bj}, \lambda \bar{S}_{Mj}$ is the unique 'steady state' solution of the system when s_j retains the value s_j^0, but S_M is assigned the new value λS_m^0 (λ being any positive constant). From this it follows immediately that, in equilibrium, relative commodity prices, the rate of interest and real asset balances are all invariant with respect to changes in the aggregate stock of money. Alternatively, it may be noted that the statical system obtained from S2 by setting $\Delta S_{Bj} = \Delta S_{Mj} = 0$ can be solved uniquely to yield

8. It should be remarked that, by virtue of the constraint equation 9, the aggregate stock of money, S_M, may be regarded as a 'structural parameter' in the dynamical system S2. The constraint equation 8, on the other hand, does not fix the value of the aggregate stock of outstanding bonds $S_B \equiv \frac{1}{2} \sum |S_B|$.

reduced form identities from which the aggregate money stock parameter, S_M, is altogether absent; thus

$$
\left.
\begin{aligned}
\bar{p}_i/P &\equiv g_i(s_1, \ldots, s_m) && (i = 1, \ldots, n) \\
\bar{r} &\equiv g(s_1, \ldots, s_m) && \\
\bar{d}_{ij} &\equiv h_{ij}(s_1, \ldots, s_m) && (i = 1, \ldots, n; j = 1, \ldots, m) \\
\bar{D}_{Bj}/P &\equiv h_{Bj}(s_1, \ldots, s_m) && (j = 1, \ldots, m) \\
\bar{D}_{Mj}/P &\equiv h_{Mj}(s_1, \ldots, s_m) && (j = 1, \ldots, m) \\
\bar{S}_{Bj}/P &\equiv h_{Bj}(s_1, \ldots, s_m) && (j = 1, \ldots, m) \\
\bar{S}_{Mj}/P &\equiv h_{Mj}(s_1, \ldots, s_m) && (j = 1, \ldots, m)
\end{aligned}
\right\} \text{S3}
$$

These conclusions have to be modified if one considers a model in which the total (nominal) stock of bonds is fixed in advance (i.e. in which $S_B \equiv \frac{1}{2} \sum_{j=1}^{m} | S_{Bj} | \equiv$ constant). For in this case it can be shown that the ratio between the aggregate stock of bonds and the aggregate stock of money, i.e. S_B/S_M, appears as an explicit parameter in the reduced form equations corresponding to S3. Even in this instance, however, all 'real' quantities are invariant with respect to equiproportionate changes in the aggregate stock of money *and* bonds. This emphasizes what is perhaps the most interesting feature of the system S2, namely that the stock of bonds is 'geared' to the stock of money *via a market adjustment mechanism* in such a fashion that induced changes in the aggregate stock of bonds are, *ceteris paribus*, directly proportional to changes in the stock of money.

Results precisely analogous to the above can be obtained for an economy containing fixed supplies of physical assets (which yield an income in 'kind'). Provided no trader suffers from 'money illusion', and provided individual traders are permitted to issue new securities and to retire outstanding debts in the light of changing market conditions, the effects of a change in the aggregate stock of money can and will be entirely offset by an equiproportionate rise in money prices and in nominal asset balances.

More generally, if we consider an economy in which all commodities except money are produced, consumed and held in the form of assets, and if the relevant supply and demand functions of the system depend only on relative prices and other real variables, then it can be shown that the equilibrium demand for commodities, for real-bond income, for physical assets and for real-money balances are all invariant against a change in the nominal stock of money. To put the matter another way, *the equilibrium distribution of real wealth and real income in such an economy is determined by 'tastes and technique' and is otherwise independent of historical accidents.* This, it appears, is the most general statement of the Archibald–Lipsey 'invariance principle'.[9]

References

1. G. C. ARCHIBALD and R. G. LIPSEY, 'Monetary and value theory: a critique of Lange and Patinkin', *Review of Economic Studies*, vol. 26, 1958, pp. 2–9.
2. C. E. V. LESER, 'The consumer's demand for money', *Econometrica*, vol. 11, 1943, pp. 123–40.
3. D. PATINKIN, *Money, Interest and Prices*, Row Peterson, 1956.
4. D. W. BUSHAW and R. W. CLOWER, *Introduction to Mathematical Economics*, Irwin, 1957, pp. 36, 76, 128–34, 160–63, 166–71.
5. R. W. CLOWER, 'An investigation into the dynamics of investment', *American Economic Review*, vol. 44, March 1954, pp. 69–71, 73–7.

9. A rigorous demonstration of these and related results would require more space than can be devoted to them here. The interested reader may pursue the matter further by consulting relevant portions of Bushaw and Clower (4) and Clower (5).

12 P. A. Samuelson

Classical and Neo-classical Monetary Theory

P. A. Samuelson (1968), 'What classical and neo-classical monetary theory really was', *Canadian Journal of Economics*, vol. 1, no. 1, pp. 1–15.

To know your own country you must have travelled abroad. To understand modern economics it is good to have lived long enough to have escaped competent instruction in its mysteries. When Archibald and Lipsey try to draw for Patinkin a picture of what a 'classical' monetary theorist believed in, they are pretty much in the position of a man who, looking for a jackass, must say to himself, 'If I were a jackass, where would I go?'

Mine is the great advantage of having once been a jackass. From 2 January 1932 until an indeterminate date in 1937, I was a classical monetary theorist. I do not have to look for the tracks of the jackass embalmed in old journals and monographs. I merely have to lie down on the couch and recall in tranquillity, upon that inward eye which is the bliss of solitude, what it was that I believed between the ages of 17 and 22. This puts me in the same advantageous position that Pio Nono enjoyed at the time when the infallibility of the Pope was being enunciated. He could say, incontrovertibly, 'Before I was Pope, I believed he was infallible. Now that I am Pope, I can *feel* it.'

Essentially, we believed that in the longest run and in ideal models the amount of money did not matter. Money could be 'neutral' and in many conditions the hypothesis that it was could provide a good first or last approximation to the facts. To be sure, Hume, Fisher and Hawtrey had taught us that, under dynamic conditions, an increase in money might lead to 'money illusion' and might cause substantive changes – e.g. a shift to debtor-entrepreneurs and away from creditor-rentiers, a forced-saving shift to investment and away from consumption, a lessening of unemployment, a rise in wholesale prices relative to sticky retail prices and wage rates, *et cetera*.

170

But all this was at a second level of approximation, representing relatively transient aberrations. Moreover, this tended to be taught in applied courses on business cycles, money and finance, and economic history rather than in courses on pure theory. In a real sense there *was* a dichotomy in our minds; we were schizophrenics. From 9 to 9.50 a.m. we presented a simple quantity theory of neutral money. There were then barely ten minutes to clear our palates for the 10 to 10.50 discussion of how an engineered increase in M would help the economy. In mid-America in the mid-1930s, we neo-classical economists tended to be mild inflationists, jackasses crying in the wilderness and resting our case essentially on sticky prices and costs, and on expectations.

Returning to the 9 o'clock hour, we thought that *real* outputs and inputs and price ratios depended essentially in the longest run on real factors, such as tastes, technology and endowments. The stock of money we called M (or, to take account of chequable bank deposits, we worked in effect with a velocity-weighted average of M and M'; however, a banking system with fixed reserve and other ratios would yield M' proportional to M, so M alone would usually suffice). An increase in M – usually we called it a doubling on the ground that after God created unity he created the second integer – would cause a proportional increase in *all* prices (tea, salt, female labour, land rent, share or bond prices) and values (expenditure on tea or land, share dividends, interest income, taxes). You will hardly believe it, but few economists in those days tried to write down formal equations for what they were thinking. Had we been asked to choose which kinds of equation system epitomized our thinking, I believe at first blush we would have specified:

A. Write down a system of real equations involving *real* outputs and inputs, and *ratios* of prices (values), and depending essentially on real tastes, technologies, market structures and endowments. Its properties are invariant to change in the stock of money M.

B. Then append a fixed-supply-of-M equation that pins down (or up) the absolute price level, determining the scale factor that was essentially indeterminate in set A. This could be a quantity equation of exchange ($MV = PQ$) or some other non-homo-

171

geneous equation. More accurately, while A involves homogeneity of degree zero in *all* Ps, B involves homogeneity of degree one of Ps in terms of M.

I have purposely left the above paragraphs vague. For I doubt that the typical good classical monetary theorist had more definite notions about the *mathematics* of his system.

Moreover, I must leave room for an essential strand in our thinking. Our expositions always began with barter and worked out fundamental pricing in barter models. But then we, sensibly, pointed out the *real* inconvenience of barter and the real convenience of an abstract unit of money. Here we made explicit and tacit reference to the real facts of brokerage or transaction charges, of uncertainties of income and outgo, and so on. In short, we did have a primitive inventory theory of money holding, but we were careful to note that true money – unlike pearls, paintings, wine and coffee – is held only for the *ultimate exchange* work it can do, which depends upon the scale of *all* Ps in a special homogeneous way.

So there was another dichotomy in our minds, a very legitimate one. We had, so to speak, *qualitative* and *quantitative* theories of money. According to our qualitative theory, money was not neutral; it made a big difference. Pity the country that was still dependent upon barter, for it would have an inefficient economic system. But once this qualitative advantage had been realized by the adoption of market structures using M, the *quantitative* level of M was of no particular significance (except for indicated transient states and uninteresting resource problems involved in gold mining or mint printing). We liked the image of John Stuart Mill that money is the *lubricant* of industry and commerce. As even women drivers know, lubrication is important. But M is quantitatively a special lubricant: a drop will do as well as a poolful. So an even better image was the post-Mill one: money is like a catalyst in a chemical reaction, which makes the reaction go faster and better, but which, like the oil in the widow's cruse, is never used up. To push the analogy beyond endurance, only an iota of catalyst is needed for the process.

What I have just said makes it unmistakably clear that a classical monetary theorist would not go the stake for the belief that the real set of equations A are independent of M, depending essentially only on price ratios as in barter. If time were short on a quiz, I might carelessly write down such an approximation. But if asked specifically the question 'Is Set A really independent of M?', I and my classmates would certainly answer 'No' and we would cite the qualitative aspects mentioned earlier.

In a moment we shall see that this considered qualitative view requires that M enter *quantitatively in Set A in certain specified homogeneous ways*. But first let us investigate how those of us who were mathematically inclined would have handled the Set A and Set B problem. The economists interested in mathematics tended to be specialists in value theory. They had a big job just to describe the real relations of A, whether under barter or otherwise. They wanted to simplify their expositions, to sidestep extraneous complication. Hence, many would have followed the practice (which I seem to connect with Cassel's name, at least) of writing Set A purely in barter terms, and essentially giving enough equations to determine real quantities and price ratios as follows:

(A′) $f_i(Q_1, \ldots, Q_n, P_1, \ldots, P_n) = 0 \ (i = 1, 2, \ldots, 2n)$

where there are n inputs or outputs, with n prices. However, the f_i functions are made to be homogeneous of degree zero in all the Ps, and, luckily, the $2n$ functions f_i are required to involve one of them as being dependent on the other, thus avoiding an over-determination of the $2n$ functions. This homogeneity and dependence postulate enables us to write A′ in the equivalent form:

(A′) $f_i(Q_1, \ldots, Q_n, \lambda P_1, \ldots, \lambda P_n)_\lambda \equiv 0 \ (i = 1, 2, \ldots, 2n).$

This formulation does not contain price ratios explicitly. But since λ is arbitrary, it can be set equal to $1/P_1$ to give us price ratios, $P_i/1$. Or if you have an interest in some kind of average of prices, say $\pi (P_1, \ldots, P_n) = \pi (P)$, where π is a homogeneous function of degree one, you can rewrite A′ in terms of ratios $P_i/\pi(P)$ alone, by suitable choice of λ. Hence, Set A′ involves $2n-1$ independent functions which hopefully determine a unique (or multiple) solution to the $2n-1$ real variables $(Q_1, \ldots, Q_n, P_2/P_1, \ldots, P_n/P_1)$. With the special structure of A′, we are now free to add any non-homogeneous B′ we like, of the following types:

$P_1 = 1$, good 1 being taken as *numéraire*, or

(B′)
$P_1 + P_2 = 3 \cdot 1416$,
$P_1 + P_2 + \ldots + P_n = 1$,

$P_1[Q_1^* + (P_2^*/P_1)Q_2^* + \ldots + (P_n^*/P_1)Q_n^*]$
$= \bar{M} \times$ Fisher's constant,

where Q_i^*, $(P_i/P_1)^*$ are solutions of A′.

Of course, the last of these looks like the Fisher–Marshall formulation of the 'quantity equation of exchange'. But, since some Q_i are inputs, my way of writing it recognizes the realistic fact that money is needed to pay factors as well as to move goods.[1]

I do not defend this special (A′, B′) formulation. I am sure it was often used. And even today, if I am behind in my lectures, I resort to it in courses on pure theory. But we should admit that it is imperfect. And we should insist that the classical writers, when they did full justice to their own views, did not believe that this formulation was more than a provisional simplification.

What is a minimal formulation of (A, B) that does do full justice? I am sure that I personally, from 1937 on at least, had a correct vision of the proper version. It is as if to understand Gary, Indiana, I had to travel to Paris. I began to understand neoclassical economics only after Keynes' *General Theory* shook me up. But I am sure that I was only learning to articulate what was intuitively felt by such ancients as Ricardo, Mill, Marshall, Wicksell and Cannan. I regret that I did not then write down a formal set of equations. I did discuss the present issue at the Econometric Society meetings of 1940, of which only an incomplete abstract appeared, and also at its 1949 meetings, where Hickman, Leontief and others spoke; and there are fragmentary similar remarks in half a dozen of my writings of twenty years ago. The nub of the matter is contained in my 1947 specification (1, p. 119) that the utility function contain in it, along with physical quantities of good consumed, the stock of M and all money Ps, being homogeneous of degree zero in $(M, P_1, \ldots, P_n)$

1. An equation like the last one could be split into two equations without altering the meaning:

$$(B_1'); \; (1/FC) \sum_{j=1}^{n} (P_j/M)Q_j^* = 1 \text{ and } (B_2'); \; M = \bar{M},$$

a prescribed total. The important thing to note is that B_1', even if it looks a little like some A′ equations, is completely decomposable from Set A′.

P. A. Samuelson

in recognition of money's peculiar 'neutral' quantitative properties.

Frankly, I was repelled by the abstract level at which Lange, Hicks, and others carried on their discussion of Say's law, staying at the level of equation counting and homogeneity reckoning, without entering into the concrete character of the models. And this was one of the few continuing controversies of economics from which I steadfastly abstained.

For the rest of this discussion, what I propose to do is to get off the couch and go to the blackboard and write down an organized picture of what we jackasses implicitly believed back in the bad old days.

The Way Things Are

I abstract heroically. We are all exactly alike. We live for ever. We are perfect competitors and all-but-perfect soothsayers. Our inelastic labour supply is fully employed, working with inelastically supplied Ricardian land and (possibly heterogeneous) capital goods. We have built-in Pigou–Böhm rates of subjective time preference, discounting each next-year's independent utility by the constant factor $1/(1 + \rho)$, $\rho > 0$. We are in long-run equilibrium without technical change or population growth: the stock of capital goods has been depressed to the point where all own-interest-rates yielded by production are equal to r, the market rate of interest; in turn, r is equal to the subjective interest rate ρ, this being the condition for our propensity to consume being 100 per cent of income, with zero net capital formation.

We equally own land and such capital goods as machinery and material stocks. We own, but legally cannot sell, our future stream of labour earnings. We hold cash balances, because we are *not* perfect soothsayers when it comes to the uncertainty of the timing of our in-and-out payments, which can be assumed to follow certain probability laws in the background; this lack of synchronization of payments plus the indivisible costs of transactions (brokerage charges, need for journal entries, spread between bid and ask when earning assets are converted into or out of cash, etc.) requires us to hold money. To keep down inessential complications, while not omitting Hamlet from the

175

scenario, I am neglecting the need for cash balances for corporations; it is as if consumer families alone need cash balances for their final consumption purchases, whereas in real life cash is needed at every vertical stage of the production process. Later we can allow our holdings of earning assets – titles to land and machines – to economize on our need for M balances, just as does the prospect of getting wage increases.

Our system is assumed to come into long-run equilibrium. This equilibrium can be deduced to be unique if we add to our extreme symmetry assumptions the conventional strong convexity assumptions of neo-classical theorizing – constant returns to scale with smooth diminishing returns to proportions, quasiconcave ordinal utility functions that guarantee diminishing marginal rates of substitution, and so on.

We should be able to *prove rigorously* what is probably intuitively obvious – doubling all M will exactly double *all* long-run prices and values, and this change in the absolute price level will have absolutely no effect on real output–inputs, on price ratios or terms of trade, on interest rate and factor shares generally.

For this system, it is not merely the case that tautological quantity equations of exchange can be written down. Less trivially, a simple 'quantity theory of prices and money' holds exactly for the long-run equilibrium model. Although Patinkin has doubts about the propriety of the concept, I think our meaning was unambiguous – and unobjectionable – when we used to say that the 'demand curve for money' (traced out by shifts in the vertical supply curve of M) plotted in a diagram containing, on the x-axis, M and, on the y-axis, the 'value of money', (as measured by the reciprocal of *any* absolute money price $1/P_i$ or any average price level) would be a rectangular hyperbola with a geometrical Marshallian elasticity of exactly minus one.

To prove this I write down the simplest possible set of equations. These do split up into two parts, showing that there is a legitimate 'dichotomy' between 'real elements' and 'monetary elements which determine only the absolute level of prices'. Call these two parts A and B. Now this legitimate dichotomy will not be identical with the over-simple dichotomy of A' and B' mentioned earlier. If Patinkin insists upon the difference, I am in complete agreement with him. If he should prefer not to call the

(A, B) split a dichotomy, that semantic issue is not worth arguing about so long as enough words are used to describe exactly what the (A, B) split is, and how it differs from the (A', B') split. If Patinkin insists on saying that my A equations do have in them a 'real-balance effect', I see no harm in that – even though, as will be seen, my formulation of A need involve no use of an average price index, and hence no need to work with a 'deflated M' that might be called a real balance. Peculiarly in the abstract neo-classical model with its long-run strong homogeneity properties, all Ps move together in strict proportion when M alone changes and hence no index-number approximations are needed. By the same token, they do absolutely no harm: Patinkin is entitled to use any number of average price concepts and real-balance concepts he wishes. If Patinkin wishes to say that the principal neo-classical writers (other than Walras) had failed to *publish* a clear and unambiguous account of the (A, B) equation such as I am doing here, I would agree, and would adduce the worth and novelty of Patinkin's own book and contributions. On the other hand, the present report on my recollections claims that the best neo-classical writers did *perceive* at the intuitive level the intrinsic content of the (A, B) dichotomy which I am about to present. All the more we should regret that no one fully set down these intuitions thirty years ago!

Now what about Archibald and Lipsey?[2] I want to avoid semantic questions as to what is meant by real-balance effects being operative. If they claim that the (A', B') dichotomy does justice to the tacit neo-classical models of 1930, I think they are wrong. If they think an (A', B') dichotomy does justice to a reasonably realistic long-run model of a monetary economy, I think they are also wrong. Whether, as a *tour de force*, some special, flukey (A', B') model might be found to give a representation of some monetary economy is a possibility that I should hate to deny in the abstract; but I should be surprised if this issue turned out to be an interesting one to linger on or to debate. For what a casual opinion is worth, it is my impression that Patinkin's general position – which I interpret to be essentially identical to my (A,

2. Don Patinkin's *Money, Interest and Prices* (2), summarizes his path-breaking writings on money over the last twenty years. A critique of aspects of its first (1954) edition, is given by Archibald and Lipsey (3).

B) dichotomy *and* to the tacit neo-classical theory of my youth – is left impregnable to recent attacks on it. There is one, and only one, legitimate dichotomy in neo-classical monetary theory.

Abjuring further doctrinal discussion, I proceed now to the equations of my simplest system.

Structure of the Model – Production Relations

To keep down inessentials, let land T, real capital K (assumed homogeneous merely as a preliminary to letting K stand for a vector of heterogeneous capital goods) and labour L, produce real output which, because of similarity of production factors in all sectors, can be split up into the linear sum of different physical consumption goods $\pi_1 q_1 + \ldots + \pi_n q_n$ and net capital formation $\dot{K}(= dK/dt)$, namely: $\dot{K} + \pi_1 q_1 + \pi_2 q_2 + \ldots + \pi_m q_m = f(K, \bar{L}, \bar{T})$ where F is a production function of the Ramsey–Solow type, homogeneous of first degree, and where the π_i are constants, representing marginal costs of the ith goods relative to machines. From this function, we can deduce all factor prices and commodity prices relative to the price of the capital good P_K, namely:

$$(\text{A}_{1,1}) \quad \frac{P_i}{P_K} = \pi_i \ (i = 1, 2, \ldots, n)$$

$$(\text{A}_{1,2}) \quad \frac{W}{P_K} = \frac{\partial F(K, \bar{L}, \bar{T})}{\partial L}, \text{ the marginal productivity wage,}$$

$$\frac{R}{P_K} = \frac{\partial F(K, \bar{L}, \bar{T})}{\partial T}, \text{ the marginal productivity rent,}$$

$$r = \frac{\partial F(K, \bar{L}, \bar{T})}{\partial K}, \text{ the marginal productivity interest rate.}$$

Bars are put over L and T because their supplies are assumed to be fixed. To determine the unknown stock of capital K we need:

$r = p$, the subjective time preference parameter,[3]

$\text{A}_{\text{II}};$ $\dot{K} = 0$, the implied steady-state long-run equilibrium condition,

$r = R/P_T$, the implicit capitalization equation for the price of land.

Hence, $\rho = \partial F(\bar{K}, \bar{L}, T)/\partial K$ henceforth gives us our fixed $\bar{K}$.

3. In unpublished memos and lectures, using a Ramsey maximum analysis I have shown how the long-run steady-state condition where

The above relationships determine for the representative man the wage and interest income (inclusive of land rentals expressed as interest on land values) which he can spend on the $(q_1, q_2, \ldots, q_n)$ goods and on holding of M cash balances which bear no interest and thus cost their opportunity costs in terms of interest foregone (or, to a net borrower, the interest on borrowings). What motive is there for holding any M? As I pointed out in *Foundations*, one can put M into the utility function, along with other things, as a real convenience in a world of stochastic uncertainty and indivisible transaction charges.[4]

If, however, one does put M directly into U, one must remember the crucial fact that M differs from every other good (such as tea) in that it is not really wanted for its own sake but only for the ultimate exchanges it will make possible. So along with M, we must always put all Ps into U, so that U is homogeneous of degree zero in the set of monetary variables $(M, P_1, \ldots, P_m)$, with the result that $(\lambda M, \lambda P_1, \ldots, \lambda P_m)$ leads to the same U for all λ.

In *Foundations*, I wrote such a U function:

$$U(q_1, q_2, \ldots, q_n; M, P_1, P_2, \ldots, P_n)_\lambda \equiv$$
$$U(q_1, \ldots, q_m; \lambda M, \lambda P_1, \ldots, \lambda P_n),$$

where Ps are prices in terms of money. Here I want merely to add a little further cheap generality. The convenience of a given M depends not only on Ps, but also upon the earning assets you hold and on your wage prospects. It is not that we will add to M the earning-asset total EA, which equals $P_T \bar{T} + P_K \bar{K}$. Nor shall we add EA after giving the latter some fractional weight to take account of brokerage and other costs of liquidating assets into

---

$r = \rho$ is approached so that $\dot{K}$ (or $K^{t+1} - K^t$) is zero. The steady-state analysis of $U(q; M, \ldots)$ here is shorthand for the perpetual stream $\sum_{t=0}^{\infty} U(q^t; M^{t+1}, \ldots)/(1 + \rho)^t$, etc. My colleague, Professor Miguel Sidrauski, has independently arrived at such dynamic formulations.

4. This is not the only way of introducing the real convenience of cash balances. An even better way would be to let U depend only on the time stream of qs, and then to show that holding an inventory of M does contribute to a more stable and greatly preferable stream of consumptions. The present oversimplified version suffices to give the correct general picture.

cash in an uncertain world. Rather, we include such new variables in U to the right of the semicolon to get:

$$U(q_1, \ldots, q_n; M, EA, W\bar{L}, P_1, \ldots, P_n) = U(q; x) = U(q; \lambda x).$$

That is, increasing all Ps, including those of each acre of land and machine and of hourly work along with M, will not make one better off. Thus U ends up homogeneous of degree zero in M and *all* prices ($M, P_K, P_T, W, P_1, \ldots, P_n$) by postulate.

Now, subject to the long-run budget equation indicated below, the representative man maximizes his utility:

$$U(q_1, \ldots, q_n; M, P_K\bar{K} + P_T\bar{T}, W\bar{L}, P_1, \ldots, P_n)$$

subject to

$$P_1q_1 + \ldots + P_nq_n = W\bar{L} + r \text{ (Total Wealth} - M)$$

or

$$P_1q_1 + \ldots + P_nq_n + rM = W\bar{L} + r \text{ (TW)} = \\ W\bar{L} + r(P_K\bar{K} + P_T\bar{T} + M^*),$$

where each representative man has Total Wealth defined as:

$$\text{Total Wealth (in money value)} = EA + \text{Money Endowment} \\ = P_K\bar{K} + P_T\bar{T} + M^*,$$

where M^* is the money created in the past by gold mining or by government.

The maximizing optimality conditions give the demand for all q_i and for M in terms of the variables prescribed for the individual, namely:

$$(P_1, \ldots, P_n, W, P_K, P_T; r, \bar{K}, \bar{L}, \bar{T}, M^*).$$

The optimality equations can be cast in the form:

$$\frac{\partial U/\partial q_1}{P_1} = \ldots = \frac{\partial U/\partial q_n}{P_n} = \frac{\partial U/\partial M}{r}$$

or

$$(A_{\text{III},1}) \quad \frac{\partial U/\partial M}{\sum_{i=1}^{n} q_j \dfrac{\partial U}{\partial q_i} + M \dfrac{\partial U}{\partial M}} = \frac{r}{W\bar{L} + r(P_K\bar{K} + P_T\bar{T} + M^*)}$$

$$(A_{\text{III},2}) \quad \frac{\partial U/\partial q_i}{\sum_{j=1}^{n} q_j \dfrac{\partial U}{\partial q_j} + M \dfrac{\partial U}{\partial M}} = \frac{P_i}{W\bar{L} + r(P_K\bar{K} + P_T\bar{T} + M^*)}$$

$$(i = 1, 2, \ldots, n).$$

But for society as a whole (and hence for the representative man who, even if he does not know it, represents $1/N$th of the total in our symmetrical situation) total money demanded, M, must end up equalling total money endowment, M^*:

$(A_{III,3})$ $M = M^*$.

An important comment is in order.[5] Although $A_{III,3}$ holds for society as a whole, being essentially a definition of demand-for-money equilibrium, each representative man (one of thousands of such men) can*not* act in the belief that his budget equation has the form:

$$P_1 q_1 + \ldots + P_n q_n + rM = W\bar{L} + r(P_K \bar{K}_t + P_T \bar{T} + M),$$

even though substituting $A_{III,3}$ into the earlier budget equation would yield this result. What is true for all is not true for each. Each man thinks of his cash balance as costing him foregone interest and as buying himself convenience. But for the community as a whole, the total M^* is there and is quite costless to use. Forgetting gold mining and the historical expenditure of resources for the creating of M^*, the existing M^* is, so to speak, a free good from society's viewpoint, Moreover, its *effective* amount can, from the community's viewpoint, be indefinitely augmented by the simple device of having a lower absolute level of *all* money prices. To see this in still another way, with fixed labour L, land T and capital K big enough to give the interest rates equal to the psychological rate ρ, the community can consume on the production possibility equation:

$$P_1 q_1 + \ldots P_n q_n = F(\bar{K}, \bar{L}, \bar{T}) = W\bar{L} + r(P_K \bar{K} + P_T \bar{T})$$

and to *each* side of this could be added rM of any size without affecting this true physical menu.

Evidently we have here an instance of a lack of optimality of *laissez-faire*: there is a kind of fictitious internal diseconomy from holding more cash balances, as things look to the individual. Yet if all were made to hold larger cash balances, which they turned over more slowly, the resulting lowering of absolute price would end up making everybody better off. Better off in what sense? In the sense of having a higher U, which comes from having to

5. The next few paragraphs can be skipped without harm.

make fewer trips to the bank, fewer trips to the brokers, smaller printing and other costs of transactions whose only purpose is to provide cash when you have been holding too little cash.

From society's viewpoint, the optimum occurs when people are satiated with cash and have:

$$\partial U/\partial M = 0, \text{ instead of } r \times \text{ (positive constant)} > 0.$$

But this will not come about under *laissez-faire*, with stable prices (4, pp. 517–36).

Now let us return from this digression on social cost to our equations of equilibrium. Set A consists of the A_I equations relating to production and implied pricing relations, and of the A_{II} equations relating to long-run equilibrium of zero saving and investment, where technological and subjective interest rates are equal and provide capitalized values for land and other assets. Finally, A_{III} are the demand conditions for the consumer, but generalized beyond the barter world to include explicitly the qualitative convenience of money *and to take into account the peculiar homogeneity properties of money resulting from the fact that its usefulness is in proportion to the scale of prices.* Though the exact form of A_{III} is novel, its logic is that implied by intuitive classical theories of money.

All of equations A have been cast in the form of involving ratios of prices, values, and M^* only (to put A_{III} in this form, multiply M into the numerators on each side). That means they are homogeneous functions of degree zero in all Ps, and M^* or M, being capable of being written in the general form:

(A) $\quad G_i\left(q_1, \ldots, q_n, K, L, \bar{T}, r; \dfrac{P_K}{M}, \dfrac{W}{M}, \dfrac{R}{M}, \dfrac{P_1}{M}, \ldots, \dfrac{P_n}{M}, \dfrac{\text{TW}}{M}\right) = 0$

where all the magnitudes to the left of the semicolon are 'real' and all those to the right are *ratios* of a price or a value to the quantity of money. If a price ratio like P_i/P_j appears in an equation and no M, we can rewrite the ratio as $\dfrac{P_i/M}{P_j/M}$.

To the set A, we now append a decomposable single equation to fix the supply of money:

(B) $\qquad\qquad M \text{ or } M^* = \bar{M}$, an exogenous supply.

This single equation is not homogeneous of degree zero in Ps and M and therefore it does pin down the absolute scale of all Ps and values in direct proportion to the quantity of M^*. Why? Because Set A consists of as many independent equations as there are unknown real quantities and ratios. Let us check this. Omitting fixed $(\bar{L}, \bar{T})$, we count $n + 2 + n + 5$ unknowns in G_i when we ignore both $\dot{K}$ and the $\dot{K} = 0$ equation. We count $n + 3$ equations in A_I, 2 equations in A_{II}, and $n + 2$ equations in A_{III}. Thus $2n + 7 = 2n + 7$. Another way of looking at the matter is this: A_I and A_{II} determine all Ps as proportional to P_K. Then for fixed P_K and M^*, A_{III} determines all qs and M, the latter doubling when P_K and M^* double.

Summarizing, Set A determines all real quantities and all prices and values in ratio to the stock of M^*. Then equation B determines $M^* = \bar{M}$ and hence the absolute level of all prices in proportion to $\bar{M}$.

Where in A or B is the quantity theory's 'equation of exchange' to be found? Certainly not in B. If anywhere, an $MV = PQ$ equation must be found in A. Where? Certainly not in A_I or A_{II}. In A_{III}, equation $A_{III,1}$ deals with the relative marginal utility of the cash balance. By itself, it is not an $M = PQ/V$ equation. Only after all the A_{III} equations are solved, can we express M in a function that is proportional to any (and all) P_i:

$$M = P_i \psi_i (\ldots)$$

where the ψ functions depend on a great variety of real magnitudes.

This suggests to me that the late Arthur Marget was wrong in considering it a fault of Walras that, after the second edition of his *Elements*, he dropped a simple $MV = PQ$ equation. Classical and neo-classical monetary theory is much better than a crude quantity theory, although it can report similar results from special ideal experiments. In particular, correct neo-classical theory does not lead to the narrow anti-Keynesian view of those Chicago economists who allege that velocity of circulation is not a function of interest rates.

How M Gets Allocated

Symmetry plays an important role in the model given here. With every man exactly alike, it does not matter where or how we introduce new money into the system; for it gets divided among people in exactly the same proportions as previous M. We classical writers were aware that the strict (A, B) dichotomy held only when every unit's M (say $M^1, M^2, \ldots$) stayed proportional to total $\bar{M} = \sum M^k$. But being careless fellows, we often forgot to warn that this was only a first approximation to more complicated incidents of gold inflations and business cycle expansions.

Can this rock-bottom simplicity be retained if we relax this extreme symmetry assumption (which renders the problem almost a Robinson Crusoe one)? Providing all income elasticities, including that for M, are (near) unity, it never matters (much) how things are divided among people. Collective indifference curves of the Robinson Crusoe type then work for all society. The simple structure of A_{III} is preserved and the uniqueness of equilibrium is assured. Again, it matters not how the new M is introduced into the system.

Finally, there was an even more interesting third assumption implicit and explicit in the classical mind. It was a belief in unique long-run equilibrium independent of initial conditions. I shall call it the 'ergodic hypothesis' by analogy to the use of this term in statistical mechanics. Remember that the classical economists were fatalists (a synonym for 'believers in equilibrium'!). Harriet Martineau, who made fairy tales out of economics (unlike modern economists who make economics out of fairy tales), believed that if the state redivided income each morning, by night the rich would again be sleeping in their comfortable beds and the poor under the bridges. (I think she thought this a cogent argument against egalitarian taxes.)

Now, Paul Samuelson, aged 20 a hundred years later, was not Harriet Martineau or even David Ricardo; but as an equilibrium theorist he naturally tended to think of models in which things settle down to a unique position independently of initial conditions. Technically speaking, we theorists hoped not to introduce *hysteresis* phenomena into our model, as the Bible does when it says, 'We pass this way only once' and, in so saying, takes the subject out of the realm of science into the realm of genuine history. Specifically, we did not build into the Walrasian system the Christian names of particular individuals, because we thought that the general distribution of income between social classes, not being critically sensitive to initial conditions, would emerge in a determinate way from our equilibrium analysis.

Like Martineau, we envisaged an oversimplified model with the following ergodic property: no matter how we start the distribution of money among persons (M^1, M^2, . . .) after a sufficiently long time it will become distributed among them in a unique ergodic state (rich men presumably having more and poor men less). I shall not spell out here a realistic dynamic model but content myself with a simple example.

Half the people are men, half women. Each has a probability propensity to spend three quarters of its today's money on its own products and one quarter on the other sex's. We thus have a Markov transitional probability matrix of the form

$$A = \begin{bmatrix} \frac{3}{4} & \frac{1}{4} \\ \frac{1}{4} & \frac{3}{4} \end{bmatrix} = \begin{bmatrix} \frac{1}{2} + \frac{1}{2}a & \frac{1}{2} - \frac{1}{2}a \\ \frac{1}{2} - \frac{1}{2}a & \frac{1}{2} + \frac{1}{2}a \end{bmatrix},$$

with $a = \frac{1}{2}$

and $A^t = \begin{bmatrix} \frac{1}{2} + \frac{1}{2}a^t & \frac{1}{2} - \frac{1}{2}a^t \\ \frac{1}{2} - \frac{1}{2}a^t & \frac{1}{2} + \frac{1}{2}a^t \end{bmatrix}.$

$\lim\limits_{t \to \infty} A^t = \begin{bmatrix} \frac{1}{2} & \frac{1}{2} \\ \frac{1}{2} & \frac{1}{2} \end{bmatrix}$, the ergodic state.

Suppose we start out with men and women each having M of ($100, $100). Now introduce a new $100 to women only. Our transitional sequence in dollars will then be ($200, $100), ($175, $125), ($162$\frac{1}{2}$, 137\frac{1}{2}$), ($156$\frac{1}{2}$, 143\frac{3}{4}$), ($151$\frac{9}{16}$, 148\frac{7}{16}$), . . . with the obvious limiting ergodic state ($150, $150) since the divergence from this state is being halved at each step. Such an ergodic system will have the special homogeneity properties needed for the (A, B) dichotomy.[6]

6. Let me warn that this discussion in terms of a Markov probability matrix is meant to be only indicative. The temporal sequence of decisions to exchange money for goods and services and goods for money, with all that is implied for the distribution among units of the stock of M at any time, is more complicated than this. In our most idealized models, we

None of this denies the fact that the leading neo-classical economists often recognized cases and models in which it does make a difference, both in the short and the long run, how the new money is introduced and distributed throughout the system. One of the weaknesses of a crude quantity theory is that it treats M created by open-market purchases by the central bank as if this were the same as M left over from last century's (or last minute's) mining. A change in M, accompanied by an opposite change in a near-M substitute like government short-term bonds, is *not* shown in my Set A.

Indeed, when all men are alike and live for ever, we have too simple a model to take account of the interesting effect upon the system of permanent interest-bearing public debt which we as taxpayers know we will not have to pay off or service beyond our lifetimes.[7]

Epilogue

With the positive content of traditional monetary theory now written down concretely for us to see, kick and kick at, a few comments on some controversies of the last twenty years may be in order.

---

assumed that, whatever the complexity of the process, after enough time had elapsed the M would get distributed in a unique ergodic way. This does not beg the question, since there are models in which this is a theorem. In our more realistic moods, we tacitly used models involving *hysteresis*: Spain would never be the same after Columbus; Scarlett O'Hara would be permanently affected by the Confederate inflation, just as Hugo Stinnis was by the 1920–23 German inflation. Obviously, in such models all real variables do not end up unchanged as a result of certain unbalanced introductions of new M into the system. In that sense realistic equations do not seem to have the homogeneity properties in $(M, P, \ldots)$ of my Set A; but if we were to write in A the variables $(M^1, M^2, \ldots)$ and not merely their sum $\sum M^k$, it is still possible that homogeneity properties would hold – so that doubling *all* M^k together would be consistent with doubling all Ps. But this is too delicate a question to attempt in brief compass here.

7. My *Economics* (5, p. 342) shows that $(M,$ public debt) and $(\lambda M,$ λ public debt) play the role in more complicated systems that (M) and (λM) play in the simple classical system given here. Crude quantity theorists should take note of this distinction, which Franco Modigliani has also insisted on.

Oskar Lange began one line of reasoning on price flexibility in 1939 which culminated in his 1944 Cowles book, *Price Flexibility and Employment* (6). Hicks' *Value and Capital* (7), with its attempt to treat bonds and money just as some extra $n + 1$ and $n + 2$ goods along with n goods like tea and salt, had, I fear, a bad influence on Lange. It led to his suppressing possible differences between stocks and flows, to attempts to identify or contrast Say's law with various formalisms of Walrasian analysis (such as the budget equation), and to discussion in the abstract of functions of many variables possessing or not possessing certain abstract homogeneity properties. There are many interesting points raised in Lange's book, and several analytical contributions to nonmonetary economic theory. But only about a dozen pages grapple with the key problem of money (e.g. pp. 5–19), and these stay at a formalistic level that never deals with the peculiar properties and problems of cash balances. I do not say that this approach of Lange's cannot be used to arrive at valid results, but in fact it remained rather sterile for twenty years.

I had thought that Don Patinkin's work from 1947 on, culminating in his classic *Money, Interest and Prices* was much influenced by the Lange approach, and I thought this a pity. But, on rereading the book, I am not sure. What Patinkin and Lange have in common is a considerable dependence upon the *Value and Capital* device of lumping money in as an extra good. This approach has not kept Patinkin from arriving at a synthesis consistent with what I believe was the best of neo-classical theory, or from going beyond anything previously appearing in the literature. But it may help to account for his attributing error to earlier thinkers when a more sympathetic reading might absolve them from error. When we become accustomed to approaching a problem in a certain way and using a certain nomenclature, we must not confuse the failure to use this same language and approach with substantive error. Still, beyond that, Patinkin scores many legitimate points: monetary economists had better intuitions than they were able to articulate. Thus I suspect that my (A, B) dichotomy is really very similar to what Cassel had in mind, but the only form in which he could render it mathematically was (A′, B′), which is inadequate (as Patinkin insists, though perhaps not for all the reasons he insists on). In what sense can one say that a man believes one thing when he says something else? In this non-operational sense: if one could subpoena Cassel, show him the two systems and the defects in one, and then ask him which fits in best with his over-all intuitions. I believe he would pick (A, B) and not his own (A', B').[8] I might add that Cassel is not Walras; and it seems to me that Walras comes off better on Patinkin's own account than he is given credit for.

Some will interpret Archibald and Lipsey as defending an (A', B') dichotomy against Patinkin's rejection of that dichotomy. If that is their primary intention – and I am not sure that it is – I fear I must side with Patinkin. Logically, one can set up (A', B'), as I did here and as Cassel did. But I think it is bad economics to believe in such a model. *All* its good features are in the (A, B) dichotomy and none of its bad ones.

On the other hand, there is certainly much more in Archibald and Lipsey than a defence of (A', B') and this important part of their paper seems to me to be quite within the spirit of Patinkin's analysis and my own. Here, however, I shall comment the two different dichotomies.

I begin with (A', B').

(A') $F_i(q, P) \equiv F_i(q, \lambda P)$ \hfill $(i = 2, \ldots, 2n)$

(B') $P_1 = 1$ or $\sum_{j=1}^{n} q_j P_j = \bar{V} M$; $M = \bar{M}$.

Suppose that we can solve n of the A' equation to eliminate the qs, ending up with the independent homogeneous functions

(A') $f_i(P)_\lambda \equiv f_i(\lambda P) \equiv f_i(1, P_2/P_1, \ldots, P_2/P_1)$ $(i = 2, \ldots, n-1)$

(B') $\sum q_j^*(P_J/M) = \bar{V}, M = \bar{M}.$

Although f_i involve actually money Ps, it is not logically or empirically mandatory to interpret them as 'excess-demand' functions which drive up (or down) the *money* Ps. Some students of Hicks, Lange and Patinkin fall into this presupposition.

8. Needless to say, the test is not whether Aristotle, apprised of Newton's improvements over Aristotle, would afterwards acquiesce in them; the test is whether in Aristotle's writings there are non-integrated Newtonian elements. If so, we credit him only with non-integrated intuitions.

Logically, there *could* be dynamic adjustments of price ratios – as e.g. P_i/P_1 or P_i/P_j, either of which could be written as $\dfrac{P_i/M}{P_j/M}$ – of the type

(a') $\quad \dfrac{d(P_i/P_1)}{dt} = k_i f_i(1, P_2/P_1, \ldots, P_n/P_1) \quad (i = 2, \ldots, n)$

(b') $\quad \dfrac{d(P_1/M)}{dt} = k_M[\bar{M} - \sum (P_j/P_1)(P_1/M)q_j^*(1/V)], k_j, k_m > 0$

where the ks are positive speed constants of adjustment and where the q^* and V may be functions of relative Ms. Such a system could dynamically determine *relative* prices within a decomposable real Set A' and then determine the absolute price level in Set B. Note that no version of Walras' law relates B' to A' or b' to a'. Walras' law in the form that merely reflects the budget equation of each consumer is expressed in the functional dependence of the $f_1(1, P_2/P_1, \ldots)$ function (which we can ignore) on the rest – namely

$$f_1(1, P_2/P_1, \ldots) \equiv - \sum_{j=2}^{n} (P_j/P_1)f_j(1, P_2/P_1, \ldots).$$

If (a', b') is dynamically stable, $P_i/M \to$ constant is in agreement with the long-run quantity theory.[9]

References

1. P. A. SAMUELSON, *Foundations of Economic Analysis*, Harvard University Press, 1947.
2. D. PATINKIN, *Money, Interest and Prices*, 2nd edn, Harper & Row, 1965.
3. G. C. ARCHIBALD and R. G. LIPSEY, 'Monetary and value theory: a critique of Lange and Patinkin', *Review of Economic Studies*, vol. 26, 1958, pp. 1–22; and articles in subsequent numbers of this journal.

9. A short-run quantity theory need not hold. Doubling M this minute or this week need not double this week's prices. But there is a sense in which homogeneity holds in *every* run. Suppose as a *fait accompli* we are all made to wake up with every dollar of M *exactly* doubled and every P (present *and* future) exactly doubled. If nought else has changed, we recognize this to be indeed a new equilibrium. And if the time-profile of equilibrium is unique, how can we have any other time-profile of prices? At the root of this paradox is the assumption of perfectly balanced changes in M, perfect foresight, and the postulate of uniqueness of equilibrium. All this is a far cry from interpreting the stream of contemporary history.

4. P. A. SAMUELSON, 'D. H. Robertson (1890–1963)', *Quarterly Journal of Economics*, vol. 77, November 1963, no. 4, pp. 517–36, esp. p. 535.
5. P. A. SAMUELSON, *Economics*, 6th edn, McGraw-Hill, 1964.
6. O. LANGE, *Price Flexibility and Employment*, Principia, 1944.
7. J. R. HICKS, *Value and Capital*, Clarendon Press, 1939.

13 F. H. Hahn

On Some Problems of Proving the Existence of an
Equilibrium in a Monetary Economy

F. H. Hahn (1965), 'On some problems of proving the existence of an
equilibrium in a monetary economy', *The Theory of Interest Rates*, edited
by F. H. Hahn and F. Brechling, Macmillan, ch. 6, pp. 126–35.

I The Problem

Recent work on the existence of an equilibrium has been concerned with a world without money while all work in monetary
theory has ignored the 'existence' question. In this paper I propose to investigate some of the problems of rectifying this
omission. Before doing so let us ask ourselves whether the task
is worth undertaking.

Most theories in economics involve the equilibrium solutions
of certain models. These solutions are used as bench-marks, or as
states to which an economic system is believed to tend or as
means for making long-term predictions. Implicitly or explicitly
most economists, whether 'practical' or 'airy fairy', use the notion
of an equilibrium. It will also be agreed that very few of our
models have as yet been exposed to exhaustive empirical tests. It
therefore does not seem unreasonable or useless to expose them
to some logical tests in the meantime.

Suppose we found that a given model has no equilibrium
solution. This in itself need not mean that we should reject it, but
it would surely mean that we should not continue to use it to
describe equilibrium states. Take the well-known example of an
economy with strongly increasing returns to scale. It is agreed
that in this case the assumption that all units of decision take
prices as given may mean that no equilibrium solution exists.
This, it seems to me, is valuable information to have. It means that
if we judge increasing returns to scale to be prevalent and if we
also wish to discuss the working of the price mechanism by
comparing equilibrium states, or given situations with equilibrium situations, that the perfect competition model will not be
of much use. This is textbook stuff, but it is also the kind of

question existence proofs are concerned with and which has been illuminated by them.

To take an example nearer home, consider Patinkin's model of general equilibrium. Suppose it were shown that it possessed no equilibrium solution. Can it be argued that Patinkin and economists in general could reasonably be indifferent to this result? What would become of the various exercises in comparative statics which are the flesh and bones of Patinkin's argument? As it turns out, the problem is particularly interesting in this case since we must show not only that a solution exists but also that it is one in which money has positive exchange value. It is no good saying, 'We know from everyday experience that we live in a world described by Patinkin's model'. Indeed that is precisely the point at issue. We wish to inquire whether the model satisfies the minimal requirements of everyday experience. If economists are willing to count equations they should also be willing to investigate the existence of a solution to their equations.

After these rather self-evident remarks, let us get down to work.

II Equilibrium in a Monetary Economy

1. Let us first formulate the problem in the abstract. Let $P = \{P_0, \ldots, P_n\}$, $X = \{X_0, \ldots, X_n\}$ be two vectors. Suppose that we have $X_i = X_i(P)$ where $(i = 0, \ldots, n)$ or more compactly $X = X(P)$. The following assumptions[1] are made (I give them their economic names):

A.1: homogeneity (H): $X(P) = X(kP)\ k > 0, P \geqslant 0$
 Walras' law (W): $PX(P) = 0\ P \geqslant 0$
 continuity (C): $X(P)$ is continuous over $P \geqslant 0$
 boundedness (B): $X(P)$ is bounded from below
 scarcity (S): $X(0) > 0$

Given A.1 it can then be shown that there exists $P^* \geqslant 0$ such that $X(P^*) \leqslant 0$. The following obvious points should be noted:

(i) By (W) if $P_i^* > 0$, $X_i(P^*) = 0$ while only if $P_i^* = 0$ can we have $X_i(P^*) < 0$.

---

1. The notation '$\geqslant$' denotes a weak vector inequality. E.g. $X_i \geqslant 0$ means $X_i \geqslant 0$ all i, $X_i > 0$ some i.

(ii) By (H) if P^* gives $X_i(P^*) \leqslant 0$ then so does kP^*, $k > 0$.

We refer to P^* as a solution of the system $X(P) \leqslant 0$.

2. Suppose we wished to ensure that some particular component of any solution P^* is strictly positive. Let us write $P(i)$ as the vector P with its ith component identically equal to zero. If it were true that $X_i[P(i)] > 0$ all $P(i) \geqslant 0$ then evidently $P_i^* > 0$ and our task would have been accomplished.

But now let us suppose that the 0th component of X has the property

$$X_0[P(0)] \leqslant 0 \text{ all } P(0) \geqslant 0 \qquad 2.1$$

then it can easily be shown that there exists some $P^*(0) \geqslant 0$ such that $X[P^*(0)] \leqslant 0$.

For let us set $P_0 \equiv 0$ and concentrate on the vector $P(0)$. By (H) we may confine ourselves to only those $P(0)$ contained within an n-dimensional simplex. Also by (W), $\sum_{i \neq 0} P_i X_i = 0$ all $P(0) \geqslant 0$. Also if we write $\hat{P} = \{P_1, \ldots, P_n\}$ we may substitute $X_i'(\hat{P})$ for $X_i[P(0)]$ for all i. A.1 will therefore hold for the problem $X' = \{X_1, \ldots, X_n\}$, $X'(\hat{P}) = X'$ and this has a solution $\hat{P}^* \geqslant 0$. But then evidently our original problem must have a solution $P^*(0)$ where this vector has the same components as $\hat{P}^*$ and an additional zero component.

3. We may now consider an economic interpretation of the argument in 1 and 2. Let all economic agents have a two-period horizon and let the expected price of goods be always identically equal to their current price. Let there be no price uncertainty and let the initial endowments of all the agents be given. Let one of the goods have a future market and interpret P_n as the present price for the future delivery of that good and P_{n-1} as its current price. Let all prices be expressed in fictional units of account. Assume that households maximize continuous quasi-concave utility functions and that they are not satiated at any $P \geqslant 0$ and that they have positive initial endowments of every good. Suppose that the economy's production set is compact and that production without inputs is impossible. All profits are distributed to households and production agents maximize profit. They always have the choice of not producing at all and of costless disposal. We may then interpret P as a price vector and X as an excess demand vector for the current period and A.1 will hold. Note that the

future market defines an interest rate $\dfrac{P_{n-1}}{P_n} - 1$. The solution P^* gives the equilibrium prices for the current period.

The model just given is in all respects similar to Patinkin's except that it as yet contains no money. Let us designate the good with the label '0' as fiat money. We are told that the demand for fiat money depends on its exchange value (absence of 'money illusion'). It follows that no money will be demanded if its exchange value is zero. But that means that X_0 has the property 2.1. We therefore reach the rather displeasing conclusion (based on the argument in 2), that the Patinkin model always contains a 'non-monetary' solution. Moreover it is not at once clear how we could establish that it also contains a solution with $P^* > 0$. For evidently we cannot make use of the device discussed in 2 for ensuring this. Something has gone wrong.

4. Now Patinkin – and others – assume that money always has positive exchange value and it can be argued that his model is not defined for the case where it has not. For if there were no money we would have to specify more closely the activities connected with exchange. That is we are asked to replace A.1 by

A.1′: (H), (W), (C) and (B) hold for all $P \geqslant 0$, $P_0 > 0$.

The question is: can we prove that an equilibrium exists when A.1 is replaced by A.1′? Curiously enough Patinkin introduces two further assumptions which make the answer to this question affirmative. I say curiously enough, because at least one of these assumptions was introduced with a quite different end in view. Let us examine this in a little more detail.

5. We write $\bar{x}_0$ as the initial endowment of cash of individual α and $X_{i\alpha}$ as this individual's excess demand for the ith good. Given the absence of 'money illusion' it is well known that we may write, using the notation introduced in 2,

$$X_{i\alpha} = X_{i\alpha}(\hat{P}, P_0 \bar{x}_{0\alpha}) \text{ for all } i.$$

Moreover, $X_{i\alpha}$ possesses (H) in the given arguments. Write $\bar{x}_0 = \sum_\alpha \bar{x}_{0\alpha}$. Patinkin's two further assumptions are:

A.2: we may write $X_i \equiv \sum_\alpha X_i = X_i(\hat{P}, P_0 \bar{x}_0)$ for all i.

A.3: $X_0(\hat{P}, P_0 \bar{x}_0) > 0$ for all $\hat{P} \geqslant 0$, $P_0 > 0$, $\bar{x}_0 = 0$.

A.2 states that all individuals are exactly alike so that the total excess demand for any good is independent of the distribution of initial cash balances between them. By 'exactly alike' we here mean that they all have parallel linear Engel curves going through the origin. A.3 states that the demand for money is always strictly positive for all prices admissible by A.1′.

Now using A.1′, A.2 and A.3 the existence of an equilibrium can be established. Here I shall only sketch a proof. Set $P_0 \equiv 1$ and consider the simplex

$$S = \{P, \bar{x}_0/P_i \geqslant 0 \text{ for all } i, \bar{x}_0 \geqslant 0, \sum P_i + \bar{x}_0 = 1\}.$$

A.1′ holds over S. We may now use a slightly modified mapping of S into itself first proposed by Uzawa

$$P_j = \frac{1}{k} \max [0, P_j + hX_j] \text{ for all } j \neq 0$$

$$\bar{x}_0 = \frac{1}{k} \max [0, \bar{x}_0 + hX_0]$$

$$k = \sum_{j=0} \max [0, P_j + hX_j] + \max [0, \bar{x}_0 + hX_0]$$

where h is taken sufficiently small to ensure $k > 0$. (Recall (B) of A.1′.) The mapping 5.1 can be shown to have at least one fixed point $\hat{P}^*$, $\bar{x}_0^*$. Using (W), we easily find

$$(k-1)[\sum_{i \neq 0} (P_i^*)^2 + \bar{x}_0^*] = h[\sum P_i^* X_i(P^*\bar{x}_0^*) + X_0(P^*\bar{x}_0^*)]=0$$

so that at the fixed point $k = 1$. It is now easy to see that, using A.3, $X_i(\hat{P}^*\bar{x}_0^*) \leqslant 0$ and $P_i^* X_i = 0$ all $i \neq 0$ and $X_0(\hat{P}^*\bar{x}_0^*) = 0$.

Since by A.3, $\bar{x}_0^* > 0$ and by A.2 its redistribution between individuals leaves all excess-demand functions unaffected, we may redistribute it between individuals in the ratio of their actual initial endowments. A simple scale change (of $\hat{P}^*$ and $\bar{x}_0^*$) will then give us the money stocks for each individual which he started out with and the problem is solved.

It is evident that a proof of the existence of equilibrium which turns crucially on a supposition such as A.2 is hardly acceptable. Indeed the rule of this assumption is simply to enable us to employ a technical trick to ensure that we can use a fixed point theorem and one cannot believe that it has any fundamental significance to the whole problem. The trick of course was to keep the exchange value of money strictly positive throughout so that money was always 'desirable' and to obtain the desired continuity by varying initial total stocks knowing that once an equilibrium was found the actual initial stock distribution could be restored without upsetting the equilibrium. But quite apart from A.2, A.3 too will repay further scrutiny.

6. The supposition that the demand for money will always be positive when $P_0 > 0$ is justified by Patinkin by an appeal to the alleged uncertainty of the exact instant of sales and purchases within a given time period. We are also asked to imagine there to be a 'penalty' for being out of cash when a given purchase comes due. Tobin and Baumol justify the same assumption by the existence of transaction costs (brokerage fees). All assume that no transactions are possible without the intermediate use of money. It is, I think, evident that none of these rationalizations can be taken as an explanation of the positive exchange value of money since that is already assumed.

Now explanations which turn on 'brokerage' fees and the 'inconvenience' of indirect transactions are not easy to accommodate in a model such as Patinkin's. These are all 'imperfections' which find no place in the model. Indeed the notion of 'liquidity' would be hard to accommodate in Patinkin's world for that, as Marschak has pointed out, turns rather crucially on the imperfections of markets. But even Patinkin's own preferred account is not easy to understand. We are told that there exist claims to debt. A unit of these is the promise to pay one unit of account in perpetuity. Let us suppose that they are (or have been) issued by the government which otherwise plays no role in the economy other than financing its interest payments by lump sum taxes. There is no price uncertainty. Why should transactions not be carried out by means of these claims to debt? But even if that is not granted it is not clear why when I come to make a purchase, being out of cash (having miscalculated the timing of my receipts), I could not offer to pay a little later (after I have cashed my claim), a little more (offer interest). In Patinkin's world such an offer should always be acceptable, and if trade credits cause no social embarrassment in the world we live in why should it in the abstract world of the textbook?

All this suggests that while Patinkin has rendered signal services he has failed to provide a model which can serve as an adequate foundation for a monetary theory. Such a model, it seems to me, must have two essential features beside price uncertainty. It must distinguish between abstract exchange opportunities at some notionally called prices and actual transaction opportunities. The latter requires a precise statement of the methods of transactions open to an individual with their attendant costs. Secondly it must specify rather precisely the conditions in which future markets for various commodities would arise. For if there were future markets in all goods and services and no price uncertainty there would, as in Debreu's world, be only need for one single set of transactions over an individual's lifetime and there would be no problem of the non-coincidence of payments and receipts. This involves questions of costs of storage, etc. But it also involves questions of the 'standardization' of commodities. It forces one to recognize that there is no commodity called 'a second-hand car' and makes the unsuitability of 'perfect competition models' to monetary theory rather obvious.

7. The reason why I do not propose to attempt the construction of such a model there is as follows: In the usual existence problem the 'initial' position of the participants can be described independently of prices, i.e. in terms of the initial endowment of goods, technological knowledge, etc. The interesting point of a monetary economy is that we cannot do so. For it is one of the features of such an economy that contrasts, as Keynes noted, are made in terms of money. In particular, debt obligations are of this kind. By postulating the possibility of 'recontract', etc. this difficulty could be overcome – but it would then, it seems to me, turn out to be a somewhat arid exercise. In any case it is on this aspect of the problem that I wish to dwell in the remainder of this paper.

Before doing so, however, it might just be worth while to sketch a procedure which could be used to establish the existence of an equilibrium in Patinkin's world if his basic assumptions are granted, but A.2 is not used.

We imagine a world without money. Each individual attaches certain probabilities to being able to effect a given exchange at the exchange rates 'called'. However, he may, if he wishes, take out insurance. A unit of insurance is the guarantee of being able to carry out a transaction worth one unit of account at a given moment of time. One may suppose that as long as exchange is desired at all and as long as the price per unit of insurance is not equal to unity, some insurance is demanded. Insurance is supplied by some outside agency, say the government. The price charged per unit of insurance per unit time is $\left(\dfrac{P_{n-1}}{P_n} - 1\right)$, the rate of interest. At any price the amount of insurance supplied is just equal to what is demanded. The government redistributes the proceeds from its activity to households. It can then be shown with the aid of a number of purely technical assumptions that an equilibrium exists. It can then further be shown that corresponding to this fictional economy there would exist an actual one in which individuals 'bought' the same amount of insurance as in the fictional equilibrium by holding certain stocks of cash. Notice that this procedure begs the question: is the government service the only way by means of which economic agents could insure their transactions?

III Are There Solutions of Realistic Monetary Models?

8. So far I have been concerned with the question of whether it is possible to construct an abstract model of economic exchange and activity in which money is used and whether the existence of an equilibrium can be proved for such a model. I hope to have shown that even for this task the difficulties are fairly formidable and that they have not yet been faced. I now wish to concern myself with the more interesting question of the existence of a solution to monetary models which are to be taken not as idealized but as in some sense as representing actual relationships. The most famous of these is of course the Keynesian short-period flow-equilibrium model.

It will be recalled that Keynes argued that if we set up a model which included the requirement that everyone willing to work at the going money wage should be able to do so, then whatever the money wage specified, no equilibrium solution may exist. Keynes further maintained that it was the existence of money in the economy, or more precisely the fact that wage bargains were made in terms of money and that money was always the preferred asset at a rate of interest 'low enough' which was responsible for that conclusion.

This has been widely rationalized in a way best given by a quotation taken from Modigliani. 'Since securities are inferior to money as a form of holding assets, there must be some positive level of the rate of interest (previously denoted by r) at which the demand for money becomes infinitely elastic or practically so. We have the Keynesian case when the full employment rate of interest is less than r''. . . . From the analytical point of view the situation is characterized by the fact that we must add to our system a new equation, namely $r = r''$. The system is therefore overdetermined . . .' (1).

That this way of putting the case is wrong seems quite clear. The hypothesis that the equilibrium rate of interest cannot fall below a certain minimum is not an additional restriction on our system and provides no new independent relation between any of the unknowns. It is simply a hypothesis concerning the form of one or more of the excess demand functions of the system. Provided these satisfied A.1. and there were as many excess-demand functions as unknowns the 'liquidity stop' would not prevent the existence of an equilibrium.

This has been recognized by a large number of writers although the objection is not usually put in this way. Instead it is argued that Keynes ignored the connexion between real cash balances and consumption. It is now widely believed that there always exists a level of money wages low enough which will ensure the existence of a 'full employment' solution. The argument is as follows: we are concerned with the technical problem of the existence of a solution. Thus while the 'Pigou effect' may be small in practice, by making money prices and wages low enough we can always make the Pigou effect 'large enough'. Indeed, since at zero money, wages and prices, there will always be excess demand (non-satiation and scarcity) for goods and labour, there will be some positive set of prices at which the excess demand for goods and labour is zero. I now wish to give reasons why this argument rests on some rather shaky foundations.

9. One of the main problems faced in establishing the existence of an equilibrium is to find acceptable assumptions which will

ensure that the excess-demand functions are continuous over the relevant domain. Among these the one that has caused most difficulty is the necessity of ensuring that at all admissible prices every individual can, if he wishes, participate in some exchange. Consider an individual who owns positive stocks of one good only: say $\bar{x}_1$. Let there be only two goods. Suppose that as long as he is able, our individual always prefers to have whatever quantities of the second good he can get, to the good he has. Then for all $1 > P_1 > 0$, he will demand nothing of the first good $(P_1 + P_2 = 1)$. But at $P_1 = 0$ he has no choice but to hold the good he has. There will be a discontinuity in his demand function. To exclude this possibility we can either postulate that he has strictly positive stocks of every good or that, loosely speaking, he is always capable of supplying a service which can be transformed into a good with positive price. One might equally suppose that there is some suitable redistribution mechanism at work which allows every individual to participate in exchange.

But now let us suppose that our individual has initial endowments which include debt fixed in terms of money at a rate of interest also so fixed. Then as the price of goods in terms of money is made lower and lower (i.e. in our earlier notation as $P_0 \to 1$) our individual will be unable to meet his obligations: he will go bankrupt. Since at that stage – even if the creditors get all the debtor's assets, and if the debtors and creditors are similar as in A.2 – the value of these assets may be less than the money value of the debt. For the debtor being capable of rendering services will go 'bankrupt' when he can no longer meet his interest payments. At that stage his assets may already be negative. The possibility of 'bankruptcy' is therefore also a possibility for the occurrence of some rather sharp discontinuities. In a society where contracts are made in terms of money and recontract is not possible an equilibrium solution may not exist. Of course in the 'long run' all contracts are escapable but that is another story.

10. The point just made is perhaps of more than purely academic interest since it focuses attention on what is probably one of the most important features of a monetary economy: namely that contracts are made in terms of money. The fact that money is the actual *numéraire* is of some significance. If the route from unemployment to high levels of demand is strewn with

bankruptcies then the smooth curves of the textbooks will be harder to justify. No doubt some sort of story could be invented to get over this difficulty, but it would be a curious one. Let me emphasize again that the difficulty cannot be overcome by supposing creditors and debtors to be exactly alike. For as long as any debtor is not bankrupt the real value of his debt to me increases with lower money prices. When he goes bankrupt and I take over his assets, their money value will be less than the value of the debt and so there is a discontinuous change in the real value of money assets. I conclude from all this that the assertion that the Pigou effect ensures the existence of an equilibrium is unproven.

Reference

1. F. MODIGLIANI, 'Liquidity preference and the theory of interest and money', *Econometrica*, vol. 12, 1944, pp. 45–88.

14 R. W. Clower

Foundations of Monetary Theory

R. W. Clower (1967), 'A reconsideration of the microfoundations of monetary theory', *Western Economic Journal*, vol. 6, pp. 1–9.

Modern attempts to erect a general theory of money and prices on Walrasian foundations[1] have produced a model of economic phenomena that is suspiciously reminiscent of the classical theory of a barter economy (5, 6). My purpose in this paper is to show that the conception of a money economy implicit in these constructions is empirically and analytically vacuous, and to propose an alternative microfoundation for the pure theory of a money economy.

I

For simplicity of exposition, I shall address my critique of the general equilibrium theory of money and prices to the classic statement presented in Don Patinkin's *Money, Interest and Prices*. Following Patinkin, suppose that we have to deal with an economy in which trading is rigidly synchronized within each of a series of discrete market periods. At the outset of every period, each transactor receives 'like manna from heaven' a collection of goods that may be consumed directly,[2] or traded for a preferred collection of goods or for money at rates of exchange established by an independent market authority in accordance with prevailing conditions of market excess demand.

By hypothesis, market excess demands are defined in terms of

1. I refer specifically to O. Lange, *Price Flexibility and Employment* (1) and Don Patinkin, *Money, Interest and Prices* (2); but my comment applies also to certain portions of Hicks' *Value and Capital* (3) and Samuelson's *Foundations* (4).

2. Manna commodities may be considered to include all goods and services, supplies of which are decision parameters rather than decision variables in the current period.

individual demand functions for goods and money obtained as solutions to the decision problem:

$$\text{Maximize } U_j(d_{1j}, \ldots, d_{nj}, M_j/P) \qquad \textbf{1}$$

subject to

$$\sum_{i=1}^{n} p_i(d_{ij} - s_{ij}) + M_j - M_j' = 0, \qquad \textbf{2}$$

where U_j satisfies familiar continuity and curvature conditions, s_{ij} and d_{ij} represent initial and desired quantities of goods, M_j' and M_j represent initial and desired quantities of fiat money, and P is a fixed-weight index of the money prices $p_1, \ldots, p_n$. The empirical content of the theory thus derives ultimately from behavior restrictions implicit in equations **1** and **2**. As it happens, the implications of the continuity and curvature conditions imposed on the utility functions **1** are exhausted in certain analytically subtle but empirically trivial restrictions involving the existence of demand functions and the continuity of their partial derivatives. The factual content of the theory depends very largely, therefore, on restrictions implicit in the budget equations **2**. Accordingly, the main question that we have to answer in order to appraise the empirical significance of contemporary monetary theory is: 'Do the budget equations **2** constitute an appropriate definition of choice alternatives in a money economy?'

That the appropriateness of the choice alternatives defined by **2** is open to serious question may be seen most easily by conducting a few simple conceptual experiments. First, consider an economy in which all transactors but one have a violent aversion to holding money balances. Starting from any initial distribution of money balances, market trading over one or more periods will ultimately yield a situation in which the entire stock of money is held by a single individual. Changes in initial endowments of goods or in the stock of money will generate precisely the same qualitative effects in this model as would occur in a system where all transactors were willing to hold money balances in full equilibrium; hence the model differs in no essential respect from models discussed by Patinkin and other writers. But our model is so defined that, in equilibrium, money is not used in any exchange transaction. More pointedly, that fact that $M_j' = 0$ for all but one value of j in no way prevents any transactor from exerting an influence on market excess demands for goods. For the goods variables s_{ij} enter the budget equations **2** in precisely the same manner as the money variables M'_j, which is to say that *goods are indistinguishable from money as sources of effective demand.*

Next consider a general Patinkin model in which all money prices except that of labor services are free to vary. Suppose that the economy, starting from a state of full equilibrium, experiences a reduction in its stock of fiat money (the result, let us say, of a disastrous fire). The price level of goods other than labor will decline; hence, real wages will rise and the demand for labor will fall. When equilibrium is eventually re-established, therefore, labor will be in excess supply. But the excess demand for all goods except labor will be zero. By Walras' law, therefore, the money value of unsold labor will be positive and equal to the excess demand for money balances. If in this situation the quantity of labor offered for sale by any transactor increases, the immediate effect on demand for other goods will be the same as if the transactor had experienced an increase in his stock of money. An autonomous increase in unemployment will thus generate a rise in the price level of other goods, a decline in the real wage rate, and so an increase in employment and output! It can be shown, indeed, that an increase in unsold stocks of any commodity the price of which is fixed will, in a Patinkinesque world, generate an increase in the general price level and so, indirectly, a rise in sales of the good whose price is fixed.[3] Again, therefore, we arrive at a conclusion that is offensive to our intuitive conception of the working of a money economy, a conclusion that indicates that money plays no distinctive role in economic activity.

The same result may be reached more directly by noticing that the budget equations **2** admit as feasible trades every possible combination of commodities traded in the economy; i.e., any commodity, whether a good or money, can be offered directly in trade for every other commodity. But an economy that admits of this possibility clearly constitutes what any classical economist would regard as a barter rather than a money economy (7). The fact

3. All of these conclusions are, of course, predicated on the assumption that the economic system is stable; i.e. that prices adjust so that markets for all commodities whose prices are permitted to vary ultimately clear.

that fiat money is included among the set of tradeable commodities is utterly irrelevant; the role of money in economic activity is analytically indistinguishable from that of any other commodity.

II

The answer to our query about the appropriateness of the budget constraints of established theory as a description of choice alternatives in a money economy is negative; what presently passes for a theory of a money economy is in truth descriptive of a barter economy. I turn now to the task of reformulating accepted theory to reflect relevant restrictions on transactor behaviour in a world where 'money matters'.

The natural point of departure for a theory of monetary phenomena is a precise distinction between money and nonmoney commodities. In this connexion it is important to observe that such a distinction is possible only if we assign a special role to certain commodities as means of payment. For any commodity may serve as a unit of account and standard of deferred payment: and every asset is, by its very nature, a potential store of value. If money is to be distinguished by the functions it performs, therefore, it is to the medium of exchange function that we must address our attention. The only difficulty is to express analytically what is meant when we assert that a certain commodity serves as a medium of exchange.

To resolve this difficulty, we proceed by associating with any set of commodities $C = (C_1, \ldots, C_n)$ an *exchange relation*, E, defined as a subset of the Cartesian product $C \times C$ of the commodity set C; i.e. a set of ordered pairs of commodity elements (C_i, C_j). We then say that a trade involving two commodities C_i and C_j is *feasible* if and only if the pair (C_i, C_j) is an element of the exchange relation, and we write $C_i E C_j$ (read 'commodity i can be traded directly for commodity j') to indicate that this condition is met.

The exchange relation is necessarily non-empty and reflexive, for since any commodity available for trade can be held by the individual who possesses it, the condition $C_i E C_i$ is satisfied vacuously for all possible values of i. Moreover, the exchange relation is symmetric; for if $C_i E C_j$, then by the nature of trade it must also be true that $C_j E C_i$.[4] In general, however, the exchange relation need not be transitive; that is to say, $C_i E C_j$ and $C_j E C_k$ may or may not entail $C_j E C_k$. Transitivity of the exchange relation of an economy is, in fact, characteristic of just one class of economies, namely, barter economies. This follows directly from the definition of a barter economy as one in which any commodity may be offered directly in trade for every commodity; i.e., an economy for which $C_i E C_j$ is true for all values of i and j.

Now define as a *money commodity* any element C_i of C for which $C_i E C_j$ is true for all values of j; i.e. any commodity that can be traded directly for all other commodities. It then follows that *a barter economy is one in which all commodities are money commodities*. This characterization of a barter economy may seem

Table 1 Alternative Exchange Relations

	C_1	C_2
C_1	X	X
C_2	X	X

	C_1	C_2	C_3
C_1	X	X	X
C_2	X	X	0
C_3	X	0	X

	C_1	C_2	C_3	C_4
C_1	X	X	X	X
C_2	X	X	0	0
C_3	X	0	X	X
C_4	X	0	X	X

(a) barter economy   (b) pure money economy   (c) non-pure money economy

paradoxical at first sight; but if one ponders the matter it becomes clear that the peculiar feature of a money as contrasted with a barter economy is precisely that *some* commodities in a money economy *cannot* be traded directly for all other commodities; i.e. some exchanges necessarily involve intermediate monetary transactions. More precisely, we now define a money economy as a system involving at least one money commodity but a nontransitive exchange relation. We note in passing that the simplest money economy must contain at least three commodities as illustrated in Table 1(b) (X indicates that $C_i E C_j$; 0 that $C_i F C_j$). For if it contains fewer than three, then as indicated in Table 1(a), the reflexivity and symmetry of the exchange relation implies that all elements of $C \times C$ are included in E. It follows – in keeping

4. Cf. the contrary but nonsensical opening statement of Patinkin's *Money, Interest and Prices*: 'Money buys goods, and goods do not buy money' (2).

with common sense – that every two-commodity economy is a barter economy. Similarly, the simplest money economy that admits simultaneously of certain forms of barter (i.e. direct trading of certain commodities none of which are money commodities) must contain at least four commodities, as illustrated in Table 1(c). In general, the exchange relation of a money economy may contain numerous barter subsets (trade credit, blocked currencies, credit cards, demand deposits, etc.). Such *non-pure money economies* (as I shall call them) seriously complicate the task of defining relevant choice alternatives for transactors. Accordingly, I shall restrict attention in the argument that follows to *pure money economies* in which one and only one commodity can be traded directly for any other commodity.

So much for the distinction between money and other commodities and for the characterization of money as contrasted with barter economies. A commodity is regarded as money for our purposes if and only if it can be traded directly for all other commodities in the economy. Correspondingly, a money economy is one in which not all commodities are money. It should perhaps be observed that the feasibility of particular trades is tacitly assumed to be determined by institutional and environmental rather than economic considerations. That is to say, the exchange relation of an economy either does or does not assign a special role to certain commodities as money. The distinction between money and other commodities is thus a matter not of degree but of kind. One might express this thought more elliptically by saying that money is traded in all markets in a money economy, or, alternatively, by saying that transaction costs are infinite for any market exchange that does not involve the offer of money as a means of payment.

III

Having enunciated sharp definitions of relevant primitive terms, it is now a straightforward matter to characterize the choice alternatives open to transactors in a pure money economy. We begin by recalling that the peculiar feature of a money economy is that some commodities (in the present context, all but one) are denied a role as potential or actual means of payment. To state the same idea as an aphorism: *Money buys goods and goods buy money; but goods do not buy goods.* This restriction is – or ought to be – the central theme of the theory of a money economy. The task of reformulating microeconomic analysis to accommodate those aspects of experience that are commonly supposed to distinguish a money from a barter economy consists, indeed, of little more than an elaboration of the implications of this one restriction.

Our aphorism automatically rules out the standard budget constraints of neo-Walrasian equilibrium analysis as accurate descriptions of planning alternatives open to transactors in a money economy. For, as remarked earlier, the familiar budget constraint effectively admits as feasible trades all pairwise combinations of commodities that are traded in the economy. In sharp contrast, choice alternatives in a money economy must be so defined as to satisfy the requirement that money be offered or demanded as one of the commodities entering into every trade. Analytically, what this entails is a clear separation between goods demanded for purchase (offers to sell money) and goods offered for sale (offers to buy money). This condition may be met most easily by dichotomizing the budget constraint into two branches, the first representing a constraint on money expenditure, the second representing a constraint on money income. Symbolically, we have

$$\sum_{i=1}^{n} P_i x_{ij} + M_j - M_j' = 0, \, x_{ij} \equiv d_{ij} - s_{ij}, \text{where } x_{ij} \geqslant 0 \quad 3$$

as the *expenditure constraint*, and

$$\sum_{i=1}^{n} P_i x_{ij} + m_j = 0, \text{ where } x_{ij} < 0 \quad\quad 4$$

as the *income constraint*, where m_j represents desired 'intra-period' receipts of money income and all other symbols are defined precisely as before.

The expenditure constraint asserts that all (net) purchase offers must be backed by a readiness to supply money in exchange. Note that the expenditure constraint cannot be satisfied for non-negative values of all x_{ij} unless $M_j - M_j'$ is non-positive (i.e., $0 \leqslant M_j \leqslant M_j'$). Thus M corresponds to what is commonly referred to as demand for precautionary money balances; i.e.

total initial cash balances less prospective (gross) depletions of cash balances for currently scheduled purchases of goods. It follows that the *total value of goods demanded cannot in any circumstances exceed the amount of money held by the transactor at the outset of the period.* Our definition of choice alternatives thereby captures the essential meaning of the traditional (but curiously non-modern) contention that demand in a money economy is effective only if it involves a combination of desire with money purchasing power.

The income constraint asserts that all (net) sale offers involve a demand for just one other commodity, namely money, in exchange. Thus m_j corresponds to what is commonly referred to as demand for transactions balances (to replace cash currently scheduled for disbursement from initial holdings of money balances).[5] For convenient reference, I shall refer henceforth to m_j as the income demand for money, to M as the reservation demand for money. Such a separation of income and reservation demands has no place in accepted equilibrium models, for these models invariably contain a budget constraint that permits but does not require that offers to purchase goods be backed by willingness to give, and that offers to sell goods be accompanied by willingness to receive units of money in exchange. The omission of these restrictions from contemporary monetary theory is a natural consequence of the tacit presupposition, appropriate in a world of *tâtonnement* or recontract, that money is just one of many commodities that may be bartered directly for other commodities.

Given the budget restraints 3 and 4, we may write the utility function of a typical transactor as

$$U_j(d_{ij}, \ldots, d_{nj}, M_j/P, m_j/P) \qquad 5$$

and proceed as usual to define individual demand functions, for goods, reservations balances and money income as solutions to the problem of maximizing 5 subject to the expenditure and income constraints 3 and 4. The inequality conditions that determine whether a given net demand x_{ij} enters the expenditure or the income constraint preclude us from stating precise conditions that will guarantee the existence of the required solutions.

5. The income constraint cannot be satisfied for non-positive values of x_{ij} unless $m_j > 0$; like the variable M_j, therefore, m_j is, in general, positive.

Supposing that the decision problem has a solution, however, we arrive at individual demand and excess-demand functions that differ in crucial respects from those of established theory.

As in established theory, so in our model the demand functions for goods and for real money income and real reservation balances are homogeneous of degree zero in money prices and initial money balances. In contrast with established theory, however, substitution effects of changes in price are asymmetrical unless both commodities are either offered for sale or demanded for purchase. Unlike established theory, moreover, a change in initial money balances has no 'income' effect on goods offered for sale. More significantly, changes in initial endowments of goods have no 'income' effect on commodities that are demanded for purchase; i.e. supply of goods does not create demand for other goods. All of these results are obvious consequences of dichotomizing budget constraints into separate expenditure and income branches.[6]

As in established theory, the money value of the sum of all excess demands, including the excess demand for reservation balances and for money income, is identically zero; hence a proposition analogous to what has come to be known as Walras' law applies to transactors in a money as well as to transactors in a barter economy. As noted earlier, however, in our model the money value of the sum of *gross* demands for goods and for reservation balances is identically equal to initial cash balances. Demand (and excess-demand) functions in a money economy are thus subject to much more severe restrictions than are those of a barter economy – the latter category being interpreted to include all neo-Walrasian models of money and prices.

A full statement of the implications of my proposed micro-foundation for monetary theory cannot be given here. For present purposes, it is sufficient to observe that the results given above ensure that the response of transactors to changes in prices or in initial endowments of goods or money will differ qualitatively from findings suggested by established theory. Correspondingly, the response of market prices and quantities traded to changes in

6. Certain qualifications are in order if the initial solution value of $x_{1j} = 0$, for in this case changes in M_j or s_{ij} determine which branch of the budget constraint the terminal solution value of x_{1j} enters.

tastes, initial endowments, or in the aggregate stock of money will differ qualitatively from findings associated with established doctrines.

IV

The tasks that I set myself in this paper were: firstly, to demonstrate that the conception of money economy implicit in modern accounts of the general equilibrium theory of money and prices is formally equivalent to the classical conception of a barter economy; secondly, to propose a reformulation of established microeconomic analysis suitable as a foundation for explicit analysis of the working of a money economy. The first of these tasks has, I think, been carried through to completion. The second is obviously unfinished. All I have done is to exhibit a model that is immune to the specific criticisms that can be levelled at established microeconomic analysis – a model where, in sharp contrast with established theory, money commodities play a peculiar and central role in shaping prevailing forces of excess demand. My work with this model has already yielded numerous results, including an explicit formal integration of price theory and income analysis and a wholesale reconstruction of large areas of multiple-market dynamics. These and other findings will be presented elsewhere. My central aim in this paper has been not so much to present results of finished research as to communicate to other economists what seems to me a fruitful conceptual basis for systematic theoretical analysis of large areas of experience that have hitherto eluded such treatment.

References

1. O. LANGE, *Price Flexibility and Employment*, Principia, 1944.
2. D. PATINKIN, *Money, Interest and Prices*, 2nd edn, Harper & Row, 1965.
3. J. R. HICKS, *Value and Capital*, Clarendon Press, 1939.
4. P. A. SAMUELSON, *Foundations of Economic Analysis*, Harvard University Press, 1947.
5. J. R. HICKS, 'A rehabilitation of "classical" economics?' *Economic Journal*, vol. 67, June 1957, p 278.
6. F. H. HAHN, T. NEGISHI and R. W. CLOWER, papers in *The Theory of Interest Rates*, edited by F. H. Hahn and F. Brechling, Macmillan, 1965.
7. J. S. MILL, 'Of money', *Principles of Political Economy*, Book 3, Longmans, Green & Co., 6th edn, 1888, ch. 7, pp. 293–7.

Part Four Monetary Theory and Keynesian Economics

Keynes' *General Theory of Employment, Interest and Money* is, *par excellence*, a theory of the actual working of a money economy. Unfortunately, Keynes expressed his ideas in language and relations that too easily lend themselves to interpretation within the formal framework of neo-classical equilibrium analysis. Partly for this reason, partly because the actual working of a monetary economy is inherently difficult to portray analytically, economic theorists are still arguing about the precise nature of the so-called Keynesian revolution or, as some would put it, the precise difference between a money and a barter economy. There is a vast literature on this subject, most of it having some bearing on monetary theory, much of it already available in earlier volumes of readings on macro-economics. With two exceptions, the selections reprinted here are recent enough to have benefited from previous discussion of the points at issue.

15 J. M. Keynes

The General Theory: Fundamental Concepts and Ideas

J. M. Keynes (1937), 'The general theory of employment', *Quarterly Journal of Economics*, vol. 51, pp. 209–23.

I am more attached to the comparatively simple fundamental ideas which underlie my theory than to the particular forms in which I have embodied them, and I have no desire that the latter should be crystallized at the present stage of the debate. If the simple basic ideas can become familiar and acceptable, time and experience and the collaboration of a number of minds will discover the best way of expressing them. [. . .]

I

It is generally recognized that the Ricardian analysis was concerned with what we now call long-period equilibrium. Marshall's contribution mainly consisted in grafting on to this the marginal principle and the principle of substitution, together with some discussion of the passage from one position of long-period equilibrium to another. But he assumed, as Ricardo did, that the amounts of the factors of production in use were given and that the problem was to determine the way in which they would be used and their relative rewards. Edgeworth and Professor Pigou and other later and contemporary writers have embroidered and improved this theory by considering how different peculiarities in the shapes of the supply functions of the factors of production would affect matters, what will happen in conditions of monopoly and imperfect competition, how far social and individual advantage coincide, what are the special problems of exchange in an open system, and the like. But these more recent writers like their predecessors were still dealing with a system in which the amount of the factors employed was given and the other relevant facts were known more or less for certain. This does not mean that they were dealing with a system in which change was ruled out, or even one in which the disappointment of expectation was ruled out. But at any given time facts and expectations were assumed to be given in a definite and calculable form; and risks, of which, though admitted, not much notice was taken, were supposed to be capable of an exact actuarial computation. The calculus of probability, though mention of it was kept in the background, was supposed to be capable of reducing uncertainty to the same calculable status as that of certainty itself; just as in the Benthamite calculus of pains and pleasures or of advantage and disadvantage, by which the Benthamite philosophy assumed men to be influenced in their general ethical behavior.

Actually, however, we have, as a rule, only the vaguest idea of any but the most direct consequences of our acts. Sometimes we are not much concerned with their remoter consequences, even though time and chance may make much of them. But sometimes we are intensely concerned with them, more so, occasionally, than with the immediate consequences. Now of all human activities which are affected by this remoter preoccupation, it happens that one of the most important is economic in character, namely, wealth. The whole object of the accumulation of wealth is to produce results, or potential results, at a comparatively distant, and sometimes at an *indefinitely* distant, date. Thus the fact that our knowledge of the future is fluctuating, vague and uncertain, renders wealth a peculiarly unsuitable subject for the methods of the classical economic theory. This theory might work very well in a world in which economic goods were necessarily consumed within a short interval of their being produced. But it requires, I suggest, considerable amendment if it is to be applied to a world in which the accumulation of wealth for an indefinitely postponed future is an important factor; and the greater the proportionate part played by such wealth-accumulation the more essential does such amendment become.

By 'uncertain' knowledge, let me explain, I do not mean merely to distinguish what is known for certain from what is only probable. The game of roulette is not subject, in this sense, to uncertainty; nor is the prospect of a Victory Bond being drawn. Or, again, the expectation of life is only slightly uncertain. Even the weather is only moderately uncertain. The sense in which I am using the term is that in which the prospect of a European war is uncertain, or the price of copper and the rate of interest twenty years hence, or the obsolescence of a new invention, or the position of private wealth-owners in the social system in 1970. About these matters there is no scientific basis on which to form any capable probability whatever. We simply do not know. Nevertheless, the necessity for action and for decision compels us as practical men to do our best to overlook this awkward fact and to behave exactly as we should if we had behind us a good Benthamite calculation of a series of prospective advantages and disadvantages, each multiplied by its appropriate probability, waiting to be summed.

How do we manage in such circumstances to behave in a manner which saves our faces as rational economic men? We have devised for the purpose a variety of techniques, of which much the most important are the three following:

1. We assume that the present is a much more serviceable guide to the future than a candid examination of past experience would show it to have been hitherto. In other words we largely ignore the prospect of future changes about the actual character of which we know nothing.

2. We assume that the *existing* state of opinion as expressed in prices and the character of existing output is based on a *correct* summing up of future prospects, so that we can accept it as such unless and until something new and relevant comes into the picture.

3. Knowing that our own individual judgement is worthless, we endeavor to fall back on the judgement of the rest of the world, which is perhaps better informed. That is, we endeavor to conform with the behavior of the majority or the average. The psychology of a society of individuals each of whom is endeavoring to copy the others leads to what we may strictly term a *conventional* judgement.

Now a practical theory of the future based on these three principles has certain marked characteristics. In particular, being based on so flimsy a foundation, it is subject to sudden and violent changes. The practice of calmness and immobility, of certainty and security, suddenly breaks down. New fears and hopes will, without warning, take charge of human conduct. The forces of disillusion may suddenly impose a new conventional basis of valuation. All these pretty, polite techniques, made for a well-panelled board room and a nicely regulated market, are liable to collapse. At all times the vague panic fears and equally vague and unreasoned hopes are not really lulled and lie but a little way below the surface.

Perhaps the reader feels that this general philosophical disquisition on the behavior of mankind is somewhat remote from the economic theory under discussion. But I think not. Though this is how we behave in the market-place, the theory we devise in the study of how we behave in the market-place should not itself submit to market-place idols. I accuse the classical economic theory of being itself one of these pretty, polite techniques which tries to deal with the present by abstracting from the fact that we know very little about the future.

I daresay that a classical economist would readily admit this. But, even so, I think he has overlooked the precise nature of the difference which his abstraction makes between theory and practice, and the character of the fallacies into which he is likely to be led.

This is particularly the case in his treatment of money and interest. And our first step must be to elucidate more clearly the functions of money.

Money, it is well known, serves two principal purposes. By acting as a money of account, it facilitates exchanges without its being necessary that it should ever itself come into the picture as a substantive object. In this respect it is a convenience which is devoid of significance or real influence. In the second place, it is a store of wealth. So we are told, without a smile on the face. But in the world of the classical economy, what an insane use to which to put it! For it is a recognized characteristic of money as a store of wealth that it is barren; whereas practically every other form of storing wealth yields some interest or profit. Why should anyone outside a lunatic asylum wish to use money as a store of wealth?

Because, partly on reasonable and partly on instinctive grounds, our desire to hold money as a store of wealth is a barometer of the degree of our distrust of our own calculations and conventions concerning the future. Even though this feeling about money is itself conventional or instinctive, it operates, so to speak, at a deeper level of our motivation. It takes charge at the moments when the higher, more precarious conventions have weakened. The possession of actual money lulls our disquietude; and the premium which we require to make us part with money is the measure of the degree of our disquietude.

The significance of this characteristic of money has usually been overlooked; and in so far as it has been noticed, the essential nature of the phenomenon has been misdescribed. For what has attracted attention has been the *quantity* of money which has been hoarded; and importance has been attached to this because it has been supposed to have a direct proportionate effect on the price level through affecting the velocity of circulation. But the *quantity* of hoards can only be altered either if the total quantity of money is changed or if the quantity of current money-income (I speak broadly) is changed; whereas fluctuations in the degree of confidence are capable of having quite a different effect, namely, in modifying not the amount that is actually hoarded, but the amount of the premium which has to be offered to induce people not to hoard. And changes in the propensity to hoard, or in the state of liquidity preference as I have called it, primarily affect, not prices, but the rate of interest; any effect on prices being produced by repercussion as an ultimate consequence of a change in the rate of interest.

This, expressed in a very general way, is my theory of the rate of interest. The rate of interest obviously measures – just as the books on arithmetic say it does – the premium which has to be offered to induce people to hold their wealth in some form other than hoarded money. The quantity of money and the amount of it required in the active circulation for the transaction of current business (mainly depending on the level of money income) determine how much is available for inactive balances, i.e. for hoards. The rate of interest is the factor which adjusts at the margin the demand for hoards to the supply of hoards.

Now let us proceed to the next stage of the argument. The owner of wealth, who has been induced not to hold his wealth in the shape of hoarded money, still has two alternatives between which to choose. He can lend his money at the current rate of money interest or he can purchase some kind of capital asset. Clearly in equilibrium these two alternatives must offer an equal advantage to the marginal investor in each of them. This is brought about by shifts in the money prices of capital assets relative to the prices of money loans. The prices of capital assets move until, having regard to their prospective yields and account being taken of all those elements of doubt and uncertainty, interested and disinterested advice, fashion, convention and what else you will, which affect the mind of the investor, they offer an equal apparent advantage to the marginal investor who is wavering between one kind of investment and another.

This, then, is the first repercussion of the rate of interest, as fixed by the quantity of money and the propensity to hoard, namely, on the prices of capital assets. This does not mean, of course, that the rate of interest is the only fluctuating influence on these prices. Opinions as to their prospective yield are themselves subject to sharp fluctuations, precisely for the reason already given, namely, the flimsiness of the basis of knowledge on which they depend. It is these opinions taken in conjunction with the rate of interest which fix their price.

Now for stage three. Capital assets are capable, in general, of being newly produced. The scale on which they are produced depends, of course, on the relation between their costs of production and the prices which they are expected to realize in the market. Thus if the level of the rate of interest taken in conjunction with opinions about their prospective yield raise the prices of capital assets, the volume of current investment (meaning by this the value of the output of newly produced capital assets) will be increased; while if, on the other hand, these influences reduce the prices of capital assets, the volume of current investment will be diminished.

It is not surprising that the volume of investment, thus determined, should fluctuate widely from time to time. For it depends on two sets of judgements about the future, neither of which rests on an adequate or secure foundation – on the propensity to hoard and on opinions of the future yield of capital assets. Nor is there any reason to suppose that the fluctuations in one of these factors will tend to offset the fluctuations in the other. When a more pessimistic view is taken about future yields, that is no reason why there should be a diminished propensity to hoard. Indeed, the conditions which aggravate the one factor tend, as a rule, to aggravate the other. For the same circumstances which lead to pessimistic views about future yields are apt to increase the propensity to hoard. The only element of self-righting in the system arises at a much later stage and in an uncertain degree. If a decline in investment leads to a decline in output as a whole, this may result (for more reasons than one) in a reduction of the amount of money required for the active circulation, which will release a larger quantity of money for the inactive circulation, which will satisfy the propensity to hoard at a lower level of the rate of interest, which will raise the prices of capital assets, which will increase the scale of investment, which will restore in some measure the level of output as a whole.

This completes the first chapter of the argument, namely, the liability of the scale of investment to fluctuate for reasons quite distinct (a) from those which determine the propensity of the individual to *save* out of a given income, and (b) from those physical conditions of technical capacity to aid production which have usually been supposed hitherto to be the chief influence governing the marginal efficiency of capital.

If, on the other hand, our knowledge of the future was calculable and not subject to sudden changes, it might be justifiable to assume that the liquidity-preference curve was both stable and very inelastic. In this case a small decline in money income would lead to a large fall in the rate of interest, probably sufficient to raise output and employment to the full.[1] In these conditions we might reasonably suppose that the whole of the available resources would normally be employed; and the conditions required by the orthodox theory would be satisfied.

II

My next difference from the traditional theory concerns its apparent conviction that there is no necessity to work out a theory of the demand and supply of output *as a whole*. Will a fluctuation in investment, arising for the reasons just described, have any

---

1. When Professor Viner charges me with assigning to liquidity preference 'a grossly exaggerated importance' he must mean that I exaggerate its instability and its elasticity. But if he is right, a small decline in money income would lead, as stated above, to a large fall in the rate of interest. I claim that experience indicates the contrary.

effect on the demand for output as a whole, and consequently on the scale of output and employment? What answer can the traditional theory make to this question? I believe that it makes no answer at all, never having given the matter a single thought; the theory of effective demand, that is the demand for output as a whole, having been entirely neglected for more than a hundred years.

My own answer to this question involves fresh considerations. I say that effective demand is made up of two items – investment expenditure, determined in the manner just explained, and consumption expenditure. Now what governs the amount of consumption expenditure? It depends mainly on the level of income. People's propensity to spend (as I call it), is influenced by many factors such as the distribution of income, their normal attitude to the future and – though probably in a minor degree – by the rate of interest. But in the main, the prevailing psychological law seems to be that when aggregate income increases, consumption expenditure will also increase but to a somewhat lesser extent. This is a very obvious conclusion. It simply amounts to saying that an increase in income will be divided in some proportion or another between spending and saving, and that when our income is increased it is extremely unlikely that this will have the effect of making us either spend less or save less than before. This psychological law was of the utmost importance in the development of my own thought, and it is, I think, absolutely fundamental to the theory of effective demand as set forth in my book. But few critics or commentators so far have paid particular attention to it.

There follows from this extremely obvious principle, an important, yet unfamiliar, conclusion. Incomes are created partly by entrepreneurs producing for investment and partly by their producing for consumption. The amount that is consumed depends on the amount of income thus made up. Hence the amount of consumption goods which it will pay entrepreneurs to produce depends on the amount of investment goods which they are producing. If, for example, the public are in the habit of spending nine-tenths of their income on consumption goods, it follows that, if entrepreneurs were to produce consumption goods at a cost more than nine times the cost of the investment goods they are producing, some part of their output could not be sold at a price which would cover its cost of production. For the consumption goods on the market would have cost more than nine-tenths of the aggregate income of the public and would therefore be in excess of the demand for consumption goods, which by hypothesis is only the nine-tenths. Thus entrepreneurs will make a loss until they contract their output of consumption goods down to an amount at which it no longer exceeds nine times their current output of investment goods.

The formula is not, of course, quite so simple as in this illustration. The proportion of their incomes which the public will choose to consume will not be a constant one, and in the most general case other factors are also relevant. But there is always a formula, more or less of this kind, relating the output of consumption goods which it pays to produce to the output of investment goods; and I have given attention to it in my book under the name of the *multiplier*. The fact that an increase in consumption is apt in itself to stimulate this further investment merely fortifies the argument.

That the level of output of consumption goods which is profitable to the entrepreneur should be related by a formula of this kind to the output of investment goods depends on assumptions of a simple and obvious character. The conclusion appears to me to be quite beyond dispute. Yet the consequences which follow from it are at the same time unfamiliar and of the greatest possible importance.

The theory can be summed up by saying that, given the psychology of the public, the level of output and employment as a whole depends on the amount of investment. I put it in this way, not because this is the only factor on which aggregate output depends, but because it is usual in a complex system to regard as the *causa causans* that factor which is most prone to sudden and wide fluctuation. More comprehensively, aggregate output depends on the propensity to hoard, on the policy of the monetary authority as it affects the quantity of money, on the state of confidence concerning the prospective yield of capital assets, on the propensity to spend, and on the social factors which influence the level of the money wage. But of these several factors it is those which determine the rate of investment which are most unreliable, since it is they which are influenced by our views of the future about which we know so little.

This that I offer is, therefore, a theory of why output and employment are so liable to fluctuation. It does not offer a ready-made remedy as to how to avoid these fluctuations and to maintain output at a steady optimum level. But it is, properly speaking, a theory of employment because it explains *why*, in any given circumstances, employment is what it is. Naturally I am interested not only in the diagnosis, but also in the cure; and many pages of my book are devoted to the latter. But I consider that my suggestions for a cure, which, avowedly, are not worked out completely, are on a different plane from the diagnosis. They are not meant to be definitive; they are subject to all sorts of special assumptions and are necessarily related to the particular conditions of the time. But my main reasons for departing from the traditional theory go much deeper than this. They are of a highly general character and are meant to be definitive.

I sum up, therefore, the main grounds of my departure as follows:

1. The orthodox theory assumes that we have a knowledge of the future of a kind quite different from that which we actually possess. This false realization follows the lines of the Benthamite calculus. The hypothesis of a calculable future leads to a wrong interpretation of the principles of behavior which the need for action compels us to adopt, and to an underestimation of the concealed factors of utter doubt, precariousness, hope and fear. The result has been a mistaken theory of the rate of interest. It is true that the necessity of equalizing the advantages of the choice between owning loans and assets requires that the rate of interest should be *equal* to the marginal efficiency of capital. But this does not tell us at what *level* the equality will be effective. The orthodox theory regards the marginal efficiency of capital as setting the pace. But the marginal efficiency of capital depends on the price of capital assets; and since this price determines the rate of new investment, it is consistent in equilibrium with only one given level of money income. Thus the marginal efficiency of capital is not determined, unless the level of money income is given. In a system in which the level of money income is capable of fluctuating, the orthodox theory is one equation short of what

is required to give a solution. Undoubtedly the reason why the orthodox system has failed to discover this discrepancy is because it has always tacitly assumed that income *is* given, namely, at the level corresponding to the employment of all the available resources. In other words, it is tacitly assuming that the monetary policy is such as to maintain the rate of interest at that level which is compatible with full employment. It is, therefore, incapable of dealing with the general case where employment is liable to fluctuate. Thus, instead of the marginal efficiency of capital determining the rate of interest, it is true (though not a full statement of the case) to say that it is the rate of interest which determines the marginal efficiency of capital.

2. The orthodox theory would by now have discovered the above defect, if it had not ignored the need for a theory of the supply and demand of output as a whole. I doubt if many modern economists really accept Say's law that supply creates its own demand. But they have not been aware that they were tacitly assuming it. Thus the psychological law underlying the multiplier has escaped notice. It has not been observed that the amount of consumption goods which it pays entrepreneurs to produce is a function of the amount of investment goods which it pays them to produce. The explanation is to be found, I suppose, in the tacit assumption that every individual spends the whole of his income either on consumption or on buying, directly or indirectly, newly produced capital goods. But, here again, while the older economists expressly believed this, I doubt if many contemporary economists really do believe it. They have discarded these older ideas without becoming aware of the consequences.

225

16 H. G. Johnson

Monetary Theory and Keynesian Economics

Excerpt from H. G. Johnson (1964), *Money, Trade and Economic Growth*, Allen & Unwin, ch. 5, pp. 107–25.[1]

What is the subject-matter of monetary theory? What is monetary theory about? This question brings us directly to the heart of the Keynesian revolution. Monetary theory before the Keynesian revolution was concerned primarily with the theory of the price level, the determination of the general level of prices. Associated with the price level was the question of economic fluctuations, which were connected with movements in the price level through the effects of rising prices in redistributing income from rentiers to entrepreneurs, increasing profit expectations and stimulating investments. Falling prices, on the other hand, redistributed income from entrepreneurs to rentiers, reduced profit expectations and depressed investment.

It is to be observed that classical monetary theory was not directly concerned with the level of employment, which entered only incidentally in connexion with economic fluctuations. The classical theorists assumed a tendency to full employment of the economic system as a consequence of flexibility in wages and prices, and attributed unemployment to rigidity of wages and prices. We might note that, contrary to what some Keynesians have alleged, the classical economists did not assume automatic full employment. In their system full employment was a deduction from wage-price flexibility. On the other hand, they did not – as the Keynesians have shown – adequately investigate the effects of wage-price flexibility on employment and wrongly applied the analysis of a single commodity or factor to the economy as a whole.

Nor did classical theory investigate directly the theory of the rate of interest, which was held to be determined by real forces

1. Originally published in the *Pakistan Economic Journal* (1).

and not by monetary forces. The classical theorists did, however, introduce monetary forces to explain price trends and fluctuations, for example in the well-known form of the analysis of the effects of a divergence between the real and the market rate of interest.

To summarize, the classical theory was mainly concerned with the determination of the price level and with economic fluctuations, and was not directly concerned with the level of employment and the theory of interest. The essence of the Keynesian revolution was to shift the subject-matter of monetary theory, placing the emphasis on the level of employment as the central subject of monetary theory and posing the determination of the rate of interest as a specifically monetary problem. In the Keynesian theory, monetary forces influence the equilibrium rate of interest and do not merely, as in classical theory, exercise a transitional influence on market rates during periods of disequilibrium. On the other hand, in Keynesian theory the theory of the price level is reduced to a relatively minor role. Keynes took the level of money wages as given (through measuring all his variables in wage units) and assumed a closed economy. On this assumption there could be only three causes of a change in the price level: a change in the level of employment, a change in the wage unit and a change in technique of production, that is, a change in productivity. Of these three, Keynes was not concerned with changes in productivity, and the use of the wage unit left only variation in the level of employment as a cause of changes in the price level.

In addition to reducing the theory of the price level to a minor role, Keynes practically removed economic fluctuations from the picture. Although Keynesian concepts have since provided the means of clarifying considerably the mechanism of economic fluctuations and cycles, the theory, as Keynes presented it, was not concerned with cycles: it was a static theory.

In summary, Keynes shifted the determination of the level of employment and the rate of interest from real theory into monetary theory, and reduced the former subject-matter of monetary theory – the price level and the economic fluctuations – to a minor position. In what follows I shall be concerned with various arguments centering on the question whether Keynes was right or not in doing this; with subsequent developments of Keynesian concepts as a result of theoretical discussion and practical experience; and with an evaluation of the present position of Keynesian theory in the light of experience over the past twelve years.

First, let me summarize briefly Keynes' theory. Its essence was an attack on the classical assumption of a tendency towards full employment and substitution for it of the possibility of underemployment equilibrium. The argument centred on the independence of decisions to save from decisions to invest. In a modern economy decisions to save are taken by a large number of individual households and firms but decisions to invest are taken by a specialized group of entrepreneurs. There is, therefore, no guarantee that the desire to save will find expression in investment, or that an increased desire to save will be matched by increased investment. Instead, the increased desire to save may run to waste through unemployment, the increased savings of some being offset by reduction in the savings of others brought about by increased unemployment, total saving being made to correspond with the amount of investment that entrepreneurs want to do by a reduction of aggregate income.

Now according to classical theory, this could not happen: it would be prevented by a change in the rate of interest which would reduce saving and increase investment so as to make them balance at full employment. But, Keynes argued, the classical theory of interest involved indeterminacy, because it neglected the dependence of saving on income. Through variations in the level of income, savings and investment could be equated at any level of the rate of interest, and would not necessarily be equated at the full-employment level of income. (I shall return to this question of indeterminacy later on.)

So much for Keynes' attack on the classical theory; let us now turn to his own theory. I shall begin with a simple version of that theory which may be put as follows: output and employment are determined by the demand for output, which comes from two sources – consumption demand and investment demand. Investment decisions, which depend on entrepreneurial profit expectations and other factors, are taken for granted at this stage. Consumption demand depends largely on the level of income (other influences, including the rate of interest, are recognized but dismissed from the argument) and when income rises, consumption is certain to rise but not as much as income – in other words, as income rises, saving rises.

On this assumption the level of income is determined by the level of investment. Investment is taken as given by factors lying

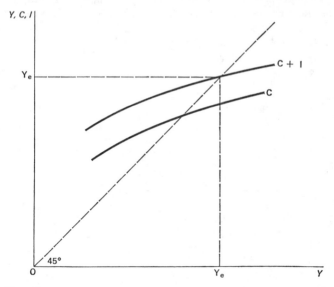

Figure 1

outside the theory; income must be such that saving equals investment and income is the sum of the consumption from this level of income and investment.

This theory of income determination may be represented by two diagrams which are commonly employed in the literature: in Figure 1 we measure income and output Y along both axes and draw a 45° line; at any point on this line the quantities measured on the two axes are equal. We then draw a curve to represent the relation between consumption C and income. The vertical distance between this line and the 45° line represents saving (the unconsumed part of income). The diagram assumes that below

229

some level of income the community will consume more than its income, that is, it will dissave; and that as income rises, consumption will increase but less than income. We now add the fixed amount of investment to the consumption that would take place at various levels of income, thus obtaining the curve $C + I$ which represents the demand for output at different levels of income. The intersection of this line with the 45° line determines the equilibrium level of income Y_e. At a lower level of income and

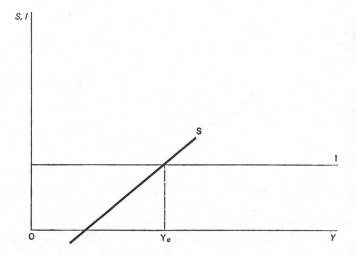

Figure 2

output demand for output will exceed output, and output and income will rise: conversely, at a higher level of income, demand for output will fall short of output, so output will fall. Another version of the same diagram is presented in Figure 2, which plots saving S as a function of income; the equilibrium level of income is that for which saving is equal to the given level of investment I. The second diagram is more commonly used and has been described by Schumpeter as the 'Keynesian cross' (by analogy with the Marshallian cross of the demand and supply curves).

This diagram shows the determination of the level of output and employment. For some purposes we are concerned with the relation between an initial change in demand for output and the total change in income to which it gives rise. This is the theory of the multiplier. Since an increase in investment will raise income and the increase in income will raise consumption, thereby raising the demand for output still further, the total increase in income will be some multiple of the initial increase in investment. In the simple theory just presented, the multiplier will be the reciprocal of the marginal propensity to save. In the early years after the publication of the *General Theory*, a great deal of the literature was devoted to elaboration of the theory of the multiplier. This literature, however, is not relevant to my main theme, so I shall not attempt to deal with it.

What I have just presented is a very simple version of the Keynesian theory. It is incomplete and unsatisfactory because it leaves both the rate of investment and the rate of interest undetermined. In the full version of the Keynesian theory, the rate of investment is determined by the balancing of the rate of return on investment, which Keynes termed 'the marginal efficiency of capital', against the rate of interest, the rate of investment being determined by the condition that, at the margin, the rate of interest and the marginal efficiency of capital should be equal. The rate of interest, in turn, is determined by the quantity of money and the demand for it, which Keynes analysed under the description of 'liquidity preference'.

The quantity of money is assumed to be determined by the monetary authorities. The demand for money is divided into two parts – the transactions demand (including the demand for precautionary balances) which depends on the level of money income, and the speculative demand. The speculative demand arises from the fact that, if the rate of interest is expected to rise, an owner of cash may do better not to invest it in securities immediately, but to wait until he can buy those securities at a lower price (higher yield). The lower the actual rate of interest relative to some 'normal' level, the less the sacrifice of interest in not investing immediately, and the more likely a rise in the rate in the near future; consequently the greater the relative attraction of holding cash, and the greater the demand for money to hold as speculative balances. (Keynes, and even more so his followers, tended to write of the speculative demand for money as depending only on the actual rate of interest, and varying with it; this has given rise to confusion and misunderstanding, since it leaves implicit the role of expectations of future rates.) Keynes also held that at some low rate of interest, the demand for idle balances might become completely interest elastic, thus putting a bottom stop to the rate of interest.

Notice that this theory seems to imply a one-way chain of causation: the rate of interest is determined by the demand for

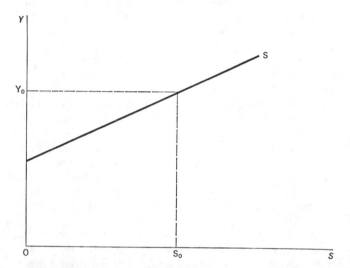

Figure 3a The relation between saving and income

and supply of money: the level of investment is determined by the rate of interest and the marginal efficiency of capital; and the level of income and consumption is determined by the level of investment and the propensity to save. There is, apparently, no reverse influence of saving and investment on the rate of interest; and this feature has led to much discussion and criticism of Keynes' theory. But the appearance is misleading: in fact, the Keynesian system is an interdependent system, in which all the variables influence each other, for the reason that the transactions part of the demand for money depends on the level of income, which in

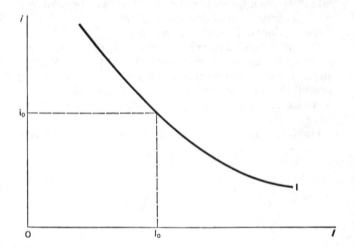

Figure 3b The relation between investment and the rate of interest

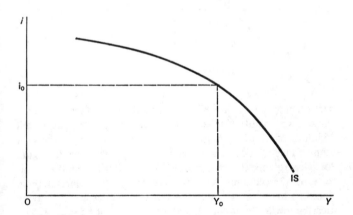

Figure 3c The IS curve

turn depends on the desires to save and invest. Appreciation of this interdependence dispels much of the startling novelty of Keynes' theory of interest as he presented it.

The full Keynesian theory, in which the interest rate, income, saving and investment, demand for money and supply of money are all mutually interdependent, can be represented very conveniently by a diagram developed by Professor J. R. Hicks (2), which has proved so useful that it has become a standard tool of monetary theory.

From the two relations (Figures 3a and 3b) may be deduced the

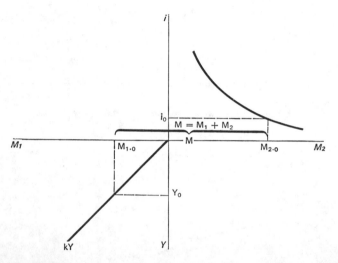

Figure 4a

relation between the rate of interest and the level of income which will ensure equality between saving and investment, that is, will maintain equilibrium between the demand for and supply of output. This relation, known as the IS curve, is shown in Figure 3c; it represents the requirements of equilibrium in the 'real' sector of the economy. The IS curve will be downward-sloping, since at a lower rate of interest investment will be greater, saving must be greater, and consequently income must be greater.

Figure 4a represents the relation between the demand for and the supply of money. The upper right-hand quadrant represents the speculative demand for money, or the demand for speculative balances, M_2, as a function of the rate of interest. The lower left-hand quadrant represents the transactions demand for money, M_1, on the assumption that the transactions requirement is a fraction k of national income. The actual amount of money in existence $M(= M_1 + M_2)$ is represented by a bar, which can be

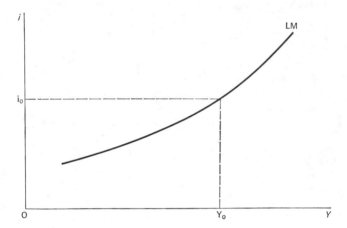

Figure 4b

shifted along the $M_1 M_2$ axis to derive the relation between the rate of interest and the level of income at which the demand for money will just equal the amount of it available, that is, which will maintain equilibrium between the demand for and supply of money. This relation, known as the LM curve, is shown in Figure 4b; it represents the requirements of equilibrium in the 'monetary' sector of the economy. The LM curve will be upward-sloping, since at higher levels of national income more money will be required for transactions, leaving less available for idle balances, and to induce speculators to hold less idle money, the rate of interest must rise.

The IS and LM curves are combined in Figure 5, which shows the determination of the rate of interest and the level of income at the levels which ensure simultaneous equilibrium in the monetary and real sectors. This diagram may be described as 'the Hicksian cross' after its inventor; it can be adapted to take account of more general assumptions than Keynes made – for example, that saving depends partly on interest rates and investment partly on income, and that both demands for money depend on both income and the interest rate; and it can be used to expound a number of important propositions and solve a number of problems in monetary theory.

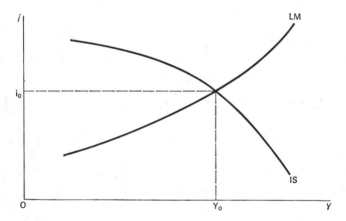

Figure 5

For completeness, I shall fill out this diagrammatic picture of Keynesian theory with two further diagrams which illustrate significant aspects of his analysis, namely the determination of the price level and the concept of 'involuntary unemployment'. Figure 6 depicts the supply curve of output X_s, on Keynes' assumptions that labour is the only variable factor, diminishing returns prevail, and competition ensures that supply is determined by the equality of price and marginal cost. The different combinations of real output and price level consistent with a given value of output may be represented by a rectangular hyperbola; the equilibrium price level output are given by the intersection with the aggregate supply curve of the hyperbola representing the level of income determined from Figure 5. (I neglect

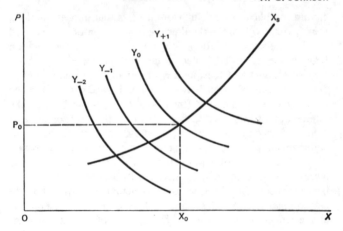

Figure 6

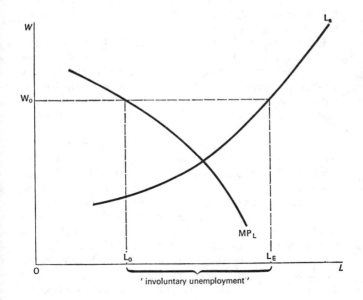

Figure 7

certain complications arising from the fact that movement along the X_s-curve will probably alter the distribution of income, and the income-saving relation.) Figure 7 represents the relation between the real wage earned by labour (the marginal productivity of labour) and the quantity of labour employed (the MP_L curve); and the relation between the real wage earned and the quantity of labour supplied (the L_s-curve). In classical theory, the intersection of these two curves determines the levels of employment and income; in Keynesian theory, however, the levels of employment and the real wage are determined by aggregate demand, the level of employment L_O being derived from the level of output (Figure 6) by means of the technological relation between them. The difference between actual employment at the real wage so determined, L_O, and the labour that would be offered at the real wage, L_E, measures the amount of 'involuntary unemployment' $(L_E - L_O)$. (The diagrams, though not the economics, could be simplified by measuring unemployment in terms of the additional output it could produce, recognizing that the price level varies inversely with the real wage, and inserting a supply curve of labour in Figure 6.)

Let me now turn from exposition of the Keynesian theory to discuss some of the arguments and controversies to which it has given rise, and some of the recent developments of Keynesian concepts. In discussing the former, I shall ignore most of the minor controversies which have figured in the literature, and confine myself to what I consider the important issues.

The chief argument pertaining to Keynes' theory of employment relates to the question whether Keynesian under-employment equilibrium depends on the assumption of rigid wages, which Keynes introduced into the theory by measuring all magnitudes in wages units. The answer to this question hinges on the effect on employment of a larger volume of money, since the effect of a wage cut in the system is the same as the effect of an increase in money supply (with a fall in wages and prices, less money is required for transactions, more is available for speculative balances). With a larger quantity of money, the rate of interest will tend to be lower and the level of investment higher; the question is whether a sufficient increase in the money supply (wage cut) will lead to full employment; if so, under-employment equilibrium is dependent on rigidity of wages.

Within the Keynesian framework, two cases in which increased money supply will not lead to full employment can be distinguished. Firstly, liquidity preference may set a bottom limit to the rate of interest at a level above that required for a full-employment level of investment. Secondly, the IS curve may be so interest-inelastic that, at positive interest rates, investment does not increase, or savings fall, to a level consistent with full employment. (Since a negative interest rate is impossible when people have the alternative of holding money, we need not consider this possibility, which would require a policy of subsidizing investment or taxing savings.) The two cases mentioned can be combined in one statement: full employment will not be achieved by monetary expansion (wage cuts) if savings from a full-employment income would exceed investment at the lowest rate of interest the money market will allow.

The foregoing argument, however, assumes Keynes' own view of the factors which determine consumption. Against it may be brought an argument originated by Pigou (3, 4), which incorporates the assumption that consumption depends on wealth (assets) as well as income. The argument is that, as money wages and prices fall, the real value of cash balances rises, and the increasing real wealth of cash-holders will lead them eventually to increase their consumption. This is the so-called 'Pigou effect'; I should point out that it assumes token money or money backed by gold, since in the case of money backed by private debt the debtor becomes poorer in real terms as the cash-holder becomes richer, and the net effect on consumption is unpredictable. However, if we are prepared to assume that the government is indifferent to changes in the real value of its debts, the Pigou effect can be extended to the public's holdings of government debt, or of cash backed by government debt.

In my opinion, though not, I should add, in the opinion of all Keynesians, the Pigou effect finally disposes of the Keynesian contention that under-employment equilibrium does not depend on the assumption of wage rigidity. It does. How serious a criticism of Keynesian theory is this? Not, I think, a very important one. The heat engendered by the argument over it can largely be attributed to the desire of Keynes and his followers to reject the idea that cuts in wage rates are the appropriate way to cure depressions. That argument is a policy argument, involving political and dynamic considerations not relevant to the consideration of Keynesian theory as a purely static theory.

The criticism does have significance in a broader context, though this is a consequence of the challenging way in which Keynes presented his theory – as a general theory of which the classical theory was a special case. It turns out that Keynes' theory is a special case of the classical – or rather of the neoclassical theory, since a satisfactory 'classical' theory was not worked out until after the Keynesian revolution. But this sort of argument about a theory is not particularly interesting; what is more important is that Keynes' theory started from an empirically relevant special assumption, derived some important meaningful results from it, and provided an approach which has since proved its usefulness for a wide range of problems.

Let me now turn from the Keynesian theory as a theory of employment to the Keynesian theory as a theory of interest. Here there have been several interesting controversies. The most fundamental has been the debate, initiated by Keynes, over whether the rate of interest is a real or a monetary phenomenon (the latter, of course, being Keynes' own view). This debate has two versions, of which the less important is the Cambridge battle over whether real or monetary (speculative) factors dominate actual credit markets (5, 6 and 7). That is really an empirical question; I shall confine myself to two remarks on it. The first is that, since Keynes' speculative demand for money is based on the relation between actual and expected rates of interest, there is nothing to prevent 'real' forces, in the shape of the profitability of investment, from entering into liquidity preference. On the other hand, it is not valid in my opinion to dismiss the Keynesian liquidity preference theory on the grounds that it is a 'bootstrap' theory of interest (8, p. 164)[2] – since interest is a relation between the present and the future, expectations must inevitably influence the rate as determined in the market.

The theoretically more important version of the debate has centred around the proposition that the so-called 'classical

2. Contrast R. F. Kahn (7).

dichotomy' is invalid (9 to 15). In classical theory (the argument runs) relative prices and the rate of interest are determined independently of the quantity of money, whereas the quantity of money influences the general price level (money prices) but not relative prices. This independence of relative price determination from absolute price determination has been shown to be invalid. The argument has been complex and mathematical, but its essence can be simply put: if people are to hold money, their demands for goods must depend in part on the value of their money holdings, which must therefore influence relative prices as well as the absolute price level.

If it is assumed that utility depends on the quantities of goods consumed and on the *real* value of cash balances, it is possible to retain the classical result that an increase in the (nominal) quantity of money will raise the price level but leave relative prices and the rate of interest unchanged. But this conclusion is not very relevant or interesting for a modern economy, where money is created by the banking system against debt and its quantity is altered by open-market operations (16, 17). In general, the quantity of money must be regarded as influencing all decisions; and the rate of interest is inevitably 'a monetary phenomenon'.

Let me now deal briefly with two other controversies about Keynesian interest theory. The first is the 'loanable funds *versus* liquidity preference' debate – the argument as to whether the rate of interest is determined by the demand and supply of money, as Keynes maintained, or by the demand and supply of securities, as Robertson and others maintain (5, 18, pp. 153–62, and 19 to 26). We can approach this question by dividing the economy into three markets – the markets for output, cash and securities. According to a principle known as Walras' law, the sum of the excess demands in these three markets must be identically equal to zero; in symbols,

$$X_g + X_m + X_s = 0.$$

It is clear that if the market for goods is in equilibrium ($X_g = 0$), equilibrium in either of the other markets implies equilibrium in the remaining one, so that on this assumption it makes no difference whether we say that the equilibrium rate of interest is that which equates the demand for and supply of cash, or that which equates the demand for and supply of securities – the two theories amount to the same thing. To put the same point another way, in full-equilibrium positions the rate of interest equates both the demand and supply of money and the demand and supply of securities. But if the market for output is not in equilibrium, we can no longer say that the rate of interest is determined in either one of the other two markets, unless we assume that the remaining market behaves in such a way that we can lump it together with the commodity market – 'liquidity preference' assuming that excess demand for output (investment greater than saving) is financed by bond sales, and 'loanable funds' assuming it is financed by running down cash balances.

A similar controversy relates to the allegation recently made by Professor Hansen, that the Keynesian theory as well as the classical theory is indeterminate (27–30). Whereas Keynes charged the classics with neglecting the dependence of saving on income, Hansen charges Keynes with neglecting the dependence of the transactions demand for money on income. In my opinion, Professor Hansen's argument is invalid: as I have already pointed out, the Keynesian theory appears to be one of one-way causation but is in fact a theory of interdependence and mutual determination; it is determinate.

Let me now turn from the controversies stirred up by the Keynesian revolution to post-Keynesian developments of Keynesian concepts. The most interesting developments have been those relating to the consumption function, which were stimulated by the failure of the prediction of a major post-war slump, and the apparent contradiction between Kuznets' finding that in the long run the proportion of income saved is constant, and the evidence of time-series and budget studies that saving is a rising proportion of income in the short run.[3] The effort to reconcile the short-run and the long-run propensities to save has stimulated several reformulations of the theory of the consumption function: Tobin has introduced the influence of assets (as well as income) on consumption, Duesenberry has employed the hypothesis that individual consumption behaviour depends on relative rather than absolute income, Friedman that consumption is governed

3. On the failure of the forecasts, see L. R. Klein (31); for Kuznets' data (32).

by 'normal' rather than actual income, Modigliani and Brumberg that consumption is governed by maximization of utility over the consumer's whole life (33-6). These and other contributions all have in common the reintroduction of utility maximization into the theory of the consumption function.

On the side of the inducement to invest, the most important development has been the introduction of the relation between capital-stock and output (in the form either of the accelerator or of the capital–output ratio) as a determinant of investment decisions. This has permitted the conversion of the static equilibrium Keynesian system into cycle and growth models. Useful work has also been done on inventory cycles – Keynes himself tended to think in terms of fixed capital investment as the dominant determinant of income (37-43).

The theory of liquidity preference has been improved in a variety of ways by closer analysis of the motives for holding money. The most important development, however, has been the extension of the liquidity-preference concept to take account of more alternatives than the simple bonds – cash choice assumed by Keynes. Generally speaking, the tendency has been to move towards a generalized theory of asset-holding, suitable for application to the analysis of monetary and fiscal policy. In this connexion the Keynesian assumption of a fixed quantity of money has been modified to permit the banking system to exercise a liquidity preference of its own.

Before concluding I should like to say something about how well Keynesian theory has stood up to the experience of war-time economic problems and the war and post-war inflation. It is agreed, I think, that Keynesian theory provided a far better basis for understanding the nature of the war-time economic problem and the causes of inflation than did previous theory. It made it clear that the war-time economic problem is not the financing of the war effort but the adjustment of aggregate demand to the capacity of the economy to produce; and that the source of inflation is an excess demand for output. (Both of these propositions are applicable to the problems of development planning.)

On the other hand, Keynesian theory has shown definite weaknesses as a theory of prices. In Keynesian theory, the level of money wages is taken as given, and alterations in it are not explained by the theory. Inflation models have been built by assuming relations between aggregate demand and the rates of wage or price change or between wage and price changes; but while they describe the inflationary process they do not explain it very well. The problem of explaining the differing price histories of different countries during and since the war has led to a certain tendency to return to the quantity theory of money as an explanation of inflation, and to explain post-war inflation as a result of the war-time expansion of the money supply. (See, for example, Brown (44).) It is clear that the accumulation of money during the war has had an important effect; but I would myself prefer to employ a neo-Keynesian explanation, based on the accumulation of assets relative to income (these assets including both money and government debt) rather than one which stressed the quantity of money *per se*.

I conclude with a general evaluation of the Keynesian revolution. As a theory for dealing with problems of employment, inflation and economic planning, it constitutes, in my opinion, a great and pervasive advance, the essence of which is to look at the relations between aggregate demand for and availability of resources, rather than at the quantity of money. In monetary theory, its main contribution has been to emphasize the function of money as an asset, alternative to other assets, and to break the quantity-theory assumption that there is a direct connexion between money quantity and aggregate demand. On the other hand, the theory as Keynes presented it is misleading in many ways, and needs much adaptation to fit non-depression conditions; and the Keynesian approach does tend to play down the influence of monetary conditions, which may at times be very important.

References

1. H. G. JOHNSON, 'Money, trade and economic growth', *Pakistan Economic Journal*, vol. 8, 1958, no. 2, pp. 56–70.
2. J. R. HICKS, 'Mr Keynes and the "Classics": a suggested interpretation', *Econometrica*, vol. 5, 1937, no. 2. pp. 147–59.
3. A. C. PIGOU, 'The classical stationary state', *Economic Journal*, vol. 53, 1943, no. 212, pp. 343–51.
4. D. PATINKIN, 'Price flexibility and full employment', *Readings in Monetary Theory*, American Economic Association, Allen & Unwin, 1951, ch. 13, pp. 252–88.

5. D. H. ROBERTSON, 'Mr Keynes and the rate of interest', *Essays in Monetary Theory*, Staples, 1940, ch. 1, pp. 11–49.

6. JOAN ROBINSON, 'The rate of interest', *Econometrica*, vol. 19, April 1951, no. 2, pp. 92–111, reprinted in *The Rate of Interest and Other Essays*, Macmillan, 1952, ch. 1, pp. 3–21.

7. R. F. KAHN, 'Some notes on liquidity preference', *The Manchester School of Economic and Social Studies*, vol. 22, 1954, no. 3, pp. 229–57.

8. J. R. HICKS, *Value and Capital*, 2nd edition, Clarendon Press, 1946.

9. D. PATINKIN, 'The indeterminacy of absolute prices in classical economic theory', *Econometrica*, vol. 17, 1949, no. 1, pp. 1–27.

10. D. PATINKIN, 'The invalidity of classical monetary theory', *Econometrica*, vol. 19, 1951, no. 1, pp. 134–51.

11. D. PATINKIN, *Money, Interest and Prices*, Row Peterson, 1956.

12. W. B. HICKMAN, 'The indeterminacy of absolute prices in classical economic theory', *Econometrica*, vol. 18, 1950, no. 1, pp. 9–20.

13. W. LEONTIEF, 'The consistency of the classical theory of money and prices', *Econometrica*, vol. 18, 1950, no. 1, pp. 21–4.

14. C. G. PHIPPS, 'A note on Patinkin's "Relative prices"', *Econometrica*, vol. 18, 1950, no. 1, pp. 25–6.

15. K. BRUNNER, 'Inconsistency and determinacy in classical economics', *Econometrica*, vol. 19, 1951, no. 1, pp. 152–73.

16. L. A. METZLER, 'Wealth, saving and the rate of interest', *Journal of Political Economy*, vol. 59, 1951, no. 2, pp. 93–116.

17. D. PATINKIN, 'Keynesian economics and the quantity theory', *Post-Keynesian Economics*, Kurihara (ed.), Allen & Unwin, 1955, pp. 123–52.

18. J. R. HICKS, *Value and Capital*, Clarendon Press, 1938, ch. 12, pp. 153–62.

19. W. FELLNER and H. M. SOMERS, 'Alternative monetary approaches to interest theory', *Review of Economic Statistics*, vol. 23, 1941, no. 1, pp. 43–8.

20. W. FELLNER and H. M. SOMERS, 'Note on "stocks" and "flows" in monetary interest theory', *Review of Economics and Statistics*, vol. 31, 1949, no. 2, pp. 145–6.

21. L. R. KLEIN, *The Keynesian Revolution*, Macmillan, pp. 117–23.

22. L. R. KLEIN, 'Stock and flow analysis in economics', *Econometrica*, vol. 18, 1950, no. 1, pp. 236–41.

23. W. FELLNER and H. M. SOMERS, 'Stock and flow analysis: comment', *Econometrica*, vol. 18, 1950, no. 1, pp. 241–5.

24. L. R. KLEIN, 'Stock and flow analysis: further comment', *Econometrica*, vol. 18, 1950, no. 1, p. 246.

25. K. BRUNNER, 'Stock and flow analysis: discussion', *Econometrica*, vol. 18, 1950, no. 1, pp. 247–51.

26. W. FELLNER and H. M. SOMERS, 'Stock and flow analysis: note on the discussion', *Econometrica*, vol. 18, 1950, no. 1, p. 252.

27. A. H. HANSEN, 'Classical loanable funds and Keynesian interest rate theories', *Quarterly Journal of Economics*, vol. 65, 1951, no. 3, pp. 429–32.

28. A. H. HANSEN, *A Guide to Keynes*, McGraw-Hill, 1953, ch. 7, pp. 140–53.

29. E. T. NEVIN, 'Professor Hansen and the Keynesian interest theory', *Quarterly Journal of Economics*, vol. 69, 1955, no. 4, pp. 637–41.

30. A. H. HANSEN, 'Comment', *Quarterly Journal of Economics*, vol. 69, 1955, no. 4, pp. 641–3.

31. L. R. KLEIN, 'A post-mortem on transition predictions of national product', *Journal of Political Economy*, vol. 54, 1946, no. 1, pp. 289–304.

32. S. KUZNETS, 'Capital formation, 1879–1938', *Studies in Economics and Industrial Relations*, W. C. Mitchell *et al.*, University of Pennsylvania Press, 1941, pp. 53–78.

33. J. TOBIN, 'Relative income, absolute income and savings', *Money, Trade and Economic Growth, in honor of John Henry Williams*, Macmillan, 1951, pp. 135–56.

34. J. S. DUESENBERRY, *Income, Saving and the Theory of Consumer Behavior*, Harvard University, 1949.

35. M. FRIEDMAN, *A Theory of the Consumption Function*, Princeton University Press, 1957.

36. F. MODIGLIANI and R. BRUMBERG, 'Utility analysis and the consumption function: an interpretation of cross-section data', *Post-Keynesian Economics*, Kurihara (ed.), Allen & Unwin, 1955, pp. 383–436.

37. M. KALECKI, *Essays in the Theory of Economic Fluctuations*, Allen & Unwin, 1939, pp. 116–49.

38. N. KALDOR, 'A model of the trade cycle', *Economic Journal*, vol. 50, 1940, no. 1, pp. 78–92.

39. R. M. GOODWIN, 'Econometrics in business-cycle analysis', *Business Cycles and National Income*, Hansen (ed.), Allen & Unwin, 1951, pp. 417–68.

40. P. A. SAMUELSON, 'Interaction between the multiplier analysis and the principle of acceleration', *Review of Economic Statistics*, vol. 21, 1939, no. 2, pp. 75–8.

41. J. R. HICKS, *A Contribution to the Theory of the Trade Cycle*, Clarendon Press, 1950.

42. R. F. HARROD, *Towards a Dynamic Economics*, Macmillan, 1948.

43. L. A. METZLER, 'The nature and stability of inventory cycles', *Review of Economic Statistics*, vol. 23, 1941, no. 2, pp. 113–29.

44. A. J. BROWN, *The Great Inflation: 1939–1951*, Oxford University Press, 1955.

17 B. P. Pesek and T. R. Saving

The Demand for Money: Some post-Keynesian Confusions

Excerpt from B. P. Pesek and T. R. Saving (1967), *Money, Wealth and Economic Theory*, Macmillan, ch. 14, pp. 323–31.

From our [earlier] analysis of consumer behavior, we concluded that the demand for money will depend on income and on the rate of interest. However, money demanded for speculative purposes was excluded from our analysis. Were we to put it in, the determinant of the speculative demand for this good – just as the determinant of a speculative demand for any other good – would surely be some function containing expectations about future interest rate and price changes:

$$m = m_1 + m_2 = l_1(y, r) + l_2(x). \qquad 1$$

On the other hand, the Keynesian demand for money function (1, p. 199), while also containing income and the rate of interest as determinants, reads as follows:

$$M = M_1 + M_2 = L_1(Y) + L_2(r). \qquad 2$$

The fact that one equation is stated in real terms and the other in money terms is of no interest to us at present. Other differences, however, are worth discussing because the manner in which Keynes wrote his demand function for money gave rise to what we consider to be a serious confusion in monetary theory. This confusion results from accepting the Keynes function as stated above and from several subtle, almost imperceptible, shifts in interpretation, terminology and emphasis. Firstly, the fact that Keynes split up the two determinants of the demand for transaction money and the demand for speculative money fostered the notion, so frequent in the literature, that we may distinguish between these two demands by referring to the determinants: that demand for money determined by income is transaction demand and that demand for money determined by the interest rate is

247

speculative demand. Secondly, the term 'speculative' has come to be replaced with terms very misleading in their implications: 'the asset demand', 'demand for money to hold', etc. Thirdly, Keynes wrote the demand for money equation as *the sum* of the two demands. Although this is harmless when we talk about 'transaction money' and 'speculative money', it becomes most confusing once we start to speak about 'money demanded for transactions' and 'money demanded to hold'. The additive feature of Keynes' equation then leads directly to the notion that money demanded for transactions may not be held at all and that there may be demand for money to hold with money not used for transactions at all. Once this view is established, it becomes easy to conclude that when we attempt to provide an operationally meaningful *definition* of money to which the above equations pertain, we may concentrate on assets that are being held – regardless of whether or not they happen to facilitate transactions. Ultimately, we end up with the declared inability of economists to distinguish between money and debts. Before we grasp this nettle, it might be useful to go back to the *General Theory* to see to what extent Keynes is responsible for all this.

As far as the consumption function is concerned, Keynes carefully spelt out all the factors affecting it and then dashed off an equation completely unrelated to his discussion. Similarly, the demand-for-money equation reproduced above has little relation to his verbal analysis of the determinants of the demand for money. Firstly, he disposes of the additive feature of his equation by stating that these two demands 'are *largely* [emphasis ours] independent of one another' and even that statement he declares to be merely 'a safe first approximation'. Secondly, about the transaction demand he states that it will depend on income *and*, among other factors, on 'the effective cost of holding idle cash'; i.e. on the rate of interest. However, strangely enough for a book containing 'interest' in the title and a discussion of the effects of changes in the rate on the page following, he adds correctly but irrelevantly and misleadingly that, 'if we have a short period of time in view and can safely assume *no material change* [emphasis ours] in any of these factors', we can ignore them. Thirdly, about the speculative demand Keynes states the following:

... *uncertainty* as to the future course of the rate of interest is the sole intelligible explanation of [speculative demand]. ... It follows that a given [amount of speculative money] will not have a definite quantitative relation to a given rate of interest of *r* – what matters is not the *absolute* level of *r* but the degree of its divergence from what is considered a fairly *safe* level of *r*, having regard to those calculations of probability which are being relied on (1, p. 201).

While he goes on to make the speculative demand depend simply on the level of the rate of interest, this is explicitly merely a simplifying assumption. Obviously, by now nothing is left of equation 2 in his verbal analysis, Keynes comes up with a demand for money function that is identical with the one expressed in equation 1 (except for the difference that one is stated in nominal and the other in real terms).

Let us now return to the notion that money may be demanded for transaction purposes but not held or that money may be demanded for asset purposes but not for transaction purposes. Keynes himself starts this trend in thinking when he uses interchangeably the concept of the speculative demand and the concept of the propensity to hoard. By the time that Franco Modigliani wrote his well-known mathematical version of the Keynesian model, the transition from the speculative demand to the demand for money to hold was completed. Modigliani distinguishes between 'the transaction demand for money' and 'the demand for money as an asset'; later, he analyses 'the classical case when the equilibrium rate of interest is sufficiently high to make the *demand for money to hold* zero or negligible' (2, p. 223). Here we meet the notion that money may be held or not held at will and that there may be money used for transactions while none is 'held'. As time goes by, such statements become more and more explicit until we reach analyses such as the one presented by James Tobin. Under certain conditions, he states:

Even though money is required as a medium of exchange, transactors will suffer no cost or inconvenience by holding more lucrative assets at all times except the negligible microseconds before and after transactions (3, p. 26).

As a result, as Tobin puts it, 'no one will hold [money]'. On the opposite side of the spectrum, we find analyses of the demand for money only for asset purposes and not at all for transaction purposes. For instance, Paul A. Samuelson considers 'the social contrivance of money' as a store of value in a society 'with ideal clearing arrangements [where] money as a medium of exchange might have little function' (4, p. 481). In what follows we intend to show that neither one of these two polar positions can survive careful analysis:

A. We cannot have transaction money unless money is held between transactions. This can be shown by proceeding from two opposite directions. Firstly, we may assume that money does not exist and inquire into the conditions for its existence. Secondly, we may assume that money does exist and inquire into the conditions which, if they prevail, will cause money to cease to exist:

(a) If the consumer can get rid of the good he does not want and acquire the good he wants instantaneously, money is not needed and will not exist since barter is the only efficient means of undertaking exchanges. However, if a chain of barter transactions is required to accomplish the consumer's purpose, the existence of money becomes possible – but even then it is not certain. It becomes possible because the use of money reduces the chain of transactions necessary to only two: the initial and the final one. This shows that transactions undertaken by the use of money cannot be, purely conceptually, instantaneous since, if they could be, money would not exist.[1]

(b) Now let us approach the problem from the other side: let us assume that money exists and let us assume that consumers make a decision not to hold it and merely to use it for transactions. If no one holds money, where will the transactors acquire money needed for transactions? Money becomes the proverbial hot potato: as the time during which money is held in between

1. Note that if it were *always* possible to sell an unwanted good for money and, within microseconds, sell money for ultimately wanted goods, why should money exist? Merely to add one extra futile step to the transacting activity? The mere fact that money exists is conclusive evidence that barter is not, in general, economically feasible. Of course, once money exists, habits and customs may make it used even in cases in which barter would do. But such cases do not prove that money exists so as to complicate barter any more than an observation of a man carrying a bicycle proves that bicycles exist so as to burden pedestrians.

transactions approaches zero, the price of money approaches zero (the general price level approaches infinity). Given the relationship between the price of money and the real value of money, money ceases to exist.

Thus we have just shown that (a) money will not exist unless held in between transactions and (b) if not held in between transactions, money will cease to exist. Consequently we can say that an unavoidable property of money is that it is held. In the case of money, these periods of inactivity are unavoidable conceptually; in the case of many nonmoney capital goods, they are unavoidable technically. In all cases, the consumer will exert an effort to minimize these periods of inactivity of all capital goods. The intensity of this effort to minimize these idle periods (or, what is saying the same thing, to minimize the average money holding in a given period) will depend on the ability of the consumer to afford these inactive periods (i.e. on his income) and on the cost of these periods (i.e. on the rate of interest). The holding of money – or of any other capital goods that cannot be operated continuously – becomes less attractive the higher the rate.[2] If this

2. In contrast, loans of resources become more attractive the higher the rate. But then, since an increase in the rate of interest makes (a) holding of wealth of a given productivity (currency and demand deposits) less attractive and (b) lending of wealth (e.g. purchases of time deposits) more attractive, we would expect on *a priori* grounds that a negative relationship between interest rate and item (a) will be weakened (indeed, may be reversed and become positive) if we shift to a composite consisting of items (a) plus (b).

It is thus easy to understand that Allan H. Meltzer's investigation of this issue led to the conclusion that '. . . the effect of a rise in the rate of interest on the percentage change in the quantity of money demanded is much greater when time deposits are excluded from M than when they are included in it.' (5, p. 239.)

Similarly, Milton Friedman and Anna Jacobson Schwartz stated that '. . . the velocity of currency plus demand deposits adjusted, at least in the post-war period, may be more sensitive to interest-rate changes than velocity of money is.' (Note that in both cases the definition of 'money' includes time deposits.) The same authors prepared a bibliography of many other studies yielding the same results (6, p. 652). For definition of 'money', cf. 6, p. 640. For the above mentioned bibliography, cf. 6, p. 646, note 6. For cases in which the relation between the rate of interest and the composite of items (a) plus (b) reversed itself and became positive, cf. 6, p. 842, index item 'Interest rates, changes in the velocity of money and inverse relation of'.

rate is so high as to reduce the amount of money held down to zero, it cannot be true as stated by Franco Modigliani that

$$L_r = 0 \text{ and } M = L(y);$$

it must be true that $\qquad M = 0.$

A rate that makes the demand for money to hold equal to zero makes it, simultaneously, worthless for the performance of the task that money performs, that of facilitating exchanges. Thus, money disappears from the economy completely. Precisely the same is true about any other capital good that cannot be, for whatever reason, operated twenty-four hours per day. If the level of the rate of interest makes it impossible to bear the cost of the period of inactivity, these capital goods will simply not exist.

B. The converse proposition cannot hold either: there cannot exist a demand for money to hold if there is not a demand for money for the purpose of undertaking transactions. The ability of any good to serve as a store of value is a derived one; derived from the economic value of the good in its prime task. In a society with perfect clearing arrangements, money is not needed and thus will not exist; as a result, it will not perform the store-of-value role either. Why does it nevertheless exist in Samuelson's model discussed earlier? He believes that he has specified a model in which wealth does not exist, in which provision of retirement income is impossible, and in which social coercion is necessary to maximize welfare.[3] The collectivity in his model prints pieces of

3. The article analyses and solves the problem of determining the rate of interest and of providing for retirement income in a society in which non-human wealth is assumed not to exist. However, reading of this article indicates that Samuelson neglects the existence of human wealth.

(a) Should human wealth also be assumed away (implicitly), the whole problem becomes insoluble since one cannot draw blood out of a turnip.

(b) Actually, human wealth is implicitly assumed to remain in the model. But then, since wealth exists, the problem which the article purports to solve does not exist. Human income is either produced by human capital during working years or is assured to humans as rent (say, manna from heaven) during those years. In either case, the capitalized value of this income *is wealth*, human wealth. If slavery is permitted, this wealth may be purchased outright; if it is forbidden, demanders may purchase titles to the income produced by human wealth, bonds or debt certificates. In either case, there *will* exist a market rate of interest and there is *no* reason

paper and 'makes a grand consensus on the use of these green-backs as a money of exchange' (4, p. 481). Unfortunately, it is left completely unexplained why consumers agree to use these pieces of paper as money – for which in this economy with ideal clearing arrangements there is no use – and why they fail to agree to use these pieces of paper as debt certificates – which in this economy of perishables are needed. Lacking explanation, all we can do here is to deny that these pieces of paper are money [. . .] and to assert that these pieces of paper are debt certificates.

References

1. J. M. KEYNES, *The General Theory of Employment, Interest and Money*, Harcourt Brace, 1935.
2. F. MODIGLIANI, 'Liquidity preference and the theory of interest and money', *Readings in Monetary Theory*, Lutz and Mints (eds.) Blackiston, 1951.
3. J. TOBIN, 'Money, capital and other stores of value', *American Economic Review*, vol. 51, May 1961, pp. 26–37.
4. P. A. SAMUELSON, 'An exact consumption-loan model of interest with or without the social contrivance of money', *Journal of Political Economy*, vol. 66, December 1958, pp. 467–82.
5. A. H. MELTZER, 'Demand for money: evidence from the time series', *Journal of Political Economy*, vol. 71, June 1963, pp. 219–46.
6. M. FRIEDMAN and ANNA J. SCHWARTZ, *A Monetary History of the United States 1867–1960*, Princeton University Press, 1963.
7. A. P. LERNER and P. A. SAMUELSON, 'Consumption-loan interest and money', 'Reply' and 'Rejoinder', *Journal of Political Economy*, vol. 67, October 1959, pp. 512–25.
8. W. H. MECKLING and P. A. SAMUELSON, 'An exact consumption-loan model of interest: a comment', 'Reply' and 'Rejoinder', *Journal of Political Economy*, vol. 68, February 1960, pp. 72–84.

---

whatever why it should be 'the biological rate', identical with the rate of growth of population. Regardless of population growth, it may be positive, zero, or negative, depending on the orthodox forces of supply and demand in the (human) capital market. The seller of human wealth or titles to it may utilize the proceeds as consumption loans or as *investment loans* (education, training, production of children who will become new income receivers, etc.). The purchaser of human wealth or titles to it *is* able to provide for his retirement through the market and *no* social collusion or conspiracy is required to reach the Pareto optimality of perfect competition. The only social collusion necessary is a law enforcing private contracts – surely *no* violation of the principles of *laissez-faire*.

In other words, the analysis contained in this article is false from beginning to end (4, 7 and 8).

18 J. R. Hicks

Monetary Theory and History: An Attempt at Perspective[1]

Excerpt from J. R. Hicks (1967), *Critical Essays in Monetary Theory*, Clarendon Press, ch. 9, pp. 155–73.

I have attempted, on two previous occasions, to elucidate the relation between Keynes and those whom he called 'classics'. The method that was employed in those papers was analytical; analysis was one of the things that needed to be done; I believe that the analytical method, up to a point, did justify itself. It has nevertheless left me in some ways dissatisfied. The question is not merely analytical, it is also historical. What did the pre-Keynesian writers say, and why did they say it? In order to complete the discussion, there are some further matters in this direction which need to be explored.

'Classics', as used by Keynes, was a confusing description. Before Keynes (and even since Keynes, by those who are not specially concerned with Keynesian controversy), 'classical economics' has been used in a different and more restricted sense. What we otherwise mean by classical economics is the economics of Adam Smith, Ricardo and their contemporaries; not the economics of those whom we have now had to call the 'neo-classics' – those who flourished in the three-quarters of a century before 1936. Keynes certainly means his 'classics' to include the neo-classics; it may indeed be some of the latter whom his cap most exactly fits. But I think that he spoke of them all as 'classics' because he perceived (quite rightly perceived) that some of the things he was attacking came down from Smith and Ricardo, especially perhaps Ricardo, whom he was right in identifying as the chief originator of what he called the classical tradition.

1. Given as the Edward Shann lecture, Perth, Western Australia, in February 1967.

I

Monetary theory is less abstract than most economic theory; it cannot avoid a relation to reality, which in other economic theory is sometimes missing. It belongs to monetary history, in a way that economic theory does not always belong to economic history. Indeed it does so in two ways which need to be distinguished.

It is noticeable, on the one hand, that a large part of the best work on 'money' is topical. It has been prompted by particular episodes, by particular experiences of the writer's own time. All theorizing is simplifying, cutting out the unimportant and leaving what is thought to be important, in the hope that by simplifying we may increase understanding. Sometimes what is sought is a general understanding; but with monetary theory it is more often a particular understanding – an understanding directed towards a particular problem, normally a problem of the time at which the work in question is written. So monetary theories arise out of monetary disturbances. This is obviously true of the *General Theory*, which is *the* book of the Great Depression – the world depression of the nineteen-thirties; it is also true of Keynes' other version, the *Treatise on Money*, which differs from the *General Theory* quite largely because it is directed at a different contemporary problem. Though the *Treatise* was published in 1930, after the Depression had begun, it must largely have been written earlier. Its world is not the world of the Depression, it is the world of the *restored gold standard*. Its problem is how the restored gold standard is to be made to work. Now much the same is true of Ricardo and his contemporaries, a century earlier.

Ricardo's monetary writings (the earliest is dated 1808, and he died in 1823) cover a period of war inflation, in the last stages of the British war against Napoleon, and a period of reconstruction, and attempted stabilization, after the peace. His problems are the problems of those years. Thus his work, like Keynes', was the result of a challenge – a challenge from contemporary experience. It is possible that one reason why monetary theory did get a bit ossified in its neo-classical phase is that in that phase there seemed to be no similar challenge. At least in the seventies and eighties, when Marshall (the greatest of the neo-classicals) could have responded to a challenge, it was just not there; you could not get much of a kick out of bimetallism! You cannot get brilliant answers to a dull question paper; and the question paper that was set to Marshall by his monetary facts really was a bit dull.

That topicality is one way in which monetary theory is historically conditioned; but there is another also.

Throughout the whole time – back before Ricardo, forward after Keynes – money itself has been evolving. The change from metallic money to paper money is obvious; but there are other things which have gone with that change, of even greater importance, which are not so easy to recognize and to assess. Even if we say that metallic money has given place to credit money, we are still not getting to the bottom of what has happened. For credit money is just a part of a whole credit structure that extends outside money; it is closely interwoven with a whole system of debts and credits, of claims and obligations, some of which are money, some of which are not, and some of which are on the edge of being money. The obvious change in the money medium, from 'full-bodied' coins to notes and bank deposits, is just a part of a wider development, the development of a financial system. This has taken the form of the growth of financial institutions, not just banks, but other 'financial intermediaries' as well; it has carried with it a fundamental change in the financial activities of governments. In the course of these changes there has been a change in the whole character of the monetary system. In a world of banks and insurance companies, money markets and stock exchanges, money is quite a different thing from what it was before these institutions came into being.

This evolution has been going on ever since the time of Ricardo (its beginnings, of course, are much earlier); it clearly called, as it proceeded, for a radical revision of monetary theory. As the actual system changed, the theoretical simplification ought to have changed with it. We can now see that it did not change sufficiently; there was a lag. But the reason for the lag was not just laziness or sleepiness; there was an obstacle to be overcome.

On the theoretical level – in terms of basic principles – the evolution that was occurring had two aspects. From one of them it was a natural piece of economizing. Metallic money is an expensive way of performing a simple function; why waste resources in digging up gold from the ground when pieces of paper (or mere book entries) which can be provided, and transported, at a fraction of the cost will do as well? That is the reason why the credit system grows: that it provides a medium of exchange at much lower cost. But on the other side there is the penalty that the credit system is an unstable system. It rests upon confidence and trust; when trust is absent it can just shrivel up. It is unstable in the other direction too; when there is too much 'confidence' or optimism it can explode in bursts of speculation. Thus in order for a credit system to work smoothly, it needs an institutional framework which shall restrain it on the one hand, and shall support it on the other. To find a framework which can be relied on to give support when it is needed, and to impose restraint just when it is needed, is very difficult; I do not think it has ever been perfectly solved. Even in this day we do not really know the answer.

II

When Ricardo and his contemporaries saw this problem (some of them, as we shall see, did certainly begin to see it) it frightened them quite a bit. So they tried to hack their way out.

At their date, it must be remembered, the evolution of the credit system had not gone very far. Thus it was natural still to regard the metallic money as primary; the notes and bills (which already existed) as a tiresome, but secondary, qualification. If only the secondary money would behave like primary money, there would be no trouble! So let us try to make it behave like primary money. Then we can carry on in our thinking with a simple, easily understandable, primary money model.

That, in effect, is what Ricardo did. But it is not enough to recognize that his model is a metallic-money model. We should still ask: as a metallic-money model, for a system without developed credit, was it right? Would it be true, even in a world where all borrowing and lending was long-term borrowing and lending (for that, at the least, must be assumed if we are to have no credit) that interest rates will be entirely determined by saving and investment, that the level of activity will be solely determined by the real factors in the system and that the quantity of money will solely act upon the level of prices? These are the 'classical' doctrines, which we associate with Ricardo. It is evident that

Ricardo relied upon them as an approximation to reality; but I wonder whether even he, even for his metallic-money model, thought that they were *exactly* true.

For there are writings, serious and intelligent writings, which were available to Ricardo (which indeed we can be quite sure that he must have read), and in which some at least of the qualifications are quite clearly set out. The most striking of these is the essay 'Of money' by David Hume. Hume, of course, is most famous as a philosopher; but he was no mean economist also. He was a close friend of Adam Smith, but his work on economics is earlier than Smith's; it was Smith who learned from Hume, not the other way about. For Hume, writing in 1750, it was natural to assume a purely metallic money; for the growth of the credit system, though it had begun, was in his day at a much earlier stage than it was in Ricardo's. But his analysis of the working of a monetary system is not simply what Keynes would have called 'classical'. For Hume the quantity theory of money is *an equilibrium condition.*

Money [he says] is nothing but the representation of labour and commodities, and serves only as a method of rating or estimating them. Where coin is in greater plenty – as a greater quantity of it is required to represent the same quantity of goods – it can have no effect, either good or bad, taking a nation within itself; any more than it would make an alteration in a merchant's books, if instead of the Arabian method of notation, which requires few characters, he should make use of the Roman, which requires a great many. (1, pp. 292–3.)

That, for Hume, is the main point; the *classical* quantity theory point. But Hume goes on:

Notwithstanding this conclusion, which must be allowed just, it is certain that since the discovery of the mines in America, industry has increased in all the nations of Europe, except in the possessors of those mines; and this may justly be ascribed, among other reasons, to the increase of gold and silver. Accordingly we find that in every kingdom, into which money begins to flow in greater abundance than formerly, everything takes on a new face; labour and industry gain life; the merchant becomes more enterprising, and even the farmer follows his plough with greater alacrity and attention. . . .

To account then for this phenomenon, we must consider, that though the high price of commodities be a necessary consequence of the increase of gold and silver, yet it follows not immediately upon that increase; but some time is required before the money circulates through the whole state, and makes its effect be felt on all ranks of people. At first, no alteration is perceived; by degrees the price rises, first of one commodity, then of another; till the whole at last reaches a just proportion with the new quantity of specie which is in the kingdom. In my opinion, it is only in this interval or intermediate situation, between the acquisition of money and the rise of prices, that the increasing quantity of gold and silver is favourable to industry. (1, pp. 293–4.)

Putting the point in our language, the quantity theory is valid as a long-term equilibrium condition; but in the short period, while the supply of money is increasing, the increase can be a real stimulus. Now the interesting question is: if Ricardo had been challenged, and had been held to it, would he – could he – have said anything different?

There is one piece of evidence which suggests that after all he would not. It is evidently implied by what Hume says about the stimulus of monetary expansion that the effect of monetary contraction will be the reverse. If the supply of money is reduced, or if money is taken out of circulation by hoarding, prices will fall; but while they are falling, business will be depressed. Now though Ricardo (so far as I know) never admitted this as a principle, he acted as if he believed it. For though he was prepared to accept some fall in prices, after the war (through which he had been living for so long) was over, in order to achieve what he thought was the great good of monetary stability, he was very much concerned to ensure that the fall in prices should not be unnecessarily large. That was the purpose of his famous 'ingot plan' which was designed to prevent an excessive fall in the money in circulation (2). I do not see why he should have been so bothered upon this, if he regarded money prices – the course of money prices over time – as having no *real* importance.

Quite a number of things will fit into place if we suppose that the classical economists, of this important and in so many ways constructive period, did have some such short-period theory, somewhere at the back of their minds, though they preferred not to emphasize it. One can see several reasons why they should have preferred not to emphasize it.

There was a special reason in Ricardo's own case, that he was the great creator of the static-equilibrium method in economics; he was showing, for the first time, how much could be done with that method; it was his method, and he was reluctant to turn away from it. Not only here, but in many other applications, he tended to rush from one equilibrium to another much too quick. Then there is the point, which I have already mentioned, that the monetary theory of that time was oriented towards a particular practical problem, the restoration of a particular kind of stability, a problem that seemed eminently suitable for analysis in equilibrium terms. But there was also another reason, the most important of all. They were terribly afraid that if too much weight were given to short-period effects, it would play into the hands of crude inflationists. The long period, it would be said, is just a succession of short periods. Why not keep the stimulus going, when the first dose is exhausted, by another dose? They were afraid of that question, for they did not know the answer to it. Yet they felt in their bones that the suggestion in it was wrong.

Nowadays, I think, we know the answer. We know it in theory, and we have seen it confirmed in practice. Inflation does give a stimulus, but the stimulus is greatest when the inflation starts – when it starts from a condition that has been non-inflationary. If the inflation continues, people get adjusted to it. But when people are adjusted to it, when they *expect* rising prices, the mere occurrence of what has been expected is no longer stimulating. Nor can the fade-out be prevented by accelerating the inflation; for acceleration of inflation can be expected too. It is perfectly possible to have an 'inflationary equilibrium' in which prices go on rising, even for years, more or less as they are expected to rise; but then there is no stimulus. In real terms, in terms of production and even of employment, the economy may be very depressed. We have seen examples of this in our time, in South America and in East Asia, in Argentina and in Indonesia, for instance; they are not pretty. The 'classical' economists were quite right in refusing to look that way, though they did not quite know just why they were refusing.

You may ask for some evidence that this really was their state of mind. I can say that I know one very eminent nineteenth-century economist in whom the statement of it is almost explicit – so nearly explicit as to be readily recognizable; this is John Stuart

Mill. There is no doubt at all that Mill did have a short-period theory such as I have been describing. He has written it out for us himself, in his essay on the 'Influence of consumption upon production' (in his *Essays on Unsettled Questions*, 3). There is no doubt at all that when Mill wrote that essay he was on what we have been calling Hume's side. But it is a remarkable thing that when we turn to Mill's *Principles* (1848 – the *Essays* were published in 1844, but are stated to have been written earlier, 4), we find no reference at all to the argument of the essay. In the *Principles* (see especially the chapter on 'Excess of supply') Mill appears, on all this side, to be just a hard-boiled 'classic'. The argument of the essay is not withdrawn, but it is just not there. I feel sure that we can best explain Mill's position by supposing that he always held to what he had said in the essay, but he did not want to emphasize it, for he held that it was *dangerous*.

III

All this can be said before we come (at all seriously) to the evolution of credit. But in fact, even in Ricardo's time – and still more by the time of Mill, a generation later – the development of credit had gone quite far. In trying to treat the monetary system as if it was a metallic system, or could be forced into the mould of a metallic system, Ricardo was looking backward. The monetary system in terms of which he was thinking was already, in his day, a thing of the past.

There was at least one of his contemporaries to whom this was quite familiar. Ricardo must certainly have read the 'Enquiry into the nature and effects of the paper credit of Great Britain', by Henry Thornton (1802 – six years earlier than any of Ricardo's writings); but he passed it by. Thornton has a short-period theory, not unlike Hume's; but it is worked out in terms of a credit economy. Thornton's is in fact the best analysis of the working of a credit system which was given by any of the older economists. As a short-period theory, it can be rewritten in a form which brings it quite close to Keynes.

For Thornton does not only recognize (as Hume had done) that in the short period, monetary causes may have real effects; he also recognized that in a credit system the reverse can happen. Real causes have monetary effects. A credit system will expand automatically if there are real causes making for an expansion in activity (more or less what Keynes was later to call 'a rise in the marginal efficiency of capital'); it will contract automatically if there is a panic (involving a sharp rise in liquidity preference), or if there are changes in the demand for capital which make for contraction. Some of these expansions and contractions are desirable, some highly undesirable. Thornton accordingly held that a credit system must be *managed*. It must be managed by a central bank, whose operations must be determined by judgement, and cannot be reduced to procedure by a mechanical rule.

The objectives to which Thornton thought this management should be directed were quite complex; it is most interesting to find that the avoidance of unnecessary unemployment does find a place among them. But the weighting which he gives to different objectives is not unnaturally very different from the weighting which would have been given by Keynes. I need not go into that; the thing on which I want to insist is that Thornton does believe in the necessity of monetary management; on that crucial matter he is on the same side as Keynes – on the opposite side from Ricardo.

Now where did Mill stand on that point? In the light of what I have already said about Mill, that is quite an interesting question. Mill was writing after Ricardo, and after Thornton; there is no doubt that he was acquainted with the work of both. (There is quite a long passage from Thornton's book that is quoted in full in Mill's *Principles*.[2]) Mill was perfectly well aware that he was dealing with what had become a credit economy. Though he did not have Thornton's practical experience, he had good observers of the financial scene[3] on whose work he could draw; and that a mighty change had occurred was by his time unmistakable. Ricardo had died in 1823; there followed in 1825 the first of that notable series of credit crises which mark the economic history of nineteenth-century England (1825, 1839, 1847, 1857, 1866) – demonstrations of the instability of credit which could not be overlooked. This period of credit crises (much more distinctive as credit crises than some of those which have

2. (4, pp. 515–19 (Ashley edition).)
3. Especially Tooke and Fullarton.

marked later 'trade cycles') was the period during which Mill was writing. He had to take a line about them.

The analysis which Mill gives of the working of credit expansion is really rather good. He saw that it was likely to get started, not by an expansion of bank credit, but by an expansion of trade credit, without the banks (or the main banks) being at that stage much involved. As the boom develops, it requires to be fortified by more secure forms of credit, so the pressure is carried back from the circumference to the centre of the banking system. It is essential, at that point, that the centre should hold firm; it must protect itself, but only in order to be able to spread security around it. Because he understands that this is the way the system works, Mill is unable to follow Ricardo in looking for mechanical rules by which credit is to be controlled; it can only be controlled by quite subtle appreciation of the 'feel' of the market, by monetary *policy*. In all this Mill is on the same side as Thornton; he believes in monetary management.

Yet Mill's idea of monetary management seems oddly one-sided. He is concerned to prevent booms; but he seems much less concerned to prevent slumps. One must clearly not attribute this to any lack of sensitivity to the suffering caused by slumps; for Mill is outstanding among the older economists for his social sympathy. It does, however, seem to be explicable in terms of his particular experience. The slumps of his time followed on directly from the crises; they seemed obviously traceable to the disorganization caused by the crisis. Once that disorganization was set right, trade recovered. It was natural to conclude that if the booms could be prevented, if credit could be prevented from over-expanding, the slumps would be prevented too. That is a point (of course) on which a Keynesian economist would refuse to follow him. Mill, I think, just took it for granted; for in his time things did look just like that. It did not seem to be necessary to inquire further.

IV

I can now conclude what I have to say about these old classical economists. It is an old story; but I have tried to show that it is a significant story. There is much more to it than the formation of an orthodoxy. The classical economists did not all say the same thing. There were differences among them, and some of the differences which then came up for the first time are still important.

There were, at the least, two strands in classical economics. There was one (represented, roughly speaking, by Ricardo and his followers) which maintained that all would be well if by some device credit money could be made to behave like metallic money; there was another (represented, so far as I have taken the story, by Thornton and Mill) which held that credit money must be managed, even though (as was admitted) it is difficult to manage it. This is a major difference, and it has outlasted Keynes. In this sense we still have Ricardians among us. When Milton Friedman tells us that we should have 'a legislated rule instructing the monetary authority to achieve a specified rate of growth in the stock of money' (5, p. 54), he is being Ricardian. When Jacques Rueff [4] tries to push us into revaluing gold, in order to replace credit money (if only in international transactions) by gold transfers, he is being Ricardian. But this Ricardian strand is only one strand in 'classical' monetary theory; we have Thornton and Mill to prove the contrary.

What happened to these two strands, after the time of Mill, in the neo-classical phase? I must here be very brief. What mainly happened, I think, was this. It was the Ricardian which remained the official doctrine; or perhaps one should say that many things which only make sense in Ricardian terms remained official doctrine. It survived quite sufficiently to be presentable as *the* classical theory for Keynes to attack. Bankers talked Ricardo in their speeches. Descriptions of the monetary system were given in textbooks – in terms of cash ratios, fiduciary issues, and so on – by which the quite fully developed credit system which then existed was translated into Ricardian terms. That, however, was theory; in practice it was the Thornton–Mill school which won out. On strict Ricardian principles, there should have been no need for central banks. A currency board, working on a rule, should have been enough; but in fact, during this period, there was a growth of central banks. There was quite odd double-talk about it. The Bank of England itself was supposed to be Ricardianized by the Bank Charter Act of 1844, which divided it into

4. In many current speeches.

an Issue Department, that was just to be a Currency Board, and a Banking Department that was to differ little from an ordinary bank. But that was not in fact what happened. The Banking Department became a Central Bank, which, at least to a limited extent, did exercise monetary policy. It has to be cautious about it, since it was not in accordance with official doctrine that it should do so. I think nevertheless that there is no doubt that that is what it did (6).

This was indeed an odd situation; why did it persist? I think it suited the bankers very well to represent themselves, and even to think of themselves, as passive – just keeping to the 'rules'. For if it had been suspected that they were actively controlling, people would have asked: what right have they to control? Their actions are affecting everyone, affecting everyone (on occasion) very deeply. What right have they, who have not come up through the regular channels of democratic government, to arrogate to themselves such power? So it was useful to them to keep a screen in front of them. Once it was suspected that they were exercising control, their right to control was bound to be called in question. And so, in the end, it proved.

V

That anti-banker revolution was one aspect of the 'Keynesian revolution' as it worked out in practice; but it was mixed up with the other aspect, concerning the kind of control that should be exercised, not who should exercise it. To this I must now turn.

The kind of banking control that Mill envisaged was directed against excessive expansion, not the other way about. I have suggested that in leaning that way, Mill may have been influenced by his particular experience, by the conditions of the time when he lived; but when we come to Keynes, is there not something of a similar possibility? The *General Theory* was written in the world depression; even the twenties, when Keynes was writing the *Treatise*, were in England years of semi-slump, or of a boom that misfired. It was natural for Keynes, writing when he did, to take as his base a 'depressed' economy. His practical problem was emergence from depression; he looked at the world from a depression point of view. I am myself quite sufficiently Keynesian to be convinced the Mill kind of control (control which can be exercised by a Central Bank, if it is allowed to exercise it) is by no means enough. But the picture one so easily gets from Keynes of an economy which will always be under-functioning, unless it is boosted by deliberate expansionary policy, seems to me to be just as one-sided. Ideas which arose in the thirties, and which were appropriate in the thirties, have been carried over, through Keynes' influence, into a world where they do not at all so obviously belong.

However that may be, we have unquestionably learned from Keynes that control through banking is one-sided. It can be effective against inflation and over-expansion; against over-contraction it is relatively powerless. Banks can restrict expansion by refusing to lend; but they cannot force expansion just by offering to lend, on whatever easy terms. It can be that business is feeling so dismal that even on the most favourable possible terms (which are consistent with the banking system making any sort of a profit) loans will not be taken up. (Even so, it is possible for a follower of Mill to retort[5] that this is a very odd state of mind for businessmen to be in; it must be due to some cause. It must be due to some obstruction in the business circulation, surplus stocks that can and will be worked off, bad debts that can and will be settled; the most that is needed is some help on the way to this natural recovery.) Keynes has nevertheless clearly shown that a depressed economy can be boosted by government spending; and once that is granted, the way to the acceptance of government spending as a *general* booster is hard to resist.

Two general reflections about the post-Keynesian world, which seem to arise out of what I have been saying, may be made in conclusion.

1. There was a first phase – I think one can now say that it was just a first phase – in which it seemed to be a simple matter for the whole control of economic activity to be taken over by the government budget. This was the heyday of 'fiscal policy'. If there was a tendency to contraction, more should be spent; if there was a tendency to over-expansion, taxation should be raised. For a while this did not work badly; but it was an arrangement that had its defects. When the principle is so crudely stated, the defects are rather obvious.

5. As I think Dennis Robertson might have done, more or less.

It is easy enough for government to spend more; that is a simple and popular policy. Some sorts of taxes (taxes that will be paid by people whose votes you don't want) are also popular. But the supply of such convenient taxes tends to give out; control by unpopular taxes is a different matter. When the Keynesian prescription calls upon the minister to impose unpopular taxes, he begins to long for the old days, when he had a banker behind whom he could hide. 'This business of monetary control', he will be saying, 'is a technical matter. If I deal with it by fiscal policy, though I can say that I am taking the advice of my experts (my economic advisers and so on), I have to take the responsibility myself for these nasty decisions. It would be much better to let the experts do the job themselves.' So he makes passes to hand it back to the bankers. But he cannot really hand it back to the bankers, for everyone knows that he controls the bankers. They are no longer in a position to carry out an independent monetary policy, as they could do – to some limited extent – in former times. What happens is that the control gets lost between them. The control – the Keynesian control – cannot be properly exercised until there is a government that is strong enough to take unpopular measures, and to assume responsibility for them.

In this last passage, I (in my turn) have no doubt been influenced – perhaps over-influenced – by recent experience in Britain. Still I think that the situation is one that can occur elsewhere, and may indeed have occurred elsewhere on some occasions. It is asking quite a lot of a government that it should continue, year in and year out, to maintain a Keynesian control, in both directions.

2. The other thing on which I want to say something is the international side. This, in its turn, splits up into two parts. In one of them we are looking outwards, from the point of view of the single nation, at its international economic relations. In the other we are looking at the well-being of the international economy as a whole. This latter may appear so remote as hardly to deserve attention; but it is not in fact to the advantage of any single nation that it should be forgotten, and left to look after itself.

In the old days, when monetary control was exercised by central bankers, their primary concern was the stability of the currency in terms of foreign exchange. That objective, in the new era, has been deposed from its old position. It was recognized, even in the initial charter of the I.M.F., that stability of foreign exchange was not so sacred an object as central bankers had tried to make it in former times. Arrangements were made for agreed adjustment of exchange rates on the occasion of what was called a 'fundamental disequilibrium'. I would in no way question that this is indeed a real problem, a problem which the world has not (as yet) done much to solve. I would nevertheless maintain that it has been quite over-shadowed by another, by the inflations (active and creeping inflations) which are traceable, not to 'fundamental disequilibrium', but to the implementation of pseudo-Keynesian policies by weak and irresolute governments. It is this which has been the main cause of exchange instability, and – what maybe is even worse – of feared exchange instability. There is widespread fear of exchange instability, just because, in the Keynesian epoch, the impression has got around that exchange depreciation, or devaluation, does not matter all that much.

I think it does matter. It may sometimes be necessary, as the least evil among a choice of evils. But it is an evil, which should not be regarded, as it is so often regarded at present, as a normal and natural way out.

The reason why it is an evil becomes apparent when we look at the matter from the other angle, that of the international economy. The story which I have been telling in terms of those old characters – Thornton, Mill and Ricardo – is repeating itself, in our day, on the international stage. There is the same movement from metallic money (gold) to credit money, going on there too. There is the same problem of the instability of credit. There is the same need that international credit should be managed, in order to be secure.

We do not need, on the international plane, to feel the Keynesian fear, that purely monetary management will be unable to fight depression; on the international plane it is not depression, in the old sense, that is the danger. National governments, taught by Keynes, however indirectly, can see to that. What is liable to happen, if there is a failure of international credit, is that nations will turn in upon themselves, becoming more autarkic or more protectionist, impoverishing themselves and each other by refusing to trade with each other. (And this means, we can already see, refusing to *aid* each other.) That is the danger with which we are confronted; we can already see that it is no imaginary danger at this present time.

The remedy, my old nineteenth-century experience would tell us, would be an International Central Bank, an international bank which would underpin the credit structure, but in order to underpin it must have some control over it. That was what Keynes, who understood this international aspect very clearly, wanted to get at Bretton Woods; but all he got was a currency board (for it is little more than a currency board, being so tied up with rules and regulations) – the I.M.F. That, we are finding – and Mill could have told us, one hundred and twenty years ago, that it is what we should find – is not enough. But how should the powers, which governments have been unwilling to entrust to their own central banks (once they have realized what is involved) be entrusted to an international bank? That is the dilemma, the old dilemma, to which we have now come back, on the international plane.

Stated like that, the problem looks insoluble. In such black and white terms, it probably is. But to set rules against no rules is to make too sharp an opposition. Can we find rules that are acceptable to national pride, and to national self-interest, and which yet give scope for some minimum of management – just enough to give the international credit structure the security it so sorely needs? It will be a narrow passage, but one must hope that there will be a way through.

References

1. D. HUME, 'Of money', *Essays*, Oxford University Press, 1750.
2. R. S. SAYERS, 'Ricardo's views on monetary questions', *Papers in English Monetary History*, Ashton and Sayers (ed.), Clarendon Press, 1953.
3. J. S. MILL, *Essays on Unsettled Questions*, Longmans, 1844.
4. J. S. MILL, *Principles of Political Economy*, Longmans, 6th edn, 1848.
5. M. FRIEDMAN, *Capitalism and Freedom*, Chicago University Press, 1962.
6. R. S. SAYERS, *Bank of England Operations 1890–1914*, P. S. King, 1936.

19 R. W. Clower

The Keynesian Counter-Revolution: A Theoretical Appraisal

Excerpt from R. W. Clower (1965), 'The Keynesian counter-revolution: a theoretical appraisal', *The Theory of Interest Rates*, edited by F. H. Hahn and F. Brechling, International Economic Association Series, Macmillan, ch. 5, pp. 103–25.

Twenty-five years of discussion and controversy have produced a large and surprisingly harmonious literature on Keynes and the Classics. Although the series still has not converged to a point of universal agreement, the domain remaining open to dispute has contracted steadily with the passage of time. On one essential issue, however, contemporary opinion is still largely undecided: precisely what are the purely formal differences, if any, between Keynes and the Classics? Perhaps the clearest symptom of our uncertainty is the continued lack of an explicit integration of price theory and income analysis. Equally significant, however, is the ambivalence of professional economists towards the Keynesian counter-revolution launched by Hicks in 1937 and now being carried forward with such vigour by Patinkin and other general equilibrium theorists (1–6).[1] The elegance and generality of this literature makes it most alluring. At the same time, one can hardly fail to be impressed – and disturbed – by the close resemblance that some of its central doctrines bear to those of orthodox economics.

I do not presume at this late date either to improve the views of previous writers on Keynes and the Classics or to transform equivocations into certainties. Things are not that simple. However, I shall attempt to show that the same highly special theoretical presuppositions which led to Keynes' original attack

1. The 'counter-revolution' to which I refer is clearly not a conscious revolt against Keynesian economics, for all of the writers involved are, in a practical sense, strong supporters of what they conceive to be the Keynesian revolution. It is another question whether the same people are Keynesians in a theoretical sense. That is one of the issues on which this paper is intended to shed some light.

on orthodox economics continue to pervade contemporary price theory and that the Keynesian counter-revolution would collapse without them. Unlike Keynes, who had to deal with doctrines of which no authoritative account had ever been given, we now have an extremely clear idea of the orthodox content of contemporary theory.[2] We thus have a distinct advantage over Keynes in describing what has been said. However, our basic problem is to discover and describe what has not but should have been said – and here we are on all fours with Keynes. Like Keynes, therefore, I must begin by asking 'forgiveness if, in the pursuit of sharp distinctions, my controversy is itself too keen' (7).

I Keynes and Traditional Theory

Our first task is to express in modern idiom those aspects of orthodox economics which were of special concern to Keynes. This may be accomplished most conveniently by considering a two-sector economy comprising households on one side and firms on the other. Corresponding to this division into sectors, we distinguish two mutually exclusive classes of commodities: (a) those which are supplied by firms and demanded by households; (b) those which are supplied by households and demanded by firms. Commodities in class (a) will be distinguished by numerical subscripts $i = 1, \ldots, m$, those in class (b) by numerical subscripts $j = m + 1, \ldots, n$. Thus, quantities supplied and demanded by firms are denoted, respectively, by variables $s_1, \ldots, s_m, d_{m+1}, \ldots, d_n$, while quantities demanded and supplied by households are denoted, respectively, by variables $d_1, \ldots, d_m, s_{m+1}, \ldots, s_n$. Prevailing market prices (expressed in units of commodity n) are then represented by symbols $\mathbf{p}_1, \mathbf{p}_2, \ldots, \mathbf{p}_{n-1} (\mathbf{p}_n \equiv 1)$, or, in vector notation, $\mathbf{P}$.[3]

For ease of exposition, we shall ignore aggregation problems and suppose that the preferences of all households in the economy are adequately characterized by a community utility function,

2. For this, we have mainly to thank the counter-revolutionists, since it is their writings which have revived interest in general equilibrium theory.

3. Here and throughout the remainder of the paper, boldface symbols will invariably be used to refer to magnitudes that are to be regarded as given parameters from the standpoint of individual transactors.

$U(d_1, \ldots, d_m; s_{m+1}, \ldots, s_n)$. Similarly, we shall assume that technical conditions confronting all business firms in the economy are adequately characterized by an aggregate transformation function $T(s_1, \ldots, s_m; d_{m+1}, \ldots, d_n) = 0$. Needless to say, the functions U and T are assumed to possess all continuity and curvature properties needed to ensure the existence of unique extrema under circumstances to be specified below.

Dealing first with the orthodox theory of the firm, we obtain sector supply and demand functions, $\bar{s}_i(\mathbf{P})$, $\bar{d}_i(\mathbf{P})$ as solutions of the problem:

maximize
$$r = \sum_i^m \mathbf{p}_i s_i - \sum_j^n \mathbf{p}_j d_j,{}^4$$

subject to
$$T(s_1, \ldots, s_m; d_{m+1}, \ldots, d_n) = 0.{}^5$$

Underlying both sets of solutions are transactor equilibrium conditions of the form

$$\mathbf{p}_k + \frac{\lambda \partial T}{\partial \bar{v}_k} = 0 \quad (\bar{v} = \bar{d}, \bar{s}; k = 1, 2, \ldots, n).$$

In particular, if $n = 2$ and we interpret s_1 as goods and d_2 as labour, we easily establish Keynes' classical postulate I, namely, 'the [real] wage is equal to the marginal product of labour'. (*General Theory*, p. 5.)

In a similar fashion, the demand and supply functions of the household sector are obtained as solutions, $\bar{d}_i(\mathbf{P}, \mathbf{r})$, $\bar{s}_i(\mathbf{P}, \mathbf{r})$, of the problem

maximize
$$U(d_1, \ldots, d_m; s_{m+1}, \ldots, s_n),$$

subject to
$$\sum_i^m \mathbf{p}_i d_i - \sum_j^n \mathbf{p}_j s_j - \mathbf{r} = 0,$$

---

4. The symbols $\sum_t^m$ and $\sum_i^n$ denote, respectively, the operations $\sum_{i=1}^m$ and $\sum_{j=m+1}^n$.

5. Since $\mathbf{p}_n \equiv 1$ by assumption, we have not shown it as an explicit divisor of the price variables included in the vector $\mathbf{P}$; but it is there all the same. Thus, the demand and supply functions of the business sector are homogeneous of order zero in the n price variables $\mathbf{p}_1, \ldots, \mathbf{p}_n$. Provided $d_n \not\equiv 0$, however, the same functions are not in general homogenous in the $n - 1$ *numéraire* prices which are contained in the vector $\mathbf{P}$.

the profit variable **r** being treated as a fixed parameter in this context.[6]

Underlying these solutions are transactor equilibrium conditions of the form

$$\frac{\partial U}{\partial \bar{v}_k} + \gamma \mathbf{p}_k = 0 \ (\bar{v} = \bar{d}, \bar{s}; \ k = 1, \ldots, n).$$

Thus, if we consider the case $n = 2$ and adopt an appropriate interpretation of the variables d_1 and s_2, we readily derive Keynes' classical postulate II, namely, 'The utility of the [real] wage when a given volume of labour is employed is equal to the marginal disutility of that amount of employment.' (*General Theory*, p. 5.)

So much for the basic ideas of the orthodox theory of transactor behaviour. Let us turn next to the theory of price formation, again seeking to express matters as Keynes might have expressed them had he been less steeped in Marshallian habits of thought.

At least since the time of Adam Smith, the market mechanism has been regarded by economists as an ingenious device for reconciling the freedom of individuals to trade as they please with the ultimate necessity for individuals in the aggregate to buy neither more nor less of any commodity than is offered for sale. To accomplish this feat, the mechanism must be supplied with information about individual sale and purchase plans, which is precisely what is supposed to be furnished by the supply-and-demand functions of orthodox theory.

Assuming that all business profits accrue to accounts in the household sector, we may assert first of all that the sale and purchase plans of individual transactors at any given instant of time[7] depend only on prevailing market prices.[8] We may then argue as follows.

6. The household demand-and-supply functions are homogeneous of order zero in the $n + 1$ variables $\mathbf{p}_1, \ldots, \mathbf{p}_n$ and **r**, but not in the n variables $\mathbf{p}_1, \ldots, \mathbf{p}_{n-1}$ and **r** (provided $s_n \not\equiv 0$).

7. I have chosen to regard 'time' as a continuous rather than a discrete variable, and to confine discussion to current values of all magnitudes, in order to discourage both myself and readers from playing meretricious games with alternative lag assumptions. No part of the present or subsequent argument is affected in any essential way if time is made discrete, lags are introduced, etc.

8. Since we are performing market rather than individual experiments (Patinkin, 1, p. 15), the parameter **r** which appears in the household

If prevailing prices are such that demand differs from supply in any market, this means that individual trading plans, taken as a whole, are mutually inconsistent, which, in turn, means that at least some individual plans cannot be carried into effect at prevailing market prices. In these circumstances, it is plausible to suppose that prevailing prices tend to vary over time, rising in markets where demand exceeds supply, falling in markets where supply exceeds demand. Accordingly, the economy may be said to be in a state of disequilibrium. On the other hand, if prevailing market prices at any given instant happen to be such that demand is equal to supply in every market simultaneously, this means that individual trading plans, considered as a whole, are mutually consistent; hence, that all transactions planned at prevailing prices can, in principle, actually be carried out. In these circumstances, it is plausible to suppose that there are no extraneous forces at work tending to alter either individual trading plans or prevailing market prices, and the economy may be said to be in a state of equilibrium.

The only snag in this argument is the familiar one about the number of equations being one greater than the number of prices to be determined. From the theory of household behaviour, however, we know that

$$\sum_i^m \mathbf{p}_i\, \bar{d}_i - \sum_j^n \mathbf{p}_j\, \bar{s}_j - \mathbf{r} = 0, \qquad 1$$

and from the theory of business behaviour, we know that

$$\sum_i^m \mathbf{p}_i\, \bar{s}_i - \sum_j^n \mathbf{p}_j\, \bar{d}_j - \bar{r} = 0. \qquad 2$$

Subtracting 2 from 1, therefore, we have

$$\sum_{k=1}^n \mathbf{p}_k\, [\bar{d}_k - \bar{s}_k] \equiv \mathbf{r} - \bar{r}. \qquad 3$$

Since in general the variables $\mathbf{r}$ and $\bar{r}$ refer to completely independent individual experiments, we cannot assume that $\mathbf{r} \equiv \bar{r}$.[8] In

_____

demand and supply functions is now replaced by the function the value of

$$\bar{r} = \sum_i^m \mathbf{p}_i\, \bar{s}_i - \sum_j^n \mathbf{p}_j\, \bar{d}_j,$$

which depends only on the price vector $\mathbf{P}$.

the case of market experiments, however, it does seem plausible to suppose that $\mathbf{r} = \bar{r}$ provided that the variables $s_1, \ldots, s_m$ and $d_{m+1}, \ldots, d_n$ have assumed their equilibrium values. If this is granted, then **3** leads immediately to Walras' law (in the sense of Lange, 8, pp. 49–68).[9]

$$\sum_{k=1}^{n} \mathbf{p}_k[\bar{d}_k(\mathbf{P}) - \bar{s}_k(\mathbf{P})] \equiv 0. \qquad 4$$

Walras' law obviously implies that the *numéraire* value of one of the excess demands can be inferred from the values of the others, which rids us of the extra supply-and-demand equation. Rewritten in the form

$$\sum_k \mathbf{p}_k \, \bar{s}_k \equiv \sum_k \mathbf{p}_k \, d_k,$$

Walras' law might also be said to assert that 'supply creates its own demand' (cf. *General Theory*, p. 18) – and we shall hear more of this in the sequel. For the time being, however, it may merely be remarked that Walras' law must be valid under the circumstances assumed here.

This account of orthodox doctrine accords well enough, I think, both with modern analysis and with Keynes' conception of classical theory. For the special case $n = 2$, in particular, it is apparent that Keynes' views, as expressed in chapter 2 of the *General Theory*, are exactly equivalent to what is presented above. Granted that this is so, we may reasonably assert that orthodox economics provides a general theory of equilibrium states – that is, an adequate account of the factors determining equilibrium prices and equilibrium transaction plans in a market economy. Moreover, the same analysis may be said to provide the beginnings of a theory of disequilibrium prices and disequilibrium transaction plans. Clearly, however, orthodox analysis does not provide a general theory of disequilibrium states: firstly, because it yields no direct information about the magnitude of *realized* as distinct from *planned* transactions under disequilibrium conditions; secondly, because it tacitly assumes that the forces tending at any instant to change prevailing market prices are independent

9. The distinction drawn by Lange between Walras' law and Say's law is not relevant here; from a formal point of view, the two propositions are equivalent.

of realized transactions at the same moment (this includes as a special case the assumption, made explicitly in all '*tâtonnement*', 'recontract' and 'auction' models, that no disequilibrium transactions occur).[10]

It is instructive to compare these views with those of Keynes, as represented by the following assortment of quotations (not all of them torn out of context):

I shall argue that the postulates of the classical theory are applicable to a special case only and not to the general case . . . (*General Theory*, p. 3).

The question . . . of the volume of the *available* resources, in the sense of the size of the employable population, the extent of natural wealth and the accumulated capital equipment, has often been treated descriptively [in orthodox writings]. But the pure theory of what determines the *actual employment* of the available resources has seldom been examined in any detail. . . . I mean, not that the topic has been overlooked, but that the fundamental theory underlying it has been deemed so simple and obvious that it has received, at the most, a bare mention. (*General Theory*, pp. 4–5.)

A theory cannot claim to be a *general* theory, unless it is applicable to the case where (or the range within which) money wages are fixed, just as much as to any other case. Politicians are entitled to complain that money wages *ought* to be flexible; but a theorist must be prepared to deal indifferently with either state of affairs. (*General Theory*, p. 276.)

. . . the classical theory . . . is wholly unable to answer the question what effect on employment a reduction in money wages will have. For it has no method of analysis wherewith to attack the problem. (*General Theory*, p. 260.)

Clearly, there is nothing very novel in any of this; up to this point, at least, the belief that Keynes is 'saying nothing new' need not be confined to those '. . . who are strongly wedded to . . . the classical theory' (cf. *General Theory*, p. v). Like us, Keynes does not in any way deny the generality of orthodox equilibrium analysis; he only denies that orthodox economics provides an adequate account of disequilibrium phenomena.

10. J. R. Hicks (3), note to ch. 9, pp. 127ff. Also Patinkin (1) supplementary note B, pp. 377–85.

II The Keynesian Indictment of Orthodox Economics

Grounds for theoretical controversy first begin to emerge when we come to the stage in Keynes' argument (*General Theory*, chapter 2) at which he seeks to isolate specific instances in orthodox economics of 'lack of clearness and of generality' (*General Theory*, p. v).

The first item in his bill of particulars is embedded in a lengthy discussion of wage bargains between entrepreneurs and workers (*General Theory*, pp. 1–15). Outwardly, this item represents little more than a vigorous attack on orthodox preconceptions about the stability of a market economy. For the burden of his argument seems to be that if labour is ever forced to move 'off its supply curve' it may be unable to get back on again. If this is an accurate interpretation, we may say immediately that Keynes' criticisms are not of fundamental theoretical significance, for there is no reason to suppose that Keynes was more expert at stability analysis than his orthodox predecessors. However, the same argument might also be interpreted as a direct attack on the orthodox theory of household behaviour. This would certainly put labour off its supply curve and would also explain Keynes' categorical rejection of classical postulate II. But if this is what Keynes intended, i.e. to deny the validity of the orthodox theory of household behaviour, one can only say that he was singularly unsuccessful in providing a rationale for his attack.

The second item in Keynes' bill of particulars is essentially the same as the first: classical theory is charged with failure to recognize the existence of involuntary unemployment (*General Theory*, pp. 15–18). Again, the basic question is: Are 'involuntary unemployment' and 'chronic disequilibrium' synonymous terms for the same objective phenomenon, or is 'involuntary unemployment' a special kind of disequilibrium peculiarly associated with the breakdown of the orthodox theory of household behaviour? Here there is somewhat clearer evidence that Keynes believes his objections to orthodox analysis go very deep indeed:

. . . if the classical theory is only applicable to the case of full employment, it is fallacious to apply it to the problems of involuntary unemployment – if there be such a thing (and who will deny it?). The classical theorists resemble Euclidean geometers in a non-Euclidean world who, discovering that in experience straight lines apparently parallel often meet, rebuke the lines for not keeping straight – as the only remedy for the unfortunate collisions which are occurring. Yet, in truth, there is no remedy except to throw over the axiom of parallels and to work out a non-Euclidean geometry. Something similar is required today in economics. We need to throw over the second postulate of the classical doctrine and to work out the behavior of a system in which involuntary unemployment in the strict sense is possible. (*General Theory*, pp. 16–17.)

Again, however, we are given no compelling theoretical reason to think that the proposed reconstruction of orthodox economics is really necessary.

The third and final item in Keynes' indictment is a denial of the relevance of Walras' law (*General Theory*, pp. 18–21). Most later writers (e.g. Ohlin, 4, p. 230, footnote; Goodwin, 9; Patinkin, 1, p. 249) have argued either that this portion of Keynes' indictment is wrong, or that the proposition which Keynes attacks is not in fact the one he thought he was attacking. Most economists have opted for the second explanation (10, especially p. 113),[11] partly in deference to Keynes' acknowledged intellectual powers, partly because they recognize that if Keynes seriously meant to question the validity or relevance of Walras' law, he would have to reject the orthodox theory of household behaviour and propose an acceptable alternative – and the alternative would have to include orthodox theory as a special case, valid under conditions of full employment. Walras' law is not, after all, an independent postulate of orthodox analysis; it is a theorem which is susceptible of direct proof on the basis of premises which are typically taken as given in contemporary as well as classical price theory.

III The Post-Keynesian Dilemma

The conclusion which I draw from all this may be put in one phrase: *either Walras' law is incompatible with Keynesian economics, or Keynes had nothing fundamentally new to add to orthodox economic theory.* This may seem an unnecessarily brutal way to confront one sacred cow with another. But what other conclusion is possible? In Keynes' mind, at least, the three items in his bill of

11. But see H. Rose's note on Walras' law and the reply by Patinkin (11, 12).

particulars 'all amount to the same thing in the sense that they all stand and fall together, any one of them logically involving the other two' (*General Theory*, p. 22). As we have already seen, he could hardly hold this view seriously unless he regarded each of the three items as an attack on the orthodox theory of household behaviour. But suppose that this is not in fact Keynes' view; suppose that Walras' law is both unreservedly valid, relevant and compatible with Keynesian economics. In this event, the recent literature on monetary theory makes it perfectly evident that Keynes may be subsumed as a special case of the Hicks–Lange–Patinkin theory of *tâtonnement* economics, which differs from orthodox theory only in being more detailed and precise. We would then have to conclude that Keynes added nothing fundamentally new to orthodox economic theory.

Thus, we are caught on the horns of a dilemma. If Keynes added nothing new to orthodox doctrine, why have twenty-five years of discussion failed to produce an integrated account of price theory and income analysis? If Keynes did add something new, the integration problem becomes explicable; but then we have to give up Walras' law as a fundamental principle of economic analysis. It is precisely at this point, I believe, that virtually all previous writers have decided to part company with Keynes. I propose to follow a different course. I shall argue that the established theory of household behaviour is, indeed, incompatible with Keynesian economics, that Keynes himself made tacit use of a more general theory, that this more general theory leads to market excess-demand functions which include quantities as well as prices as independent variables and, except in conditions of full employment, the excess-demand functions so defined do not satisfy Walras' law. In short, I shall argue that there has been a fundamental misunderstanding of the formal basis of the Keynesian revolution.

IV Disequilibrium Systems: A Preliminary View

Before attempting to deal directly with the issues raised above, we must say something more about the mechanics of disequilibrium states. In our earlier discussion of orthodox analysis, it was pointed out that the whole of traditional price theory rests on the tacit assumption that market excess demands are independent of current market transactions. This implies that *income magnitudes do not appear as independent variables in the demand or supply functions of a general equilibrium model*; for incomes are defined in terms of quantities as well as prices, and quantity variables never appear explicitly in the market excess-demand functions of traditional theory. To be sure, income variables could be introduced by taking factor supplies as given parameters; but this would preclude the formulation of a general equilibrium model containing supply functions of all marketable factor services.[12] The importance of these propositions for Keynesian economics can hardly be over-emphasized, for they imply directly that the Keynesian consumption function and other market relations involving income as an independent variable cannot be derived explicitly from any existing theory of general equilibrium.[13]

The most lucid account of the role which current transactions *might* play in general equilibrium theory has been presented by Professor Hicks in *Value and Capital* (3, pp. 119ff.). The following passages are especially significant in the present connexion (pp. 127–9):

Since, in general, traders cannot be expected to know just what total supplies are available on any market, nor what total demands will be forthcoming at particular prices, any price which is fixed initially can be only a guess. It is not probable that demand and supply will actually be found to be equated at such a guessed price; if they are not, then in

12. This was apparently overlooked by Patinkin when he formulated his 'general theory' of macroeconomics (*Money, Interest and Prices*, ch. 9). It is instructive to notice that this chapter is not supplemented by a mathematical appendix. Some of the consequences of this oversight are evident in the later discussion, see especially the argument beginning at p. 216, including the footnotes to pp. 218 and 220. I do not mean to suggest that authors may not put such variables as they please into their models. My point is that such variables as can be shown to be functionally dependent on others should not then be manipulated independently.

13. Cf. Lange, *Price Flexibility and Employment* (5, ch. 9, p. 53). Lange's usage of the phrase 'propensity to consume' is perfectly legitimate, but the concept invoked by him is not in any sense a consumption function of the sort Keynes worked with since, except on the Keynesian definition, it is not possible to talk about changes in consumption in response to changes in income without at the same time talking about changes in prices.

the course of trading the price will move up or down. Now if there is a change of price in the midst of trading, the situation appears to elude the ordinary apparatus of demand-and-supply analysis, for, strictly speaking, demand curves and supply curves give us the amounts which buyers and sellers will demand and supply respectively at any particular price, if that price is fixed at the start and adhered to throughout. Earlier writers, such as Walras and Edgeworth, had therefore supposed that demand-and-supply analysis ought strictly to be confined to such markets as permitted of 'recontract'; i.e. markets such that if a transaction was put through at a 'false' price . . . it could be revised when the equilibrium price was reached. Since such markets are highly exceptional, their solution of the problem (if it can be called one) was not very convincing.'

. . . in the general case . . . gains and losses due to false trading only give rise to income effects – effects, that is, which are the same kind as the income effects which may have to be considered even when we suppose equilibrium prices to be fixed straight away. We have seen again and again that a certain degree of indeterminateness is nearly always imparted by income effects to the laws of economic theory. All that happens as a result of false trading is that this indeterminateness is somewhat intensified. How much intensified depends, of course, upon the extent of the false trading; if very extensive transactions take place at prices very different from equilibrium prices, the disturbance will be serious. But I think we may reasonably suppose that the transactions which take place at *very false* prices are limited in volume. If any intelligence is shown in price-fixing, they will be.

It is heartening to know that income effects can be ignored if they are sufficiently unimportant to be neglected; but this is hardly a solution to the problem at issue. The essential question is whether the supply-and-demand functions of traditional analysis are in any way relevant to the formation of market prices in situations where disequilibrium transactions *cannot* be ignored.

To answer this question, we must first define explicit theoretical measures of disequilibrium transaction quantities. Perhaps the simplest way to define such measures is to suppose that actual transactions in any given market are always dominated by the 'short' side of the market; that is to say, market transactions are equal to planned market supply if demand is greater than supply, to planned market demand if supply is equal to or greater than demand (13, p. 203; 14; 1, pp. 157–8). This is, of course, the procedure which has been followed by all previous writers, in so far as they have said anything at all on the subject.

Taken by itself, this addendum to traditional theory has no logical implications; but it opens the way for further analysis. For example, some writers have suggested the desirability of supposing that actual transactions exert a more or less direct influence on price adjustment via 'spillover' effects – changes in prevailing supply and demand conditions to reflect current discrepancies between planned and realized purchases and sales. The most recent expression of this view has been voiced by Patinkin (1, p. 157).[14] His suggestion is to redefine the usual price adjustment functions to make the rate of change of price in one market a function not of excess demand in that market alone, but also of excess demand in all other markets. That this is not an entirely satisfactory vehicle for expressing his basic views, however, is indicated by three considerations.

Firstly, it is not consistent with established preference analysis to suppose that transactors alter their sale and purchase plans before prevailing market prices have already varied in response to the pressure of excess demand somewhere in the economy. Secondly, the supposition that price movements in one market are governed by excess-demand conditions in all markets is logically equivalent to the supposition that individual traders respond not merely to absolute levels of prevailing prices but also to current rates of change of prices. This implies some basic changes in established preference analysis to allow prices as seen by transactors to differ from current market prices (17). Thirdly, from Walras' law (obviously applicable in this instance), the 'money' value of potential 'spillover' from any given market is measured by the aggregate 'money' value of the market excess supply of all other commodities. Thus, if 'spillover' effects from a given market are *fully* reflected in other markets, we are left with effective excess demand in the given market (and, by induction, in all other markets also) identically equal to zero; which is to say that prices never vary. Patinkin does not go to this extreme; he relies instead on a proposition of Samuelson (18, p. 42)[15] and

14. Also see Hansen (15) and Enthoven (16).

15. In fairness to Samuelson, it should be added that his discussion does not refer to spillover effects, but instead to what I have elsewhere called

supposes that 'spillover' effects in any given market are only partially reflected in transfers of demand to other markets. But this is simply *ad hoc* theorizing – inventing a solution to a problem which has actually been evaded rather than resolved.

A more promising way to bring current transactions into general equilibrium theory is by way of so-called stock-flow models. Unless we suppose that all commodities traded in the economy are highly perishable, it is clearly plausible to argue that goods will accumulate or decumulate (or both) somewhere in the economic system during periods of market disequilibrium. This forces us to consider possible extensions of traditional theory to deal explicitly with asset-holding phenomena.

There is now a reasonably adequate theoretical literature on this subject, including a number of recent papers on monetary theory and at least one important book on the theory of investment.[16] I think it fair to say, however, that this literature has made little impression on the profession at large; which is perhaps another way of remarking that the equilibrium properties of stock-flow models are essentially the same as those of traditional pure-flow models and that few economists are deeply concerned with anything else. Here, therefore, I shall merely observe that the explicit introduction of asset-holding phenomena into traditional theory entails a redefinition of market excess-demand functions to include asset as well as price arrays among the relevant independent variables and, along with this, an extension of the usual equation systems to include stock-adjustment functions. As a consequence, actual transaction quantities influence market adjustment indirectly, via their impact on existing asset stocks – which creates certain new sources of potential instability (24; 18,

---

'dynamical interdependence' among market excess-demand functions. See Bushaw and Clower (19, ch. 4, pp. 82ff.).

16. Vernon L. Smith, *Investment and Production* (20). This book includes a comprehensive bibliography on the 'real' part of the stock-flow literature. For further details of the 'monetary' part, see George Horwich, 'Money, prices and the theory of interest determination' (21). The latest in this series is the article by Archibald and Lipsey (22, October 1958), the related 'Symposium on monetary theory' (22, October 1960), and Baumol's 'Stocks, flows and monetary theory' (23). The general theory underlying such models is developed at perhaps excessive length in Bushaw and Clower (19).

pp. 170–71). Even in this type of model, however, current transactions exercise an influence only after a certain time delay. As in more usual general equilibrium models, therefore, current incomes never appear as independent variables. Thus, this potential road to the *General Theory* also turns out to be a blind alley.

The preceding discussion probably does not exhaust the list of possible ways of introducing current transactions into excess-demand functions, but we have now gone far enough to appreciate that the problem is by no means so transparent as some writers might have us believe. At this point, therefore, let us return to the route which Keynes apparently travelled before us.

V Say's Principle and Walras' Law

In our earlier account of the theory of household behaviour, we did not distinguish between planned and realized magnitudes because to have done so would not in fact have been a meaningful procedure in the context of orthodox equilibrium analysis. However, if we adopt the view that states of transactor disequilibrium are, in principle, just as admissible as states of transactor equilibrium (and how can we do otherwise?) (1, pp. 237–8; 14, pp. 318ff.), the distinction between plans and realizations becomes both meaningful and theoretically relevant. In the discussion that follows, we shall adopt just this point of view; accordingly, we shall henceforth interpret boldface symbols **d**, **s** and **r** as realized or actual magnitudes (hence, given parameters from the standpoint of individual transactors); planned or notional magnitudes will be denoted, as before, by such symbols as d, $\tilde{s}$, r, etc.

For any individual household (here, we are informally modifying our discussion to recognize that the household sector comprises a multitude of independent decision units), we may clearly assume that the realized *numéraire* value of actual purchases during any given interval of time is identically equal to the aggregate *numéraire* value of realized sales and realized profit receipts during the same interval:

$$\sum_{k=1}^{n} \mathbf{p}_k[\mathbf{d}_k - \mathbf{s}_k] - \mathbf{r} \equiv 0. \qquad 5$$

Indeed, this is just a tacit definition of the concept of a transactor, since what it asserts is that commodities are acquired through market exchange rather than theft, gifts, heavenly favours, etc. The familiar household budget constraint, although similar in form to the truism, equation **5**, asserts the rather different proposition that no transactor consciously *plans* to purchase units of any commodity without at the same time *planning* to finance the purchase either from profit receipts or from the sale of units of some other commodity. For later reference, I shall call the last and very general proposition *Say's principle*. This is essentially a rational planning postulate, not a book-keeping identity nor a technical relation. Unlike the market principle known as Walras' law, moreover, Say's principle does not depend on the tacit assumption that values are calculated in terms of current market prices, or on the equally tacit assumption that market prices are independent of individual purchases and sales. Neither does it presuppose that individual behaviour is in any sense optimal. Thus, Say's principle may indeed be regarded as a fundamental convention of economic science, akin in all relevant respects to such basic ideas of physical science as the second law of thermodynamics. Say's principle is not true in the nature of things; but unless we presuppose something of the sort, we have absolutely nothing upon which to build an account of individual decision processes.

Suppose now that we carry through the usual utility maximization procedure to arrive at household demand and supply functions, $\bar{d}_i(\mathbf{P}, \mathbf{r})$, $\bar{s}_j(\mathbf{P}, \mathbf{r})$, interpreting Say's principle to mean what it usually means in this context, namely,

$$\sum_i^m \mathbf{p}_i d_i - \sum_j^n \mathbf{p}_j s_j - \mathbf{r} = 0.$$

Must we then assert that any reasonable definition of market demand and supply magnitudes will necessarily make use of the functions $\bar{d}_i$, $\bar{s}_j$ so defined? Not necessarily, for the definition of these functions tacitly presupposes something more than Say's principle, namely, that every household expects to be able to buy or sell any desired quantity of each and every commodity at prevailing market prices (24, p. 232ff.).

Now, the rationale of the last presupposition is hardly self-evident. Keynes has been scoffed at on more than one occasion for his dichotomized account of spending and saving decisions (see *General Theory*, p. 166). As far as I can see, the only reason for making humorous comments about this view is that established preference analysis tacitly presupposes that selling, buying and saving plans are all carried out simultaneously. But what if one does not happen to consider the presuppositions of established preference analysis, tacit or otherwise, to be the final word on this subject? (25, 26.) I suggest that the question will bear further examination.

The notion that all household decision are accomplished at a single stroke seems to be an analytically convenient and intuitively plausible procedure as long as we consider each household to be an isolated performer of conceptual experiments. When households are considered to be part of a connected market system, however, the same notion assumes a rather different aspect. What is then presupposed about planned sales and purchases cannot possibly be true of realized sales and purchases, unless the system as a whole is always in a state of equilibrium; that is to say, not every household can buy and sell just what it pleases if supply exceeds demand somewhere in the economy. Do we nevertheless suppose that the facts of life never intrude upon the thought experiments of households?

The answer to this is, I think, that the matter is not of much theoretical significance if, as is usually true when we deal with competitive supply-and-demand models, we are primarily interested in comparative-statics propositions. In this event, differences between realized and planned purchases and sales of individual households may properly be supposed to occur more or less at random. If we entertain the notion of developing market models that will have practical application to situations of chronic disequilibrium, however, we must surely question the universal relevance of the 'unified decision' hypothesis and, by the same token, question whether the usual household supply and demand functions provide relevant market signals.

VI The Dual-Decision Hypothesis

For the moment, let us imagine ourselves to be involuntarily unemployed in the sense of Keynes. Specifically, imagine that we have a strong wish to satisfy our champagne appetites but that the demand for our services as economic consultants does not in fact allow us to gratify this desire without doing serious damage to our household finances. How do we communicate our thirstiness to producers of champagne; how can they be made aware of our willingness to solve their market research problems in exchange for copious quantities of their excellent beverage?

The answer is that we do so indirectly. We offer more favourable terms to potential buyers of our services (these may include some champagne merchants), leaving it to the market to provide us more employment and income and, in due time, more booze. Do we also signal our craving directly by drawing on money balances and savings accounts and sending our children out to work? In short, do we drink more even before we work more? Or do we become, at least temporarily, involuntarily abstemious and postpone our satisfaction to financially more propitious times? Clearly, this is to pose the question in a highly misleading way, for the issue is not, 'Which do we do?', but 'How much do we do of each?'

But if even this much is granted, we thereby affirm that the demand functions of orthodox theory do not provide relevant market signals. For if realized current receipts are considered to impose any kind of constraint on current consumption plans, planned consumption as expressed in effective market offers to buy will necessarily be less than desired consumption as given by the demand functions of orthodox analysis.

A formal statement of the problem will clarify matters at this point. Following the usual procedure of traditional theory, suppose that the preference function $U(d_1, \ldots, d_m; s_{m+1}, \ldots, s_n)$ is maximized subject to the budget constraint

$$\sum_i^m \mathbf{p}_i \, d_i - \sum_j^n \mathbf{p}_j \, s_j - \mathbf{r} = 0,$$

and the resulting first-order conditions are used to define the notional demand and supply functions $\bar{d}_i(\mathbf{p}, \mathbf{r})$ and $\bar{s}_j(\mathbf{p}, \mathbf{r})$.

Provided that realized current income is not less than notional current income, i.e. provided

$$\sum_j^n \mathbf{p}_j \mathbf{s}_j \geqslant \sum_j^n \mathbf{p}_j \bar{s}_j,$$

we may suppose that the functions $\bar{d}_i$ and $\bar{s}_j$ constitute relevant market signalling devices. For this is just to say that current income receipts do not impose an operative constraint on household spending decisions.[17]

In the contrary case, however, i.e. if

$$\sum_j^n \mathbf{p}_j \mathbf{s}_j < \sum_j^n \mathbf{p}_j \bar{s}_j,$$

a second round of decision making is indicated: namely, maximize

$$U(d_1, \ldots, d_m; s_{m+1}, \ldots, s_n),$$

subject to the modified budget constraint

$$\sum_i^m \mathbf{p}_i d_i - \sum_j^n \mathbf{p}_j \mathbf{s}_j - \mathbf{r} = 0.$$

Solving this problem, we obtain a set of *constrained* demand functions,

$$\hat{d}_i(\mathbf{P}, \mathbf{Y}) \quad (i = 1, \ldots, m),$$

where, by definition,

$$\mathbf{Y} \equiv \sum_j^n \mathbf{p}_j \mathbf{s}_j + \mathbf{r}.$$

The values of the constrained functions, $\hat{d}_i$, will then be equal to those of the corresponding notional functions, $\bar{d}_i$, if and only if $\sum_j^n \mathbf{p}_j(\mathbf{s}_j - \bar{s}_j) = 0$. Except in this singular case,[18] however, the

17. More generally, we might argue that an excess of current income over desired income does affect current expenditure directly; compulsory overtime might be considered a case in point. But we shall not deal with situations of that kind here. In effect, we suppose that individuals are never forced to sell more factor services than they want to sell, though they may be forced for lack of buyers to sell less than they desire.

18. The constrained demand functions are not even defined, of course, when realized income *exceeds* desired income.

constrained demand functions $\hat{d}_i(\mathbf{P}, \mathbf{Y})$ and the notional supply functions $\hat{s}_j(\mathbf{P}, \mathbf{r})$, rather than the notional functions $\bar{d}_i$ and $\bar{s}_j$, are the relevant providers of market signals.

Here and elsewhere in the argument, it may be helpful if the reader imagines that a central 'market authority' is responsible for setting all prices (using the nth commodity as an accounting unit), and that this 'authority' maintains continual surveillance over all sale and purchase orders communicated to it by individual transactors to ensure that no purchase order is 'validated' unless it is offset by a sale order that has already been executed (i.e. purchase orders are simply 'cancelled' unless the transactor has a positive balance of 'book credit' with the market authority sufficient to cover the entire value of the purchase order). It must be assumed that the market authority communicates continuously with each transactor to inform it of the precise level of its current credit balance, and further informs each transactor of the precise rate at which previously validated purchase orders currently are being executed. Sale orders are 'validated' automatically, but the rate at which such orders are executed is governed by prevailing demand conditions. It is implicit in this entire line of argument that, at some 'initial' stage in the evolution of market trading arrangements, the market authority advances a nominal quantity of book credit to one or more transactors to set the trading process in motion (without such initial advances, no sale order could ever be executed since no purchase order would ever be validated).

Established preference analysis thus appears as a special case – valid in conditions of full employment – of the present *dual-decision theory*. Considered from this point of view, the other side of involuntary unemployment would seem to be involuntary under-consumption, which should have considerable intuitive appeal to those of us who really do have unsatisfied champagne appetites.

It is worth remarking explicitly that *the dual-decision hypothesis does not in any way flout Say's principle*. It would be more accurate to say that this hypothesis assigns greater force to the principle by recognizing that current income flows may impose an independent restriction on effective demand, separate from those already imposed by prevailing market prices and current transfer receipts. Indeed, it is this theory which is invariably presented in geometrical classroom expositions of the theory of consumer behaviour. It is only in mathematical versions of preference analysis that we lose sight of realized current income as an operative constraint on effective demand.

It is another question whether Keynes can reasonably be considered to have had a dual-decision theory of household behaviour at the back of his mind when he wrote the *General Theory*. For my part, I do not think there can be any serious doubt that he did, although I can find no direct evidence in any of his writings to show that he ever thought explicitly in these terms. But indirect evidence is available in almost unlimited quantity: in his treatment of the orthodox theory of household behaviour, his repeated discussions of 'Say's law', his development of the consumption function concept, his account of interest theory, and his discussions of wage and price determination. It is also significant, I believe, that a year after the appearance of the *General Theory*, Keynes' own evaluation of the theoretical significance of the consumption function concept still differed sharply from that of his reviewers (28):

This psychological law was of the utmost importance in the development of my own thought, and it is, I think, absolutely fundamental to the theory of effective demand as set forth in my book. But few critics or commentators so far have paid particular attention to it.

Finally, it is important to notice that unless the orthodox approach to household behaviour is modified (tacitly if not explicitly) to recognize the dual-decision hypothesis, the Keynesian notion of an aggregate consumption function does not make sense, the distinction between transactions and speculative balances is essentially meaningless, the liquidity-preference theory of interest is indistinguishable from the classical theory of loanable funds, fluctuations in the demand for physical assets cannot be supposed to have more impact on output and employment than fluctuations in the demand for securities, and excess supply in the labour market does not diminish effective excess demand elsewhere in the economy. In short, Keynes either had a dual-decision hypothesis at the back of his mind, or most of the *General Theory* is theoretical nonsense.

VII From the Classics to Keynes

We remarked above that the dual-decision hypothesis already has an established position in the oral tradition of established preference analysis. We have also argued that it plays an important (if tacit) role in income analysis. Thus, it is only when we turn to contemporary general equilibrium theory that no trace of the hypothesis is anywhere to be found. Yet it is precisely in this area that the dual decision approach is most clearly relevant – and most damaging to orthodoxy.

Referring to our previous account of traditional analysis (Part I, above), we recall that the business sector supply and demand functions may, from a market point of view, be so defined as to depend solely on the price vector $\mathbf{P}$, permitting us to write Walras' law in the form

$$\sum_i^m \mathbf{p}_i[\bar{d}_i(\mathbf{P}) - \bar{s}_i(\mathbf{P})] + \sum_j^n \mathbf{p}_j[\bar{d}_j(\mathbf{P}) - \bar{s}_j(\mathbf{P})] \equiv 0.^{[19]}$$

In the context of the present discussion, the most interesting implication of Walras' law is obtained by calling the commodities $1, \ldots, m$ 'goods' and the commodities $m + 1, \ldots, n$ 'factors'. We may then assert that excess supply of factors necessarily implies the simultaneous existence of excess demand for goods. More generally, we may assert that in any disequilibrium situation, there is always an element of excess demand working directly on the price system to offset prevailing elements of excess supply.

According to the dual-decision hypothesis, however, the market relevance of the household functions $\bar{d}_i(\mathbf{P})$ and $\bar{s}_j(\mathbf{P})$ is contingent on the satisfaction of the condition that realized current income be not less than planned income.[20] Suppose, however, that

$$\sum_j^n \mathbf{p}_j[\bar{d}_j - \bar{s}_j] < 0;$$

19. Cf. equation **4**, above.

20. Profit receipts do not concern us since we are still proceeding on the assumption that the condition $\mathbf{r} = \bar{r}$ is satisfied (this is no longer essential to the argument, but is very convenient). What we are supposing, in effect, is that household receivers of profit income have perfect information about profit prospects (they may even be producer-consumers) and react to this information precisely as if corresponding amounts of *numéraire* profit were actually being received.

i.e. suppose that notational aggregate demand for factors is less than aggregate supply (in the sense indicated). Then involuntary unemployment may be said to exist since realized factor income cannot exceed the aggregate money value of planned demand for factor inputs, that is to say,

$$\sum_{j}^{n} \mathbf{p}_j[\bar{d}_j - \mathbf{s}_j] \geqslant 0.$$

In this situation, the dual-decision hypothesis requires that we replace the usual household demand functions, $\bar{d}_i$, by the constrained demand functions $\hat{d}_i(\mathbf{P}, \mathbf{Y})$, which, by definition, satisfy the condition

$$\sum_{i}^{m} \mathbf{p}_i d_i(\mathbf{P}) \geqslant \sum_{i}^{m} \mathbf{p}_i \hat{d}_i(\mathbf{P}, \mathbf{Y});$$

i.e. the aggregate money value of constrained demand for goods is at most equal to the aggregate money value of planned demand for goods in the sense of traditional preference analysis. It follows immediately that, in a state of involuntary unemployment, Walras' law must be replaced by the more general condition

$$\sum_{i}^{m} \mathbf{p}_i[\hat{d}_i(\mathbf{P}, \mathbf{Y}) - \bar{s}_i(P)] + \sum_{j}^{n} \mathbf{p}_j[\bar{d}_j(P) - \bar{s}_j(\mathbf{P})] \leqslant 0;$$

i.e. *the sum of all market excess demands, valued at prevailing market prices, is at most equal to zero.* Indeed, since the equality sign applies with certainty only in the absence of factor excess supply, the dual-decision hypothesis effectively implies that Walras' law, although valid as usual with reference to *notional* market excess demands, is in general irrelevant to any but full employment situations. *Contrary to the findings of traditional theory, excess demand may fail to appear anywhere in the economy under conditions of less than full employment.*

The common sense of the preceding analysis may be clarified by a simple geometrical illustration. Let the curve T in the accompanying figure represent the business sector transformation function, let U_1 and U_2 represent alternative household sector indifference curves, and let $L(\mathbf{p}_f/\mathbf{p}_g)$ represent, simultaneously, the profit function of firms and the budget constraint of households. In the situation illustrated, the real wage at time t, $\mathbf{p}_f/\mathbf{p}_g$, is such that $\bar{s}_f > \bar{d}_f$; hence, factors are in excess supply. Moreover, since $\bar{d}_g > \bar{s}_g$, goods are simultaneously in a state of notional excess demand. If the real wage rate is assumed to vary inversely with notional excess demand for goods (as is assumed to be the case in orthodox analysis), $\mathbf{p}_f/\mathbf{p}_g$ will tend to fall over time at time t, and the system may therefore be said to tend towards full employment (defined by reference to the point $(\bar{N}, \bar{G})$). However, if the real wage rate is assumed to vary inversely with 'effective' excess

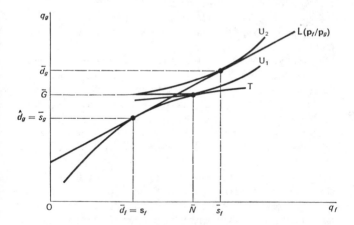

Figure 1

demand for goods, no adjustment of the real wage rate will tend to occur at time t since, as indicated, constrained demand for goods, $\hat{d}_g$, is equal to planned supply of goods at prevailing price and income levels.[21]

This illustration of how effective excess demand may be insufficient to induce price adjustment, despite the obvious sufficiency of notional excess demand, says nothing, of course, about the stability of full employment equilibrium under alternative adjustment hypotheses. For example, if the real wage rate varies in response *either* to constrained excess demand for goods *or* excess demand for factors, then in the situation illustrated the system

21. Compare Keynes' discussion of the same model, *General Theory* (7, p. 261).

may still tend towards full employment equilibrium. The point of the example is merely to illustrate that, *when income appears as an independent variable in the market excess-demand functions – more generally, when transactions quantities enter into the definition of these functions – traditional price theory ceases to shed any light on the dynamic stability of a market economy.*[22]

This line of analysis might be carried a good deal further; but I think enough has been said to justify such conclusions as are germane to the present argument:

Firstly, orthodox price theory may be regarded as a special case of Keynesian economics, valid only in conditions of full employment.

Secondly, an essential formal difference between Keynesian and orthodox economics is that market excess demands are in general assumed to depend on current market transactions in the former, to be independent of current market transactions in the latter. This difference depends, in turn, on Keynes' tacit use of a dual-decision theory of household behaviour and his consequent rejection of Walras' law as a relevant principle of economic analysis.

Thirdly, chronic factor unemployment at substantially unchanging levels of real income and output may be consistent with Keynesian economics even if all prices are flexible; this problem has yet to be investigated within the context of a Keynesian model of market price formation.

22. In an unpublished article 'A Keynesian market equilibrium model', my colleague Mitchell Harwitz considers a more general version of the rigid wages case with results that go far to anticipate the dual-decision hypothesis on which the present argument places so much weight. The following passage (Harwitz, p. 40), is particularly significant:

Suppose one market is permanently restrained from full adjustment. What does this mean in terms of the individual participants in the market? *It means that some or all of them face a binding constraint in addition to the budget constraint.* For concreteness, consider the Keynesian labour market. A worker, faced with a certain real wage, can sell *less* labour than is consistent with the usual constrained maximum. In effect, he is in equilibrium, but at a boundary [position] imposed by a quantity constraint on the labour he can sell. . . . It must be granted that these positions are equilibria by our definition; but their stability is a more delicate question. . . . A complete answer would require a theory of the dynamical behaviour of economic units both in and out of equilibrium.

VIII Conclusion

My original intention in writing this paper was simply to clarify the formal basis of the Keynesian revolution and its relation to orthodox thought. This I think I have done. In a line, Keynesian economics brings current transactions into price theory whereas traditional analysis explicitly leaves them out. Alternatively, we may say that Keynesian economics is price theory without Walras' law,[23] and price theory with Walras' law is just a special case of Keynesian economics. The bearing of my argument on the Keynesian counter-revolution is correspondingly plain: contemporary general equilibrium theories can be maintained intact only if we are willing to barter Keynes for orthodoxy.

This is not the end of the matter, for there is a choice to be made. No one can deny that general equilibrium analysis, as presently constituted, is a useful instrument for thinking about abstract economic problems, and this would hardly be so if it did not omit many realistic frills. The danger in using this instrument to think about practical problems is that, having schooled ourselves so thoroughly in the virtues of elegant simplicity, we may refuse to recognize the crucial relevance of complications that do not fit our theoretical preconceptions. As Keynes has put it, 'The difficulty lies, not in the new ideas, but in escaping from the old ones, which ramify, for those brought up as most of us have been, into every corner of our minds' (*General Theory*, p. viii).

I shall be the last one to suggest that abstract theory is useless; that simply is not so. At the same time, I am convinced that much of what now passes for useful theory is not only worthless economics (and mathematics), but also a positive hindrance to fruitful

23. It is vacuously true, of course, that a proposition similar to Walras' law holds even in Keynesian economics if we *define* the difference between desired sales and realized sales as an excess demand for 'money income'. But the proposition then becomes an empirically meaningless tautology. In conventional value theory, the total value of commodities (goods and money) offered for sale is always equal to the total value of commodities (goods and money) demanded for purchase because all purchase orders are presumed to be effective regardless of prevailing demand-and-supply conditions. But in the present discussion, purchase orders are not validated automatically, sale orders thus do not necessarily generate effective demand for other commodities (effective demands are constrained by purchase orders *executed*, not purchase orders *placed*).

theoretical and empirical research. Most importantly, however, I am impressed by the worth of Keynesian economics as a guide to practical action, which is in such sharp contrast to the situation of general price theory. As physicists should and would have rejected Einstein's theory of relativity, had it not included Newtonian mechanics as a special case, so we would do well to think twice before accepting as 'useful' or 'general', doctrines which are incapable of accommodating Keynesian economics.

References

1. D. PATINKIN, *Money, Interest and Prices*, Row Peterson, 1956.
2. J. R. HICKS, 'Mr Keynes and the Classics: a suggested interpretation', *Econometrica*, vol. 5, 1937, no. 2, pp. 147–59.
3. J. R. HICKS, *Value and Capital*, Clarendon Press, 1939.
4. B. OHLIN, 'Some notes on the Stockholm theory of savings and investment', *Economic Journal*, vol. 47, 1937, pp. 53–69, 221–40.
5. O. LANGE, *Price Flexibility and Employment*, Principia, 1944.
6. F. MODIGLIANI, 'Liquidity preference and the theory of interest and money', *Econometrica*, vol. 12, 1944, pp. 45–88.
7. J. M. KEYNES, *The General Theory of Employment, Interest and Money*, Harcourt Brace, 1935, pp. v ff.
8. O. LANGE, 'Say's law: a restatement and criticism', *Studies in Mathematical Economics and Econometrics*, edited by Lange, McIntyre and Yntema, University of Chicago Press, 1942, pp. 49–68.
9. R. M. GOODWIN, 'The multiplier as matrix', *Economic Journal*, vol. 59, 1949, pp. 537–55.
10. H. ROSE, 'Liquidity preference and loanable funds', *Review of Economic Studies*, vol. 24, February 1957, pp. 111–19.
11. H. ROSE, 'The rate of interest and Walras' law', *Economica*, vol. 26, 1959, pp. 252–3.
12. D. PATINKIN, 'Reply to R. W. Clower and H. Rose', *Economica*, vol. 26, 1959, pp. 253–5.
13. L. R. KLEIN, *The Keynesian Revolution*, Macmillan, 1952.
14. R. W. CLOWER, 'Keynes and the classics: a dynamical perspective', *Quarterly Journal of Economics*, vol. 74, 1960, pp. 318–20.
15. B. HANSEN, *A Study in the Theory of Inflation*, Allen & Unwin, 1951.
16. A. C. ENTHOVEN, 'Monetary disequilibrium and the dynamics of inflation', *Economic Journal*, vol. 66, 1956, pp. 256–70.
17. F. H. HAHN, 'The Patinkin controversy', *Review of Economic Studies*, vol. 28, October 1960, p. 42, n.l.
18. P. A. SAMUELSON, *Foundations of Economic Analysis*, Harvard University Press, 1947.
19. D. W. BUSHAW and R. W. CLOWER, *Introduction to Mathematical Economics*, Irwin, 1957.
20. V. L. SMITH, *Investment and Production*, Harvard University Press, 1961.

21. G. Horwich, 'Money, prices and the theory of interest determination', *Economic Journal*, vol. 67, 1957, pp. 625–43.

22. G. C. Archibald and R. G. Lipsey, 'Monetary and value theory: a critique of Lange and Patinkin', *Review of Economic Studies*, vol. 26, October 1958, pp. 1–22, and 'Symposium on monetary theory', vol. 28, October 1960, pp. 50–56.

23. W. J. Baumol, 'Stocks, flows and monetary theory', *Quarterly Journal of Economics*, vol. 76, February 1962, pp. 46–56.

24. T. Negishi, 'General equilibrium models of market clearing processes in a monetary economy', *The Theory of Interest Rates*, Macmillan, 1965.

25. W. J. Baumol, *Economic Theory and Operations Analysis*, Prentice-Hall, 1961.

26. R. H. Strotz, 'The empirical implications of a utility tree', *Econometrica*, vol. 25, April 1957, pp. 269–80.

27. I. F. Pearce, 'A method of consumer demand analysis illustrated', *Economica*, vol. 28, November 1961, pp. 371–94.

28. J. M. Keynes, 'The general theory of employment', *Quarterly Journal of Economics*, vol. 51, February 1937, pp. 209–23.

20 A. Leijonhufvud

Keynes and the Keynesians: A Suggested Interpretation

A Leijonhufvud (1967), 'Keynes and the Keynesians: a suggested interpretation', *American Economic Review*, vol. 57, no. 2, pp. 401–10.

I

One must be careful in applying the epithet 'Keynesian' nowadays. I propose to use it in the broadest possible sense and let 'Keynesian economics' be synonymous with the 'majority school' macroeconomics which has evolved out of the debates triggered by Keynes' *General Theory* (GT). Keynesian economics, in this popular sense, is far from being homogenous doctrine. The common denominator, which lends some justification to the identification of a majority school, is the class of models generally used. The prototype of these models dates back to the famous paper by Hicks (6) the title of which I have taken the liberty of paraphrasing. This standard model appears to me a singularly inadequate vehicle for the interpretation of Keynes' ideas. The juxtaposition of Keynes and the Keynesians in my title is based on this contention.

Within the majority school, at least two major factions live in recently peaceful but nonetheless uneasy coexistence. With more brevity than accuracy, they may be labeled the 'revolutionary orthodoxy' and the 'neo-classical resurgence'. Both employ the standard model but with different specifications of the various elasticities and adjustment velocities. In its more extreme orthodox form, the model is supplied with wage rigidity, liquidity trap and a constant capital–output ratio, and manifests a more or less universal 'elasticity pessimism', particularly with regard to the interest elasticities of 'real' variables. The orthodoxy tends to slight monetary in favor of fiscal stabilization policies. The neo-classical faction may be sufficiently characterized by negating these statements. As described, the orthodoxy is hardly a very reputable position at the present time. Its influence in the currently most fashionable fields has been steadily diminishing, but it seems to have found a refuge in business cycle theory – and, of course, in the teaching of undergraduate macroeconomics.

The terms of the truce between the two factions comprise two propositions: (a) the model which Keynes called his 'general theory' is but a special case of the classical theory, obtained by imposing certain restrictive assumptions on the latter; and (b) the Keynesian special case is nonetheless important because, as it happens, it is more relevant to the real world than the general (equilibrium) theory. Together the two propositions make a compromise acceptable to both parties, permitting a decent burial of the major issues which almost everyone has grown tired of debating – namely, the roles of relative values and of money – and, between them, the role of the interest rate – in the 'Keynesian system'. Keynes thought he had made a major contribution towards a synthesis of the theory of money and 'our fundamental theory of value' (GT, pp. vi–vii). But the truce between the orthodox and the neo-classicists is based on the common understanding that his system was *sui generis* – a theory in which neither relative values nor monetary phenomena are 'important'.

This compromise defines, as briefly as seems possible, the result of what Clower aptly calls the 'Keynesian counter-revolution' (4).

II

That a model with wage rigidity as its main distinguishing feature should become widely accepted as crystallizing the experience of the unprecedented wage deflation of the Great Depression is one of the more curious aspects of the development of Keynesianism, comparable in this regard to the orthodox view that 'money is unimportant' – a conclusion presumably prompted by the worst banking debacle in U.S. history. The emphasis on the 'rigidity' of wages, which one finds in the 'new economics', reveals the judgement that wages did not fall enough in the early thirties. Keynes, in contrast, judged that they declined too much by far. It has been noted before that, to Keynes, wage rigidity was a policy recommendation and not a behavioral assumption, e.g. (11).

Keynes' theory was dynamic. His model was static. The method of trying to analyse dynamic processes with a comparative static apparatus Keynes borrowed from Marshall. The crucial difference lies in Keynes' inversion of the ranking of price- and quantity-adjustment velocities underlying Marshall's distinction between the 'market day' and the 'short run'. The initial response to a decline in demand is a quantity adjustment. Clower's investigation of a system, which responds to deflationary disturbances in the first instance by quantity adjustments, shows that the characteristic Keynesian income-constrained, or 'multiplier', process can be explicated in terms of a general equilibrium framework (4). Such a model departs from the traditional Walrasian full employment model only in one, eminently reasonable, respect: trading at 'false prices' – i.e. prices which do not allow the realization of all desired transactions – may take place. Transactors who fail to realize their desired sales, e.g. in the labor market, will curtail their effective demands in other markets. This implies the amplification of the initial disturbance typical of Keynes' multiplier analysis.

The strong assumption of 'rigid' wages is not necessary to the explanation of such system behavior. It is sufficient only to give up the equally strong assumption of instantaneous price adjustments. Systems with finite price velocities will show Keynesian multiplier responses to initial changes in the rate of money expenditures. It is not necessary, moreover, to rely on 'monopolies', labor unions, minimum wage laws, or other institutional constraints on the utility maximizing behavior of individual transactors in order to explain finite price velocities. Keynes, in contrast to many new economists, was adamantly opposed to theories which 'blamed' depressions on such obstacles to price adjustments. The implied proposition that, if 'competition' could only be restored, 'automatic forces' would take care of the employment problem was one of his pet hates. Atomistic markets do not mean instantaneous price adjustments. A system of atomistic markets would also show Keynesian adjustment behavior.

In Walrasian general equilibrium theory, all transactors are regarded as price takers. As noted by Arrow, 'there is no one left over whose job it is to make a decision on price' (2, p. 43). The job, in fact, is entrusted to a *deus ex machina*: Walras' auctioneer is assumed to inform all traders of the prices at which all markets are going to clear. This always trustworthy information is supplied at zero cost. Traders never have to wrestle with situations in which demands and supplies do not mesh; all can plan on facing perfectly elastic demand and supply schedules without fear of ever having their trading plans disappointed. All goods are perfectly 'liquid', their full market values being at any time instantaneously realizable. Money can be added to such models only by artifice.

Alchian has shown that the emergence of unemployed resources is a predictable consequence of a decline in demand when traders do not have perfect information on what the new market clearing price would be (1, ch. 31). The price obtainable for the services of a resource which has become 'unemployed' will depend upon the costs expended in searching for the highest bidder. In this sense, the resource is 'illiquid'. The seller's reservation price will be conditioned by past experiences as well as by observations of the prices at which comparable services are currently traded (GT, p. 264). Reservation price will be adjusted gradually as search. Meanwhile the resource remains unemployed. To this analysis one need only add that the loss of receipts from its services will constrain the owner's effective demand for other products – a feedback effect which provides the rationale of the multiplier analysis of a system of atomistic ('competitive') markets.

To make the transition from Walras' world to Keynes' world, it is thus sufficient to dispense with the assumed *tâtonnement* mechanism. The removal of the auctioneer simply means that the generation of the information needed to co-ordinate economic activities in a large system where decision making is decentralized will take time and will involve economic costs. No other 'classical' assumptions need to relinquished. Apart from the absence of the auctioneer, the system remains as before: (a) individual traders still 'maximize utility' (or profit) – one need not assume that they are constrained from bargaining on their own, nor that they are 'money illusioned' or otherwise irrational; (b) price incentives are still effective – there is no inconsistency between Keynes' general 'elasticity optimism' and his theory of unemployment. When price elasticities are assumed to be generally significant, one admits the potentiality of controlling the activities of individual traders by means of prices so as to co-ordinate them in an efficient manner. It is not necessary to deny the existence of a vector of non-

negative prices and interest rates consistent with the full utilization of resources. To be a Keynesian, one need only realize the
difficulties of finding the market-clearing vector.

III

It is a widely held view that the main weaknesses of Keynesian
theory derive from Keynes' neglect of the influence of capital and
real asset values on behavior, e.g. (8, pp. 9, 11, 17; 12, p. 636). It
is above all on this crucial point that the standard model has
proved to be a most seriously misleading framework for the
interpretation of Keynes' theory. This is readily perceived if we
compare the 'aggregative structures' of the standard model and
the *General Theory* model. In either case, we are usually dealing
with but three price relations, so that the relevant level of aggregation is that of four-good models:

Table 1

Standard Model	General Theory
commodities	consumer goods
bonds	nonmoney assets
money	money
labor services	labor services

The aggregate production function makes the standard model
a 'one-commodity model'. The price of capital goods in terms of
consumer goods is fixed. The money wage is 'rigid', and the current value of physical assets is tied down within the presumably
narrow range of short-run fluctuations in the 'real' wage rate.
Relative prices are, indeed, allowed little play in this construction. 'Money' includes only means of payment, while all claims
to cash come under the heading of 'bonds'.

The four-good structure of the *General Theory* is a condensed
version of the model of the *Treatise on Money* (TM) with its
richer menu of short-term assets. All titles to prospective income
streams are lumped together in 'nonmoney assets'. Bond streams
and equity streams are treated as perfect substitutes, a simplification which Keynes achieved through some quite mechanical

manipulations of risk and liquidity premia (GT, ch. 17). The fundamental property which distinguishes nonmoney assets both from consumables and from money is that the former are 'long' while the latter two are 'short' – attributes which, in Keynes' usage, were consistently equated with 'fixed' (or 'illiquid') and 'liquid', respectively (cf. TM, V: I, p. 248). The typical nonmoney assets are bonds with long term to maturity and titles to physical assets with a very long 'duration of use or consumption'. Basically, Keynes' method of aggregation differentiates between goods with a relatively high and a relatively low interest elasticity of present value. Thus the two distinctions are questions of degree. As a matter of course, the definition of money includes all types of deposits, since their interest elasticity of present value is zero, but 'such instruments as treasury bills' can also be included when convenient (GT, p. 167 n.).

Keynes' alleged neglect of capital is attributed to his preoccupation with the short run in which the stock of physical capital is fixed. The critique presumes that Keynes worked with the standard model in which the value of such assets in terms of consumables is a constant. But in Keynes' two-commodity model, this price is, in principle, a short-run variable and, as a consequence, so is the potential command over current consumables which the existing stock of assets represents. The current price of nonmoney assets is determined by expectations with regard to the 'stream of annuities' in prospect and by the rate at which these anticipated future receipts are discounted. The relevant rate is always the long rate of interest. In the analysis of short-run 'equilibrium', the state of expectation (alias the marginal efficiency of capital) is assumed to be given, and the price of assets then varies with *the* interest rate.

In Keynes' short run, 'a decline in the interest rate' and 'a rise in the market prices of capital goods, equities and bonds' are interchangeable descriptions of the same event. Since the representative nonmoney asset is very long-lived, its interest elasticity of present value is quite high. The price elasticity of the output of augmentable income sources is very high. The aggregative structure of this model leaves no room for elasticity pessimism with regard to the relationship between investment and the (long) rate of interest. It does not even seem to have occurred to Keynes that investment might be exceedingly interest inelastic, as later Keynesians would have it. Instead, he was concerned to convince the reader that it is reasonable to assume that 'a moderate change in the prospective yield of capital assets or in the rate of interest will not involve an indefinitely great change in the rate of investment' (GT, p. 252).

The relationship between saving and the interest rate is of less quantitative significance, but Keynes' ideas on the subject are of considerable interest and give some clues to his theory of liquidity preference. The criticisms of his supposed neglect of wealth as a variable influencing behavior have been directed in particular against the *ad hoc* 'psychological law' on which he based the consumption-income relation. This line of criticism ignores the 'windfall effect' which 'should be classified amongst the major factors capable of causing short-period changes in the propensity to consume' (GT, pp. 92–4). This second psychological law of consumption states simply that the propensity to consume out of current income will be higher the higher the value of household net worth in terms of consumer goods. A decline in the propensity to consume may, therefore, be caused either by a decline in the marginal efficiency of capital (GT, p. 319) or by a rise in the long rate (GT, p. 94; TM, V: I, pp. 196–7). In the short run the marginal efficiency is taken as given and, so, it is the interest rate which concerns us.

The usual interpretation focuses on the passages in which Keynes argued that 'changes in the rate of time discount' will not significantly influence saving. In my opinion, these well-known passages express the assumption that household preferences exhibit a high degree of intertemporal complementarity, so that the intertemporal substitution effects of interest movements may be ignored. Consequently, the windfall effect of such changes must be interpreted as a wealth effect.

Hicks has shown that the wealth effect of a decline in interest will be positive if the average period of the income stream anticipated by the representative household exceeds the average period of its planned 'standard stream' (7, esp. pp. 184–8). Households who anticipate the receipt of streams which are, roughly speaking, *longer* than their planned consumption streams are made wealthier by a decline in the interest rate. The present value of net worth increases in greater proportion than the present cost of the old consumption plan, and the consumption plan can thus be raised throughout.

This brings our discussion of the *General Theory* into pretty unfamiliar territory. But Keynes' 'vision' was of a world in which the indicated conditions generally hold. In this world, currently active households must, directly or indirectly, hold their net worth in the form of titles to streams which run beyond their consumption horizon. The duration of the relevant consumption plan is sadly constrained by the fact that 'in the long run, we are all dead'. But the great bulk of the 'fixed capital of the modern world' is of a very long-term nature (e.g. TM, V: II, pp. 98, 364), and is thus destined to survive the generation which now owns it. This is the basis for the wealth effect of changes in asset values.

Keynes' *Gestalt* conception of the world resembles Cassel's. Cassel used the wealth effect to argue the 'necessity of interest' (3), an argument which Keynes paraphrased (GT, p. 94). The same conception underlies Keynes' liquidity-preference theory of the term structure of interest. Mortal beings cannot hold land, buildings, corporate equities, British consols, or other permanent income sources 'to maturity'. Induced by the productivity of roundabout processes to invest his savings in such income sources, the representative, risk-averting transactor must suffer 'capital uncertainty'. Forward markets, therefore, will generally show a 'constitutional weakness' on the demand side (7, p. 146). The relevance of the duration structure of the system's physical capital has been missed by the modern critics of the Keynes–Hicks theory of the term structure of interest rates (10, pp. 14–16; 9, pp. 347–8).

The recent discussion has dealt with the term structure problem as if financial markets existed in a vacuum. But the 'real forces of productivity and thrift' should be brought in. The above references to the productivity of roundabout processes (GT, ch. 16) and the wealth effect indicates that they are not totally ignored in Keynes' general theory of liquidity preference. The question why short streams should command a premium over long streams is, after all, not so different from the old question why present goods should command a premium over future goods. Keynes is on classical ground when he argues that the essential problem with which a theory of asset prices must deal derives from the postponement of the option to consume, and that other factors influencing asset prices are subsidiary: 'we do not devise a productivity theory of smelly or risky processes as such' (GT, p. 215).

IV

Having sketched Keynes' treatment of intertemporal prices and intertemporal choices, we can now consider how 'changing views about the future are capable of influencing the quantity of employment' (GT, p. vii). This was Keynes' central theme.

'It is by reason of the existence of durable equipment that the economic future is linked to the present' (GT, p. 146). The price of augmentable nonmoney assets in terms of the wage unit determines the rate of investment. The same price in terms of consumables determines the propensity to consume. This price is the focal point of Keynes' analysis of changes in employment.

If the right level of asset prices can be maintained, investment will be maintained and employment at the going money wage stabilized. If a decline in the marginal efficiency of capital occurs, maintenance of the prices of long-lived physical assets and equities requires a corresponding drop in the long rate and thus a rise in bond prices. To Keynes, 'the sole intelligible explanation' (GT, p. 201) of why this will normally not occur is that bear speculators will shift into savings deposits. If financial intermediaries do not 'operate in the opposite direction' (TM, V: I, pp. 142–3), bond prices will not rise to the full extent required and demand prices for capital goods and equities will fall. This lag of market rate behind the natural or 'neutral' rate (GT, p. 243) will be associated with the emergence of excess demand for money – which always spells contraction. 'The importance of money essentially flows from its being a link between the present and the future' (GT, p. 293).

Contraction ensues because nonmoney asset prices are 'wrong'. As before, 'false prices' reveal an information failure. There are two parts to this information failure. (a) Mechanisms are lacking which would ensure that the entrepreneurial expectations guiding current investment mesh with savers' plans for future consumption: 'If saving consisted not merely in abstaining from present consumption but in placing simultaneously a specific order for future consumption, the effect might indeed be quite different' (GT, p. 210). (b) There is an alternative 'circuit' by which the appropriate information could be transmitted, since savers must demand stores of value in the present. But the financial markets cannot be relied upon to perform the information function without fail. Keynes spent an entire chapter in a mournful diatribe on the casino activities of the organized exchanges and on the failure of investors, who are not obliged to hold assets to maturity, to even attempt 'forecasting the prospective yield of assets over their whole life' (GT, ch. 12).

Whereas Keynes had an exceedingly broad conception of 'liquidity preference', in the Keynesian literature the term has acquired the narrow meaning of 'demand for money', and this demand is usually discussed in terms of the choice between means of payment and one of the close substitutes which Keynes included in his own definition of money. Modern monetary theorists have come to take an increasingly dim view of his speculative demand, primarily on the grounds that the underlying assumption of inelastic expectations represents a 'special case' which is unseemly in a model aspiring to the status of a 'general theory' (5, pp. 145–51; 13; 8, p. 10; 9, p. 344). But it is only in the hypothetical world of Walrasian *tâtonnements* that all the information required to co-ordinate the economic activities of a myriad traders is produced *de novo* on each market day. In any other construction, traders must rely heavily on 'memory' rather than fresh information. In the orthodox model, with its interest inelasticity of both saving and investment, there is admittedly no *real* reason why traders' past experiences should be of a narrow normal range of long rates. In Keynes' model, there are reasons. In imperfect information models, inelastic expectations are not confined to the bond market. The explanation of the emergence of unemployed resources in atomistic markets also relies on inelastic expectations. To stress 'speculative behavior' of this sort does not mean that one reverts to the old notion of a Walrasian system adjusting slowly because of 'frictions'. The multiplier feedbacks mean that the system tends to respond to parametric disturbances in a 'deviation-amplifying' manner – behavior which cannot be analysed with the pre-Keynesian apparatus.

A truly vast literature has grown out of the Pigou-effect idea, despite almost universal agreement on its *practical* irrelevance. The original reason for this strange development was dissatisfaction with Keynes' assertion that the only hope from deflation lies 'in the effect of the abundance of money in terms of the wage-unit on the rate of interest' (GT, p. 253). This was perceived as a denial of the logic of classical theory. Viewing Keynes' position through the glasses of the standard one-commodity model, it was concluded that it could only be explained on the assumption that he had overlooked the direct effect of an increase in real net worth on the demand for commodities (e.g. 11, pp. 269–70; 12, note K:1). The one-commodity interpretation entirely misses Keynes' point: that the trouble arises from inappropriately low prices of augmentable nonmoney assets relative to both wages and consumer goods prices. Relative values are wrong. Absolute prices will 'rush violently between zero and infinity' (GT, pp. 239, 269–70), if price-level movements do not lead to a *correction* of relative prices through either a fall in long rates or an induced rise in the marginal efficiency of capital (GT, p. 263). It is hard to see a denial of 'our fundamental theory of value' in this argument.

V

We can now come back to the 'terms of the truce' between the neo-classicists and the Keynesian orthodox. I have argued that, in Keynes' theory: (a) transactors do maximize utility and profit in the manner assumed in classical analysis, also in making decisions on saving and investment; (b) price incentives are effective and this includes intertemporal price incentives – changes in interest rates or expected future spot prices (GT, p. 263) will significantly affect present behavior; (c) the existence of a hypothetical vector of non-negative prices and interest rates which, if once established, would bring full resource utilization is not denied.

The only thing which Keynes *removed* from the foundations of classical theory was the *deus ex machina* – the auctioneer which is assumed to furnish, without charge, all the information needed

A. Leijonhufvud

to obtain the perfect co-ordination of the activities of all traders in the present and through the future.

Which, then, is the more *general* theory and which the *special* case? Must one not grant Keynes his claim to having tackled the more general problem?

Walras' model, it has often been noted, was patterned on Newtonian mechanics. On the latter, Norbert Wiener once commented: 'Here there emerges a very interesting distinction between the physics of our grandfathers and that of the present day. In nineteenth-century physics, it seemed to cost nothing to get information' (14, p. 29). In context, the statement refers to Maxwell's demon – not, of course, to Walras' auctioneer. But, *mutatis mutandis*, it would have served admirably as a motto for Keynes' work. It has not been the main theme of Keynesian economics.[1]

References

1. A. A. ALCHIAN and W. R. ALLEN, *University Economics*, Wadsworth, 1964.
2. K. J. ARROW, 'Towards a theory of price adjustment', *The Allocation of Economic Resources*, Stanford University Press, 1959, pp. 41–51.
3. G. CASSEL, *The Nature and Necessity of Interest*, Frank Cass, 1957. First published 1903.
4. R. W. CLOWER, 'The Keynesian counter-revolution: a theoretical appraisal', *The Theory of Interest Rates*, edited by Hahn and Brechling, Macmillan, 1965, pp. 103–25.
5. W. FELLNER, *Monetary Policies and Full Employment*, California University, 1946.
6. J. R. HICKS, 'Mr Keynes and the Classics: a suggested interpretation', *Econometrica*, vol. 5, 1937, no. 2, pp. 147–59.
7. J. R. HICKS, *Value and Capital*, Clarendon Press, 2nd edn, 1946.
8. H. G. JOHNSON, 'The General Theory after twenty-five years', *American Economic Review*, vol. 51, May 1961, pp. 1–17.
9. H. G. JOHNSON, 'Monetary theory and policy', *American Economic Review*, vol. 52, June 1962, pp. 335–84.
10. D. MEISELMAN, *The Term Structure of Interest Rates*, Prentice-Hall, 1962.
11. D. PATINKIN, 'Price flexibility and full employment', *American Economic Review*, vol. 38, 1948, pp. 543–64.
12. D. PATINKIN, *Money, Interest and Prices*, 2nd edn, Harper & Row, 1965.

1. [On this, see A. Leijonhufvud, *Keynesian Economics and the Economics of Keynes*, New York, Oxford University Press, 1968.]

13. J. Tobin, 'Liquidity preference as behaviour towards risk', *Review of Economic Studies*, vol. 25, February 1958, pp. 65–8.
14. N. Wiener, *The Human Use of Human Beings*, 2nd edn, 1964.
GT—J. M. Keynes, *The General Theory of Employment, Interest and Money*, Harcourt Brace, 1936.
TM—J. M. Keynes, *A Treatise on Money*, vols. 1 and 2, Macmillan, 1930.

Part Five Money and Economic Growth

The neutrality of money in comparative statics – that is, the long-run invariance of the demand for real money balances with respect to changes in the nominal quantity of money – is a familiar character-istic of all accepted models of the monetary mechanism. It is tempting to carry this same characteristic over into models that deal with economic growth; to argue that *per capita* real balances will be invariant with respect to changes in the *rate of increase* in the nominal stock of money in an economy where factor supplies are increasing at a constant exponential rate. However, recent attempts to introduce money explicitly into standard growth models suggest that money is anything but neutral in these circumstances. It would no doubt be premature to attach great significance to conclusions from theoretical models that bear little more relation to reality than does Aristotelian physics. Meantime these selections offer additional evidence of the intellectual ferment and analytical uncertainties of contemporary monetary theory.

21 A. L. Marty

The Neutrality of Money in Comparative Statics and
Growth

Excerpt from A. L. Marty (1961), 'Gurley and Shaw on money in a theory
of finance', *Journal of Political Economy*, vol. 69, February, pp. 56–62.

The recent volume by Gurley and Shaw[1] presents a theory of the
role of financial institutions in a growing economy. A neo-
classical world is assumed in which prices are flexible, employment is full, and money illusion is absent. The authors' procedure
is to begin with a rudimentary economy which contains only one
financial market, that for money, and one financial institution,
the government monetary system. Their second model adds a
financial market for homogeneous business bonds, issued by
private firms, which are purchased by both the government
banking system and the public. The third model introduces a
third financial market: that for non-monetary indirect assets
which are issued by a group of non-monetary financial intermediaries that purchase business bonds. In a final chapter the
governmental monetary system is replaced by a private banking
system, and the quantity of money outstanding reflects profit
considerations of the private banking system, which is subject to
control by a central bank. [. . .]

I shall use Gurley and Shaw's first and simplest model as a
basis for criticizing their conclusions about the neutrality of
money in a growing economy. My strictures, however, are fully
applicable at every level of their analysis.

The first model divides the economy into three sectors. One is
a consumer sector, which receives income by selling labor services
to the business sector and can spend it either on consumption

1. I am indebted to Professor Milton Friedman for exceedingly helpful
substantive comments. I should also like to express my gratitude to
Professors Harry G. Johnson and Jacob Weissman for constantly pressing
me to greater rigor and clarity. The usual caveat with respect to responsibility holds.

goods or on acquiring real-money balances. A second sector is the business sector, which can invest by accumulating real assets. There is no market for real assets, and no lending or borrowing is allowed to take place between the consumer and business sectors. Finally, the government sector creates money which it uses either to purchase goods and services or to make transfer payments. It is not allowed to collect taxes. In this world any excess of *ex-ante* savings over *ex-ante* investment is identically equal to an excess real demand for money balances.

Gurley and Shaw argue that monetary policy is trivial if money is issued by transfer payments. The governmental banking system determines the nominal stock of money; the public determines the real stock. If we break into the growth path of the economy at any point in time and introduce a once-and-for-all increase in the nominal stock of money, this will have no effect on the real variables since all nominal values adjust so as to leave the real variables unchanged. As the economy moves along its growth path, the real quantity of money demanded will increase as a result of the growth of real income. This increase may be accomplished either by an increase in the nominal stock of money or by a fall in prices, or by some combination of both. In the neoclassical framework Gurley and Shaw conclude that the rate of growth of the money supply had neutral effects on the real variables and that there is no rational basis for choosing between alternative rates of growth of the money supply (1, pp. 41, 236).

This conclusion is not correct. Gurley and Shaw are examining the role of money in an economy growing through time. As a first step they break into the economy at an instant of time and ask what would happen if there were a once-and-for-all change in the nominal quantity of money. Suppose money is neutral at this level of analysis. It does not follow, as Gurley and Shaw assert, that different rates of growth of the money stock are neutral in their effects on the real variables. At any instant of time the public's demand for real balances is determined by comparing the marginal productivity of real balances with the money rate of interest. Different rates of growth of the money stock are associated with different rates of change of prices, which are reflected in the level of the money rate of interest. It follows that the stock of real balances relative to income that people choose to hold, and therefore the velocity of circulation, is a function of the rate of change of prices. Since different levels of velocity imply the use of different amounts of real resources in sustaining the payments matrix, the effect of the rate of change in the nominal quantity of money on the real variables will not be neutral. The logical counterpart in a growing economy to the neutrality of once-and-for-all changes in the quantity of money in a stationary economy would be a change in the quantity of money which did not alter the rate at which the money supply is growing.

There is in logic an optimal rate of growth of the money supply which maximizes social utility through time. From society's point of view, real balances are produced at zero marginal costs. In order to maximize social utility, people should be induced to hold the satiety level of real balances at each instant of time. This can be done by maintaining a rate of price decrease equal to the natural rate of interest, thereby reducing the money rate to zero.[2]

Suppose that money is issued by the authorities not to make transfer payments but to command real resources. Gurley and Shaw conclude that the neutrality of money will not be violated if the government allocates its expenditures among goods in precisely the same way as would private spending units (1, p. 41). However, even if the government spends in this manner, neutrality of money is violated. The proportion of real income the government desires to command determines the rate at which it chooses to inflate the money supply, and this choice, as we have seen, has non-neutral effects.

The exposition by the authors of this case is not complete. There is no discussion of the factors that determine the proportion of real resources the government can command by issuing money. It is not true that the more money the government issues the larger the amount of resources it can command. The government is in the position of a monopolist with a zero marginal cost of production of real balances. At any instant of time there is a

2. Holding the quantity of money constant in von Neumann-like growth models would automatically reduce the money rate of interest to zero. In these models, constant returns prevail, and the supply of labor is infinitely elastic at a given level of the real wage rate. The rate of fall of prices is equal to the rate of growth of output which is equal, in turn, to the net productivity of capital (the natural rate of interest) (2, 3).

determinate demand for real balances on the part of the public. In order to command the largest volume of real resources, the rate of increase in the stock of money should be such as to induce the public to hold that quantity of real balances at which the interest elasticity of demand is unity.[3]

Gurley and Shaw choose to talk of the government, in this case, as borrowing from the public (1, p. 24). It seems preferable to talk of the government taxing holders of real balances, since a given rate of inflation is equivalent to an explicit tax on real balances. Once the matter is seen in this way, it is clear why, in a growing economy, a policy of price stability allows the government to command some proportion of real income. For, if the nominal quantity of money is held constant as real income grows, prices will fall. Therefore, increasing the nominal quantity of money so as to maintain prices can be equivalent for tax purposes to a certain rate of inflation in a static economy.

Although it is illicit to infer from the neutrality of once-and-for-all changes in the quantity of money in a stationary economy that the rate of change in the quantity of money has neutral effects, the authors make some interesting tests of neutrality on the comparative-static level. For example, they consider a case in which private firms can issue bonds with fixed, nominal interest payments, which can be purchased by both the public and the governmental banking system. Suppose the total nominal stock of money which is a liability of the banking system is matched on the asset side of the balance sheet by nominal bond holdings. Money based on domestic primary securities is called 'inside money' by the authors. Then, all money is inside money, and Gurley and Shaw correctly conclude that, given the nominal stock of money, the price level is determinate. Moreover, any open-market operation is neutral in its effect on the real variables.

The authors further complicate the banking system by assuming that nominal money is composed of both inside and outside money (money that is backed by foreign or government securities or gold or fiat money issued by the government is called 'outside money'). Suppose that the banking system increases the nominal quantity of money through an open-market purchase of bonds

3. Cf. Milton Friedman's discussion of the inflationary gap in his *Essays in Positive Economics* (4, p. 257).

from the public. There are now real effects of this policy, as Gurley and Shaw prove. For example, a 10 per cent increase in total nominal money adds to the banking system's holdings of bonds by more than 10 per cent. Consequently, the open-market operation decreases the ratio of real bonds to real balances in the hands of the public. The decrease in this ratio is acceptable to private portfolio-owners only at a low rate of interest. The same result would follow if all money were inside money but were backed by private bonds and private bills. Then, by changing the proportion of bonds to bills, the banking system could affect the ratio of real bonds to real bills in the hands of the public, with consequent effects on the structure of interest rates.

Many such models are investigated in order to determine whether money is neutral. The conclusions reached are presented formally in an elegant mathematical appendix contributed by Alain C. Enthoven. The basic result is that the greater the variety of financial assets in the community, the greater is the scope for changes in the quantity of money to vary the ratios among financial assets in the public's portfolios and thereby permanently to influence the real variables in the economy.

References

1. J. G. GURLEY and E. S. SHAW, *Money in a Theory of Finance*, The Brookings Institution, 1960.
2. J. VON NEUMANN, 'A model of economic equilibrium', *Review of Economic Studies*, vol. 13, 1945, no. 1, pp. 1–9.
3. JOAN ROBINSON, *The Accumulation of Capital*, Macmillan, 1956, Book 2, ch. 8, pp. 73–84.
4. M. FRIEDMAN, *Essays in Positive Economics*, University of Chicago Press, 1953.

22 H. G. Johnson

Money in a Neo-Classical One-Sector Growth Model

Excerpt from H. G. Johnson (1967), *Essays in Monetary Economics*, Allen & Unwin, ch. 4, pp. 143–8 and 161–78.

The neo-classical one-sector growth model[1] has become a standard piece of equipment in the economic theorist's tool kit. Nevertheless, most of the available expositions of it are needlessly complicated and mathematical, and tend to obscure the simplicity of the central analytical proposition. Moreover, these expositions are for the most part confined to the case of a non-monetary economy. The purpose of this essay is to present a geometrical exposition of the one-sector growth model for the simplest possible case[2], and to apply it to the analysis of the role of money in such a model. [. . .]

The Simple Model

The simplest possible growth model assumes that production requires the use of two factors of production, labour and capital, which are employed in a production function that is subject to constant returns to scale and diminishing returns to increases in the ratio of one factor to the other; that capital is physically the same product as consumption goods, and that when output is used to add to capital stock, it lasts for ever; that labour grows at a

1. This essay draws on and elaborates the analysis of my 'The neo-classical one-sector growth model: a geometrical exposition and extension to a monetary economy' (1). Unfortunately, as James Tobin has pointed out to me, that article contained a crucial error in the treatment of the Keynesian savings assumption, which is corrected in the present version. I am indebted to Tobin also for helpful comments on this version.

2. The simple model, and the use of it to establish the golden rule conditions, are due to A. L. Marty (2). For other geometrical expositions of growth theory (see 3 to 8).

constant percentage rate, n; and that saving (equals investment) is a constant fraction of income.

On these assumptions – particularly that of constant returns to scale, which enables output per factor and the marginal products of factors to be expressed as functions of the ratios of factors – the economics of growth can be summarized in the diagram of Figure 1. The abscissa of the Figure represents capital per worker,

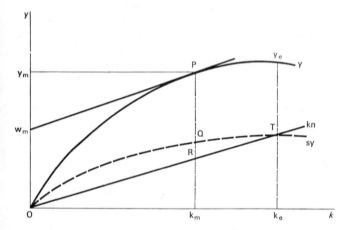

Figure 1

k, and the ordinate represents output, y, and other income magnitudes per worker. Oy graphs output per worker as a function of capital per worker, and Osy graphs savings per head as a function (via income per head) of capital per worker. The line Okn, with slope n (the rate of growth of population) graphs the investment required to supply the new additions to the labour force with the same capital per head as the existing labour force.

The first proposition to be established is that the economy will converge in the long run on a rate of growth equal to the rate of growth of the labour force, n. To prove this, it is sufficient to establish that the economy will converge on an equilibrium stock of capital per head and therefore output per head, since if output per head is constant, total output must grow at the same rate as the number of heads. As the diagram shows, there will be such an equilibrium stock of capital per head (capital–labour ratio in the economy), that saving per head is just sufficient to equip the new workers with the same stock of capital per man as the pre-existing workers possess. This equilibrium stock Ok_e, is indicated by the intersection of Osy with Okn at T. To prove that the economy's growth must converge on T, suppose that the economy began with the stock of capital per head represented by k_m less than the equilibrium stock k_e; with this stock, output would be k_mP and savings k_mQ, whereas k_mR would be sufficient to equip the additional workers with the same capital per man as existing workers, so that the QR would be available to increase capital per head. Thus capital per head would increase[3] above Ok_m and would continue to do so until it reached Ok_e. Similarly, if capital per head were above Ok_e, saving would be insufficient to equip the additional labourers with the same capital per head as existing labourers command, and capital per head would fall over time to Ok_e. Thus T and k_e represent a stable equilibrium. Both the existence and the stability of this equilibrium derive from two assumptions implicit in the diagram; that there are sufficiently diminishing returns in production, and that at some output per head saving is more than sufficient to equip new workers with the capital per head available to existing workers. It should be noted that $n = s. \frac{y}{k}$ at T, that is, the growth rate is equal to the savings ratio divided by the capital–output ratio. This is the familiar Harrod–Domar growth equation; but in this model the capital–output ratio adjusts to the growth rate, and not the other way around.

In the analysis just presented, equilibrium income per head, y_ek_e, and equilibrium consumption per head, y_eT, are determined, given the growth rate of the labour force, by the savings ratio s, and can be regarded as a function of that ratio. While equilibrium income per head rises (by assumption) as capital per head rises, equilibrium consumption per head (the vertical distance between Oy and Okn) first rises and then declines as capital per head rises. There is, therefore, obviously a savings ratio which will maximize equilibrium consumption per head. This is the ratio for which the

3. The increase in capital per head would be something less than QR, approximately $QR/(1 + n)$.

long-run equilibrium capital stock per head is such that the slope of the tangent to the Oy curve at that point is equal to the slope of the Okn curve, so that a small variation of the capital–labour ratio in either direction does not alter consumption per head and a larger variation in either direction will reduce it. The maximum consumption per head situation in the diagram is represented by k_m, with consumption per head of PR, the savings ratio required to achieve it being Rk_m/Pk_m.

The behaviour requirements for achieving maximum consumption per head may be defined in two alternative ways, each economically illuminating. Firstly, the slope of Okn is n, the equilibrium rate of growth of the economy; and the slope of Oy at P is the marginal (gross and net) product of capital (owing to the assumption that capital lasts forever) and also the own-rate-of-return on capital (since units of output and capital are identical and exchange one for one on the market). Hence the condition for maximum consumption per head can be expressed as equality of the rate of return on capital with the growth rate. Secondly, the savings per head required to maintain the maximum consumption per head are measured by Rk_m, the savings ratio required being Rk_m/Pk_m; the income earned by the capital stock per head is $y_m w_m$ (the quantity of capital per head $Ok_m = y_m P$ multiplied by the marginal product of capital, the slope of the tangent at P, $w_m P$) and the share of capital in output is $y_m w_m/Oy_m$. Since (by the parallelism of $w_m P$ and Okn required for maximization of consumption) $y_m w_m = Rk_m$, the condition for maximum consumption can be expressed as equality of savings with the income of capital or of the savings ratio with the share of capital in income. This condition, it may be noted, will be automatically fulfilled if, as is assumed by a number of writers on growth theory, capitalists save all their income and workers consume all theirs.

The condition for maximum consumption per head, expressed in the second form, has been designated as 'the golden rule of accumulation'. This designation, however, is misleading, to the extent that it implies that some quality of optimality attaches to maximum consumption per head at all points of time. There is no reason to assume that maximum consumption per head would represent maximization of welfare in terms of social utility or consumers' preferences, and certainly no reason to assume that a society not on the golden-rule growth path should set itself the objective of moving itself on to that path, or that a society on the golden-rule path should stay on it, since to do either would involve rearranging its pattern of consumption and saving over time, with effects on welfare falling outside the compass of the analysis. The conditions for maximum consumption per head apply only to alternative equilibrium growth paths of the economy, and are deduced entirely from consideration of supply factors – the exogenously given rate of growth of the labour force, and the production function, which determines the functional relation between output per head and capital per head. Utility and welfare considerations do not enter into the problem. The analysis is therefore most properly conceived as establishing the technical limits on the possibility of raising consumption per head by increasing capital per head in an expanding economy.

In conclusion to this section, it should be noted that there is nothing in the foregoing analysis to prevent the savings ratio from being such that the economy overshoots the capital–labour ratio that maximizes consumption per head – in fact, this possibility rather than its more commonly assumed converse is illustrated in Figure 1. Nor is there anything to preclude a savings ratio implying, on the equilibrium growth path, a rate of return on capital that is negative, or less than some minimum demanded by capitalist investors. [. . .]

Extensions to a Monetary Economy[4]

A. *Assumptions and problems*

The model of economic growth developed in the preceding section is a 'real' model, in which the only asset available for holding by

4. This section owes a great deal to James Tobin's two classic articles on the subject, 'A dynamic aggregative model' (9), and 'Money and economic growth' (10). I am also grateful to Tobin for having convinced me that my analysis of the Keynesian model published in the *Economica* article referred to in the initial footnote was incorrect; this error led me into producing an analysis that was not only wrong but more cumbersome than the correct analysis, so that I am quite happy to scrap it. The analysis of section B below duplicates the relevant results of Tobin's second article; to my mind, the approach employed here is somewhat simpler to grasp than Tobin's, which starts from and then modifies a model in which the influence of

the public is material capital; this section extends the model to take account of the existence of money. To do so, it is assumed that money exists in the form of non-interest-bearing currency[5] (fiat money) issued by a government or issuing agency ('the monetary authority'), additions to the money supply being effected by the printing of additional currency and the distribution of it to the public.[6] The public is assumed to regard money as net wealth; in technical terms, the model is an 'outside money' model. It should be emphasized that the assumptions that money is non-interest-bearing and that it is treated as net wealth are crucial to the analysis.

Following the classical tradition of monetary theory, it is assumed that wages and prices are perfectly flexible, in the specific sense that the real value of the public's holdings of money is instantaneously adjusted to the desired level of real cash balances. The desired level of real cash balances per person is assumed to be a function, firstly, of the level of *per capita* income or *per capita* wealth, either non-human or total non-monetary wealth (in the present model this is a matter of indifference, since in the absence of technical change income per head, capital per head, and the capitalized value of human labour services are uniquely correlated); secondly, of the rate of return on material capital; and thirdly, of the expected rate of return on money balances. For simplicity, it is assumed that, *ceteris paribus*, the desired level of

---

price-level expectations is excluded by the assumption that the real value of money is fixed.

Section C below adds to the Tobin model the utility yield of real balances as an item of real income influencing saving. I am indebted to Alvin Marty and Milton Friedman for pointing out that this item should be included in the analysis.

5. This assumption could be relaxed, and 'money' allowed to bear interest at some fixed rate. It should be noted that while the analysis is presented in terms of monetary policy, it can – on the commonly adopted assumption that government debt is treated by the public as net addition to wealth – equally well be interpreted as an analysis of the influence of fiscal policy on growth; this is the approach of Tobin (9, 10).

6. It must be assumed that this is done in some random fashion; if distribution were proportional to existing balances held, individuals would have an incentive to increase their cash balances in order to increase their shares of new money. I am indebted to discussion with Miguel Sidrauski for this point.

real cash balances bears a fixed ratio to whichever scale variable, income or the two definitions of wealth, is assumed to determine monetary and saving behaviour, so that this ratio is a function of the two rate of return variables. The rate of return on capital, on the assumption that capital is the same stuff as output and lasts for ever, is the marginal product of capital. The expected rate of return on money balances is the negative of the expected rate of change of prices, being negative when prices are expected to rise, zero when prices are expected to remain constant and positive when prices are expected to fall. It is assumed that the expected rate of change of prices is equal to the actual rate of change of prices; the actual rate of change of prices, in its turn, is determined by the rate of growth of real output, and the rate of growth of the money supply provided by the monetary authority. Whatever the monetary authority does with the supply of money, the desired level of real balances will be secured by an appropriate movement of the price level; but the required price-level change will determine the rate of return on real balances, and hence influence desired real balances and through them the growth of the economy. Further, the increase in real balances secured in this way will influence the accumulation of real capital, the mechanism depending on the theory of saving employed.

Three alternative assumptions about saving will be explored, two being variants of the Keynesian assumption of a constant ratio of saving to income and the third being that saving behaviour is governed by a desired ratio of wealth to real output. The two variants respectively ignore and take account of the utility yield of real balances as an item of real income influencing saving. The analysis based on the first assumption includes some remarks on the Keynesian problem of a possible minimum to the rate of return at which real investment will be undertaken.

The main emphasis of the analysis is placed on two related problems: the 'neutrality' of money in the context of economic growth, and the possibility of using monetary policy to influence the growth of the economy. In all three models, money is by assumption 'neutral' in the comparative-statics sense that a once-for-all change in the quantity of money, superimposed on a trend rate of growth of the money supply maintained by the monetary authority, would produce a once-for-all change in the price level with no real effects on the economy. In the context of growth theory, however, the question arises whether money is 'neutral' in the more relevant sense that a difference in the rate of change of the money supply maintained by the monetary authority would make no difference to the speed with which the economy approaches its equilibrium growth path, and, most fundamentally, that a difference in the rate of change of the money supply would make no difference to the output and consumption per head characteristic of the equilibrium growth path. If money is not neutral in the former sense, monetary policy can accelerate or retard the economy's approach to long-run equilibrium growth, and if it is not neutral in the latter sense, monetary policy can influence the characteristics of equilibrium growth.

For analytical simplicity, the monetary authority is assumed, not to fix the rate of growth of the money supply, but to govern the rate of increase of the money supply so as to achieve a target rate of price inflation or deflation, a higher rate of inflation or a lower rate of deflation requiring a higher rate of monetary expansion *ceteris paribus*. This assumption implies that, if the economy starts below its long-run equilibrium ratio of capital to output, the money supply is expanded at a declining rate as capital accumulates, the rate of expansion converging on the rate of growth of population plus the monetary authority's target rate of price change (which may be negative). Also, the policy question of whether the monetary authority can influence the character-istics of the equilibrium growth path is cast in terms of whether it can shift the economy towards the golden-rule path. Though, as previously argued, there is no real justification for regarding such an objective as desirable, this formulation of the problem seems consistent with the spirit of growth theory.

B. *The Keynesian constant savings ratio model*[7]

On the assumption that aggregate saving is a constant proportion of aggregate income, the growth of real balances as the economy grows, whether by increasing capital per worker or by growth in

7. Contrary to the contention of my *Economica* article, it makes no difference whether aggregate saving is assumed to be a constant proportion of aggregate income, or *per capita* saving a constant proportion of *per capita* income.

the number of workers at a constant ratio of capital to labour only, appears as an addition to current real output in the reckoning of the current income from which savings are made, and therefore raises the ratio of saving to output. However, the growth of real balances also absorbs saving, since the additional real balances must be held, so that the net effect is a reduction in the ratio of savings invested in the creation of material capital to output, as compared with the ratio that would obtain in a pure barter economy. Given the rate of growth of aggregate output, the absolute increase of real balances will be greater, and therefore the reduction in the ratio of real capital investment to output will be greater, the greater is the desired ratio of real balances to output.[8] Actually, the rate of growth of aggregate output cannot be taken as given, but will be interdependent with the ratio of real investment to output; but it is intuitively evident and can be proved that, allowing for this relationship, the ratio of real investment to output will vary inversely with the ratio of real balances to output.[9]

Since the rate of return on real capital is fixed by the capital to labour ratio (or the level of output per head) the desired ratio of real balances to output will vary inversely with the rate of increase of prices maintained by the monetary authority. Thus the ratio of material capital investment to output will vary directly with the rate of increase of prices maintained by the monetary authority. This in turn implies that the more expansionary is monetary policy, the faster will the economy grow (starting from any level of output per head below the equilibrium level for a barter economy), and the higher will be the level of capital per head at which the economy arrives on its long-run equilibrium growth path.

8. Alternatively, it could be assumed that the ratio relates real balances to 'disposable income', the sum of output and receipts of real balances.

9. Output per head is $y = f(k)$. Let disposable income per head be $y' = y(1 + bg)$ where b is the ratio of real balances to output demanded and g is the growth rate. Saving will be sy', from which must be deducted savings devoted to increasing real balances bgy, leaving real savings

$$s'(y) = sy \left[1 - bg \left(\frac{1}{s} - 1 \right) \right].$$

Now $g = \frac{f'}{y} s'(y) = f's - f'bg(1 - s) = \frac{f's}{1 + f'b(1 - s)}$.

Hence $s'(y) = sy \left[1 - \frac{bf'(1 - s)}{1 + bf'(1 - s)} \right]$, and it is evident that $\frac{\partial s'(y)}{\partial b} < 0$.

The mechanics of the model are illustrated in Figure 2. In the Figure, Oy, Okn, and Osy have the same meanings as in Figure 1. Oy' is disposable income *per capita*; it is the sum (*per capita*) of output and the current increment of real balances, the latter being determined by output, the ratio of real balances to output (earned income) b, and the current rate of growth g. Total saving is Osy'

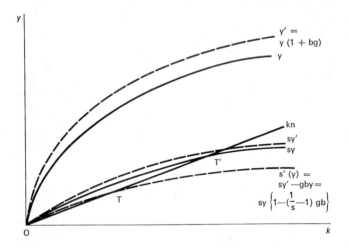

Figure 2

and the saving available for investment in real capital is Os'(y) $= \text{Osy} \cdot \left[1 - \left(\frac{1}{s} - 1 \right) gb \right]$. It should be noted that g is itself a function of s'(y), so that one cannot simply shift the Oy' curve to represent the effects of varying the level of b; however, the proof previously mentioned ensures that this heuristic procedure gives the correct answer. Moreover, the prime concern of the analysis is with the equilibrium at the point T at which Os'(y) crosses the capital requirements curve Okn, and here the rate of growth of output must be $g = n$.[10] The relation between Oy' and Oy is

10. The dynamics of the process of adjustment to the long-run equilibrium growth path, in both this and the models presented subsequently, are complex and raise awkward problems which cannot be readily handled diagrammatically.

governed by the following conflicting factors. As y rises, the rate of return on real capital must fall, tending to raise the desired ratio of real balances to income and the ratio of y' to y; on the other hand, an increase in y means a decline in the growth rate, for a constant savings ratio, since it implies a higher capital to output ratio and therefore a smaller proportionate 'deepening' of capital per unit of output; and this implies a reduction in the ratio to income of the additional real balances required by growth, and therefore of y' to y. The magnitude of b, the desired ratio of real balances to income, will (*ceteris paribus*) be greater the smaller the target rate of price increase or greater the target rate of price decrease maintained by the monetary authority. Hence the intersection at T of Os$'(y)$ with Okn must be further to the right of the diagram, the lower the target rate of price deflation or higher the target rate of price inflation set by the monetary authority. An upper limit is set by the point T$'$, which would imply a rate of inflation great enough to reduce the desired real-balance ratio to negligibility.[11]

In this model, therefore, money is neutral neither in the sense that the rate of convergence on the equilibrium growth path is independent of the rate of monetary expansion, nor in the more fundamental sense that the characteristics of the equilibrium path are independent of monetary policy. It follows that within limits monetary policy in this model can be used to move the economy towards fulfilment of the golden-rule conditions. If the economy's saving behaviour causes it to overshoot the golden-rule ratio of real investment (accumulation of material capital) to output, this can be counteracted by contraction of the money supply to generate a deflationary price trend. There may be a limit on the application of such a deflationary policy, however; if material capital is desired only for its yield, while money yields utility services, there would be a presumption that investment in real capital would cease if the rate of return on money accruing from deflation exceeded the rate of return on real investment. (In a more general portfolio-balance model, with risk attaching to both assets and risk-aversion, there would be no such presumption.) If, on the

11. This assumes that the public is precluded from issuing monetary debt to the monetary authority, an assumption that would be less reasonable in a fiscal policy model.

other hand, the economy's saving behaviour causes it to fall short of the golden-rule ratio of real investment to output, it can be nudged towards that position by an increase in the rate of expansion of the money supply. The extreme limit of such a policy would be a rate of inflation that reduced the ratio of real balances to income to negligibility and raised the ratio of real investment to output to the economy's savings ratio; this ratio might still fall short of that ratio required by the golden rule for maximizing consumption per head.

In this model, as in neo-classical growth models generally, it is assumed that the real savings produced by the savings ratio get invested in capital goods, regardless of the rate of return earned thereon. Keynesian economists frequently assume that investors demand a certain minimum rate of return on real investment, and that rather than take less they will accumulate saving in the form of cash. In this model, the results of such behaviour would be an increase in the real value of cash balances through deflation, until real balances had risen to the level per head required to reduce the ratio of real savings to output to that required for the economy to grow at its long-run equilibrium rate, with an equilibrium capital–labour ratio such as to yield the required minimum rate of return on real investment. This result could be achieved alternatively without deflation by sufficient expansion of the money supply. The assumed investor behaviour, however, is arbitrary, in that it rests on the implicit Keynesian assumption that the (actual and expected) rate of return on money balances is precisely zero; if, instead, it is assumed that the (actual and expected) return on money balances varies inversely with the rate of inflation, and that investors demand a minimum premium of the rate of return on real investment over the rate of return on cash balances, it follows that the long-run growth equilibrium of the economy would involve a rate of return on real investment equal to the required premium, plus the equilibrium growth rate of population, minus the rate of growth of the money supply (the difference between the last two being the rate of return on the money supply); and the monetary authority could, subject to the limits discussed in the previous paragraph, offset the demands of investors for a premium by operating on the rate of growth of the money supply.

To conclude the discussion of this model, it should be noted that the analysis can readily be extended to include Harrod-neutral technical progress, by redefining labour in efficiency units.

C. *The utility yield on real balances*

The model analysed in the preceding section treats income as the sum of current output and the receipts of additional real balances associated with the process of economic growth. The assumption of a demand for real balances, however, implies that such balances yield a flow of 'convenience services' or utility, which is at once a component of real consumption and real income, and should be included in the definition of the income that determines savings behaviour.

Consideration of the influence of this element of income by itself leads to conclusions about the influence of monetary policy on growth opposite to those indicated by the previous analysis of the influence of receipts of real balances. For while receipts of real balances are income that has to be saved, thereby (with a constant over-all savings ratio) reducing the proportion of output available for investment in material capital, the services of real balances are income that has to be consumed, thereby (again with a constant over-all saving ratio) reducing the proportion of physical output consumed and raising the ratio of real investment to output. Since, for any given level of output per head (and corresponding rate of return on real capital), the desired ratio of real balances to output will vary inversely with the rate of increase of prices maintained by the monetary authority, the ratio of real saving to output will be higher the less expansionary or the more contractionary is monetary policy (ignoring for the time being the influence of monetary policy on saving through its influence on additional receipts of real balances). Consequently, the less expansionary (or more contractionary) is monetary policy (defined by the target rate of price change), the faster will the economy grow, starting from any level of output per head below the long-run equilibrium level and the higher will be the long-run equilibrium level of output per head itself. This proposition, however, is subject to the possible restriction previously mentioned, that under certain conditions real investment might cease, if the rate of price deflation yielded a rate of return on real balances greater than that on real investment. (If the notion of the superior liquidity of money over real capital is admissible in a model of this kind, the maximum return on real balances allowable would in these circumstances be less than the return on real capital by the amount of the liquidity premium.) It follows that so far as the influence of monetary policy through the service yield of cash balances is concerned, money is non-neutral in the two senses of being able to influence both the current rate of growth and the characteristics of the long-run equilibrium growth path.

Since the rate of real saving (the ratio of material investment to output) is influenced by monetary policy through the influence of the latter on the magnitudes relative to income of both receipts of additional real balances and the utility of real balances held, and these influences though opposite in direction are differently determined and can be expected not to cancel out, money remains non-neutral in both the senses just mentioned when the utility yield on real balances is taken into account. However, recognition of this element in the problem has the consequence that the direction of the influence of monetary policy on the growth equilibrium of the economy is no longer unambiguous. A more inflationary policy may raise or lower the current growth rate of output and the long-run equilibrium level of output per head, depending on whether the growth-stimulating (long-run equilibrium output-raising) effect of lower real-balance receipts outweighs the growth-inhibiting (long-run equilibrium output-reducing) effect of a lower utility yield on real balances.

A more subtle and important point is that it is no longer correct to discuss the problem in terms of moving the economy towards the golden-rule situation as previously defined. When account is taken of the utility yield of real balances, the golden-rule situation has to be defined in terms of two criteria: choice of a saving ratio that satisfies the golden-rule conditions, to maximize consumption of commodities per head; and pursuit of a monetary policy of deflation at a rate equal to the golden-rule rate of return on real capital, to maximize the utility yield on real balances. (Since this rate of return is equal to the rate of growth of the economy, the latter requirement would be fulfilled by the maintenance of a constant nominal stock of money.)

Given the existence of a saving ratio different from that indicated by the golden rule, the problem is to select a monetary policy that will maximize long-run equilibrium consumption per head of commodities and real-balance services together; and since a policy may well have opposite effects on the quantity of consumable commodities available and the utility yield of real balances, it would be incorrect to assume that policy should aim to maximize the available quantity of consumable commodities, that is, to push the economy towards the golden-rule situation with respect to the output of commodities alone. Specifically, assume that the influence of monetary policy via additional receipts of real balances dominates its influence via the utility yield, so that a more inflationary policy would increase the material investment ratio, and that the economy's saving ratio would make it fall short of the golden-rule position even under barter economy conditions. An inflationary policy would raise output and consumption of commodities per head, but it might reduce the utility yield of real balances more than it increased commodity consumption. The proper policy to follow to maximize long-run equilibrium total consumption per head obviously depends on the outcome of the interaction of the relevant parameters.

To construct a geometrical version of this model, it is necessary to hypothesize a quantifiable measure of the utility yield on real balances. For this purpose it is assumed that the utility yield as a proportion of income per head is an increasing function of the ratio of real balances to income, represented by $u(b)$, where $\frac{du}{db} > 0$ and $\frac{d^2u}{db^2} < 0$ until $u(b)$ attains a maximum representing satiation with real balances.[12]

12. The logic of national income accounting suggests that the utility yield per unit of real balances be reckoned at the alternative opportunity cost of holding such balances, which is the difference between the yields on material capital and real balances, $r + \dot{p}/p$, where r is the rate of return on material capital and $\dot{p}/p$ is the rate of inflation. (The return on money, $-\dot{p}/p$, is already reckoned in the real-balance receipts portion of disposable income.) This procedure, however, produces economically nonsensical results. The imputed yield as a proportion of income is $(r + \dot{p}/p)b$, where b varies inversely with $(r + \dot{p}/p)$; if the demand for real balances is inelastic

The mechanics of this model are illustrated in Figure 3. In the Figure, Oy, Okn, and Osy have the same meanings as before. Oy″ is the revised concept of disposable income *per capita*; it is the sum *per capita* of current output y, the current increment of

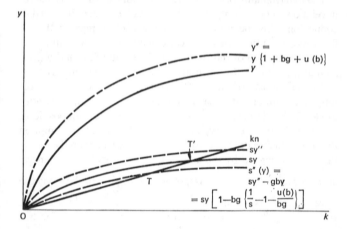

Figure 3

real balances bgy determined as in the previous model, and the imputed value of real balance services, u(b)y. Total saving is Osy″; the saving available for investment in material capital is

$$Os''(y) = Osy\left[1 - bg\left(\frac{1}{s} - 1 - \frac{u(b)}{bg}\right)\right].$$

with respect to their cost, the formula implies that real income from this source will be higher the lower is the ratio of real balances to output; and in any case it implies that if the demand for real balances is satiated ($-\dot{p}/p = r$, so that real balances cost nothing to hold), total disposable income *per capita* is lower, *ceteris paribus*, than if it is not. It seems preferable to adopt a procedure that reflects effects on economic welfare rather than on conventional accounting magnitudes.

The approach adopted here corresponds to measuring the real income derived from holding real balances by integrating the area under the demand curve subtended by the quantity of cash-balance services consumed. The usual difficulties with this approximation are disregarded on the grounds that the marginal utility of consumption of commodities may reasonably be assumed constant for the purposes of this model.

As in the previous model, it should be noted that g is a function of $s''(y)$, so that one cannot simply shift the Oy'' and $Os''(y)$ curves to represent the effects of varying the level of b; but that using the model in this way does in fact given the correct answers.

The determinants of the general behaviour of the other curves in relation to Oy as output per head rises have been discussed in connexion with the previous model, except as regards the influence of the utility yield on real balances $u(b)y$. As output per head rises the rate of return on material capital falls and b rises, so that the ratio of this portion of real income to output rises.

As the curves are drawn, $Os''(y)$ lies below Osy, so that the long-run equilibrium T lies to the left of T' as in the previous model. This relationship of the curves and equilibrium positions, however, is not necessary, but involves the implicit assumption that the influence of the utility yield of real balances on the saving ratio is outweighed by the influence of additional real balances; algebraically, that $\left(\dfrac{1}{s} - 1\right)$ is greater than $\dfrac{u(b)}{bg}$. If the converse were true, $Os''(y)$ would lie above Osy, and T would lie to the right of T'. This is an important possible alternative, for two reasons.[13]

First, it means that – confining attention to the assumption that the Oy curve does not bend down towards the horizontal axis – capital per head and output per head may be higher in a monetary economy than in a non-monetary economy with the same saving ratio. The neglect of the utility yield of real balances in the Keynesian case previously analysed produced the erroneous implication that, given the saving ratio, material capital and output per head in long-run equilibrium will always be lower in a monetary than in a non-monetary economy.[14]

Second, depending on whether the $Os''(y)$ curve lies below or

13. One should also note that, since $u(b)/b$ and g will both fall as the capital to labour ratio increases, and the relation of $Os''(y)$ to Osy depends on the relative magnitudes of $\dfrac{u(b)}{bg}$ and $\left(\dfrac{1}{s} - 1\right)$, $Os''(y)$ may cross Osy one or more times.

14. James Tobin has pointed out to me that comparison of a barter and a monetary economy in this fashion is probably unfair, since it leaves unanswered the question of how the barter economy performs the functions of money in a monetary economy.

above the Osy curve, a more inflationary policy, which will have the effect of reducing the desired ratio of real balances to output b, will raise or lower the $Os''(y)$ curve, increase or decrease the speed with which the economy approaches its long-run equilibrium growth path, and increase or reduce the long-run equilibrium levels of capital per head and output per head. Thus, as previously pointed out, while money will be non-neutral with respect to growth in the two senses of influencing the rate of growth in other than long-run equilibrium growth situations, and of influencing the characteristics of the long-run growth path, these influences will not be unidirectional as in the previous model but will depend on circumstances.

There is unfortunately no obvious simple way to extend the diagrammatic technique so as to add consumption of the services of real balances to consumption of commodities and thus permit analysis of the influence of monetary policy on total consumption in long-run growth equilibrium.

D. *The desired wealth to income ratio model*

As pointed out previously, the Keynesian assumption that a constant proportion of income is saved makes little theoretical sense. The consequences of the alternative theory that saving is motivated by the desire to achieve and maintain a certain ratio of wealth to real output are illustrated in Figure 4. The desired ratio of total wealth to output is represented by the reciprocal of the slope of OR. With real equilibrium at P_1, material capital is Ok_1, human capital is k_1K_1, and real monetary wealth is K_1W_1, total wealth being OW_1. The real value of the stock of money is equal to the desired value of cash balances, which in turn is related to total non-monetary wealth or (more complexly) to total wealth through a desired cash-balance ratio which depends on the rate of return on material capital and the rate of return on cash balances, the latter depending on the rate of growth of output and of the money supply. The ratio of real investment to output is assumed to be determined in part by the desire to maintain the current wealth-to-output ratio, and in part by the desire to increase the wealth-to-income ratio towards the desired level represented by OR. In long-run equilibrium, output is Oy_e, material capital per head Ok_e, the value of human capital per head $k_e K_e$, and real monetary wealth per head $K_e W_e$. In contrast to the real model previously discussed, the rate of return on capital must be higher than the desired ratio of income to wealth. Moreover, this rate of return will be lower, and the level of output per head prevailing in long-run growth equilibrium will be higher, the lower the ratio of monetary to total wealth desired under long-run equilibrium growth conditions.

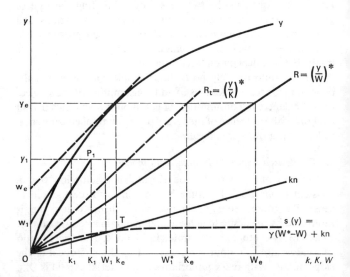

Figure 4

Since under these conditions the rate of growth of output must be equal to the rate of growth of population, the rate of return on cash balances and consequently the desired ratio of monetary to total wealth will be a decreasing function of the rate of increase of the money supply, so that total non-monetary capital per head will be an increasing function, and the rate of return on capital a decreasing function, of the rate of increase of the money supply.

This formulation of the argument, however, is somewhat misleading, since it neglects the influence of the rate of return on real capital on the desired money-to-wealth ratio. A clearer picture of the relationship, perhaps, is conveyed by considering the effect of an increase in the desired money-to-wealth ratio, starting from the initial level of non-monetary wealth K_e: this increase would be provided by a once-over change in the price level, after which prices would continue to change at the previous rate. The community would then find that its total wealth-to-income ratio was higher than desired, and it would start to decumulate wealth, including non-monetary wealth. The result of decumulation would be to raise the rate of return on material capital, and so tend to reduce the desired ratio of money to total wealth, thereby mitigating the decline in wealth that would otherwise be necessary to restore equilibrium. Alternatively, one might construct a locus OW, representing total actual wealth for the varying levels of output per head, on the assumption that monetary policy aims at a target rate of change of prices, the intersection of OW with OR indicating the characteristics of the equilibrium growth path, and OW lying further to the right the lower the target rate of price increase (higher the target rate of price decrease). This construction would, however, entail the complexity of compressing into the shape of OW the growth history of the economy, except at the intersection point.

In this model, as in the Keynesian models previously considered, money is not neutral in the long-run equilibrium sense that the characteristics of the economy on the equilibrium growth path will be independent of the rate of change of the money supply. On the contrary, the monetary authority can increase or decrease output and capital per head in growth equilibrium, by increasing or decreasing the rate of expansion of the money supply. It can thus move the economy towards the fulfilment of the golden-rule conditions, within limits set by the desired wealth to income ratio and the condition that the rate of deflation cannot exceed the rate of return on material capital. As indicated earlier, however, the services of cash balances should be included in the definitions of income and consumption; the long-run monetary policy suggested by golden-rule considerations would therefore be that which maximized the excess of disposable income (including the value of the services derived from real balance holdings) over the capital requirements of population growth, subject to the two restrictions just mentioned.

337

E. *Concluding remarks: savings behaviour and inside money*

The basic reason for the non-neutrality of money in the models explored in previous sub-sections, in the fundamental sense that monetary policy influences the characteristics of the equilibrium growth path, is that these models relate savings behaviour to other variables than the rate of return on investment. If, in line with the more traditional approach to saving as an intertemporal exchange of consumption goods, saving behaviour were represented as a willingness to accumulate assets until the rate of return on them reached a minimum set by the social rate of time preference, the long-run neutrality of money would be re-established.[15] This would, however, involve treating the rate of time preference as independent of the stock of wealth and its composition, which is an extremely questionable assumption, especially for a monetary economy in which wealth can be stored in the form of either real capital or real balances, each with its own rate of return.

The models explored have all been 'outside money' models, in which real balances constitute an addition to material wealth in the form of capital goods. If on the contrary it were assumed that money is of the 'inside' variety, created against private debts – the question of what happens to the banking profits earned by lending at interest while borrowing interest-free is temporarily ignored – real balances would not constitute a net addition to material wealth, but instead an indirect means of holding material wealth. In that case, monetary policy would not be able to influence growth through its influence (via the desired money-to-income ratio) on the magnitude of the supplement to earned income received in the form of additional real balances, and therefore on the material savings ratio. Instead, the influence of monetary policy on growth would be confined to the influence of the target rate of inflation or deflation on the utility yield of real balances.

The existence of this influence, however, results from carrying over from the outside money model the assumption that money bears no interest, so that monetary policy exercises a leverage

15. This approach is adopted in a University of Chicago Ph.D. thesis by Miguel Sidrauski.

over the real rate of return on money balances. There is no real justification for making this assumption.[16] The non-payment of interest on demand deposits, which constitute a substantially more important means of payment than currency in most advanced countries, is a consequence of legal restriction rather than natural law – and to an important extent it is evaded by the cancellation of service charges against hypothetical interest earnings. If it were not for this legal restriction, the merits of which are extremely doubtful,[17] and for the imposition of legal reserve requirements on banks, which in effect impose a special tax on the commercial banks equal to the interest they forego on assets held involuntarily in the form of non-interest-bearing central bank liabilities, competition in the commercial banking business would result in holders of demand deposits being offered a rate of interest equal to the rate of return on real capital, less the costs of the financial intermediation that allows deposit holders to hold their wealth in the more convenient form of deposits rather than real capital. In that case, the cost of holding money rather than material capital would be equal to the social cost of creating it, and money would be neutral with respect to economic growth.[18]

This conclusion leads to the final observation, that what is basically responsible for the non-neutrality of money in the models analysed is the assumption that money is a non-interest-bearing asset (or, more generally, an asset with a return fixed in nominal terms, which return has for convenience been equated to zero in this analysis). This assumption stems in part from the current institutional arrangements for the provision of the supply of money, the wisdom of which is questioned in the preceding

16. I am indebted for this point to discussion with R. A. Mundell.

17. See, for example, George J. Benston, 'Interest payments on demand deposits and bank investment behavior' (11). The case for allowing the payment of interest on demand deposits has been made cogently on numerous occasions by my colleague Milton Friedman.

18. In these conditions, there would be nothing to choose between a policy of maintaining price stability and a policy of deflating at a rate equal to the rate of interest. The recognition that modern money is mostly inside money may be partly responsible for the decline in popularity of the classical monetary theorist's recommendation of the latter policy. If money were all inside money and competition prevailed there would be an argument for price-level stability on the grounds that this would conveniently make real and nominal rates of interest equal.

paragraph, but more importantly from the convenience to the classical tradition of monetary analysis of the outside money concept, so useful in demonstrating the neutrality of money under static-equilibrium conditions. For the construction of models of growth incorporating money, it might be preferable to employ an assumption about money that, instead of ensuring non-neutrality by accepting existing monetary institutional arrangements as defining money, ensured neutrality by re-defining institutional arrangements for supplying money. Specifically, neutrality would be assured by assuming that monetary arrangements guarantee holders of money a rate of return on their real balances equal to the rate of return available on real investment.

References

1. H. G. JOHNSON, 'The neo-classical one-sector growth model: a geometrical exposition and extension to a monetary economy', *Economica*, vol. 33, 1966, no. 131, pp. 265–87.
2. A. L. MARTY, 'The neo-classical theorem', *American Economic Review*, vol. 54, 1964, no. 6, pp. 1026–9.
3. R. M. SOLOW, 'A contribution to the theory of economic growth', *Quarterly Journal of Economics*, vol. 70, 1956, no. 1, pp. 65–94.
4. T. W. SWAN, 'Economic growth and capital accumulation', *Economic Record*, vol. 32, 1956, no. 63, pp. 334–61.
5. J. BUTTRICK, 'A note on growth theory', *Economic Development and Cultural Change*, vol. 9, 1960, no. 1, part 1, pp. 75–82.
6. W. M. CORDEN, 'A brief review of some theories of economic growth', *Malayan Economic Review*, vol. 6, 1962, no. 1, pp. 1–12.
7. J. E. MEADE, *A Neo-Classical Theory of Economic Growth*, Allen & Unwin, 1961.
8. F. H. HAHN and R. C. O. MATTHEWS, 'The theory of economic growth: a survey', *The Economic Journal*, vol. 74, 1964, no. 296, pp. 779–902.
9. J. TOBIN, 'A dynamic aggregative model', *Journal of Political Economy*, vol. 63, 1955, no. 2, pp. 103–15.
10. J. TOBIN, 'Money and economic growth', *Econometrica*, vol. 33, October 1965, no. 4, pp. 671–84.
11. G. J. BENSTON, 'Interest payments on demand deposits and bank investment behavior', *Journal of Political Economy*, vol. 72, 1964, no. 5, pp. 431–49.

Further Reading

Books

M. L. BURSTEIN, *Money*, Schenkman, 1963.

M. FRIEDMAN, *Studies in the Quantity Theory of Money*, Chicago University Press, 1956.

M. FRIEDMAN, *The Optimum Quantity of Money*, Aldine, 1969.

J. G. GURLEY and E. S. SHAW, *Money in a Theory of Finance*, Brookings Institute, 1960.

F. H. HAHN and F. BRECHLING, *The Theory of Interest Rates*, Macmillan, 1965.

J. R. HICKS, *Critical Essays in Monetary Theory*, Clarendon Press, 1967.

W. S. JEVONS, *Money and the Mechanism of Exchange*, Kegan Paul, Trench Trubner, 1910, 23rd edn, ch. 1, pp. 1–7.

H. G. JOHNSON, *Essays in Monetary Economics*, Allen & Unwin, 1967.

J. M. KEYNES, *A Treatise on Money*, Macmillan, 1930.

J. M. KEYNES, *The General Theory of Employment, Interest and Money*, Harcourt Brace. 1935.

O. LANGE, *Price Flexibility and Employment*, Principia, 1945.

A. LINDBECK, *A Study in Monetary Analysis*, Almquist Wiksell, 1963.

F. LUTZ and L. W. MINTS, *Readings in Monetary Theory*, Blakiston, 1951.

A. W. MARGET, *The Theory of Prices*, Prentice-Hall, vol. 1, 1938; vol. 2, 1942.

A. MARSHALL, *Money, Credit and Commerce*, Macmillan, 1924, ch. 4.

W. L. NEWLYN, *Monetary Theory*, Oxford University Press, 1962, ch. 1, pp. 1–11.

D. PATINKIN, *Money, Interest and Prices*, Harper & Row, 1965, 2nd edn.

B. P. PESEK and T. R. SAVING, *Money Wealth and Economic Theory*, Macmillan, 1967.

A. C. PIGOU, *The Veil of Money*. Macmillan, 1949.

R. S. THORN, *Readings in Monetary Theory*, Random House, 1966.

H. THORNTON, *An Enquiry into the Nature and Effects of the Paper Credit of Great Britain (1802)*, Hayek (ed.), Frank Cass, 1962.

K. WICKSELL, *Lectures on Political Economy*, vol. 2, Routledge, 1935.

K. WICKSELL, *Selected Papers of Economic Theory*, Allen & Unwin, 1958, pp. 67–83.

Journals

Key to journal abbreviations

A.E.R. *American Economic Review*

E.J. *Economic Journal*

Further Reading

I.E.P.	*International Economic Papers*
I.E.R.	*International Economic Review*
J.A.S.A.	*Journal of the American Statistical Association*
J.F.	*Journal of Finance*
J.P.E.	*Journal of Political Economy*
N.B.R.	*National Banking Review*
O.E.P.	*Oxford Economic Papers*
Q.J.E.	*Quarterly Journal of Economics*
R.E.S.	*Review of Economic Studies*
R.E. Stats	*Review of Economics and Statistics*
S.E.J.	*Southern Economic Journal*
S.J.P.E.	*Scottish Journal of Political Economy*
W.E.J.	*Western Economic Journal*

Surveys

G. L. BACH, J. S. DUESENBERRY, M. FRIEDMAN, A. J. SCHWARTZ, F. MODIGLIANI, H. G. JOHNSON and others, 'The state of monetary economics', *R. E. Stats* Supplement, vol. 45, February 1963, pp. 3–107.

M. FRIEDMAN, 'Post-war trends in monetary theory and policy', *National Banking Review*, September 1964, pp. 1–10.

H. G. JOHNSON, 'Monetary theory and policy', *A.E.R.*, vol. 52, June 1962, pp. 335–84. Reprinted in H. G. JOHNSON, *Essays in Monetary Economics*, R. S. THORN, *Readings in Monetary Theory* and *Surveys of Economics Theory*, vol. 1, Macmillan, 1965.

R. S. SAYERS, 'Monetary thought and monetary policy in England', *E.J.*, vol. 70, December 1960, pp. 711–24.

The nature of money

W. J. BAUMOL, 'Stock, flows and monetary theory', *Q.J.E.*, vol. 7, 1962, pp. 46–56.

P. CAGAN, 'Why do we use money in open market operations?', *J.P.E.*, vol. 66, February 1958, pp. 34–46.

J. R. HICKS, 'A suggestion for simplifying the theory of money', *Economica*, vol. 2, February 1935, p. 3.

R. A. RADFORD, 'The economic organization of a P.O.W. camp', *Economica*, vol. 17, November 1945, pp. 189–201.

J. A. SCHUMPETER, 'Money and the social product', *I.E.P.*, vol. 6, 1956, no. 6, pp. 148–211.

L. B. YEAGER, 'Essential properties of the medium of exchange', *Kyklos*, vol. 21, February 1968, no. 1, pp. 45–68.

The demand for money

L. DE ALESSI, 'The demand for money: a cross-section study of British business firms', *Economica*, vol. 33, 1966, pp. 288–302.

W. J. BAUMOL, 'The transactions demand for cash: an inventory theoretic approach', *Q.J.E.*, vol. 66, November 1952, pp. 545–56.

K. BRUNNER and A. H. MELTZER, 'Predicting velocity: implications for theory and policy', *J.F.*, vol. 18, May 1963, pp. 17–54.

K. BRUNNER and A. H. MELTZER, 'Economies of scale in cash balances reconsidered', *Q.J.E.*, vol. 81, 1967, pp. 422–36.

P. DAVIDSON, 'Keynes finance motive', *O.E.P.*, vol. 17, 1965, pp. 47–65.

H. S. ELLIS, 'Notes on the demand for money', *Kyklos*, vol. 15, 1962, no. 1, pp. 216–30.

M. FLEMING, 'The timing of payments and the demand for money', *Economica*, vol. 31, May 1964, pp. 132–57.

M. FRIEDMAN, 'The demand for money', *American Philosophical Society Proceedings*, vol. 105, June 1961, pp. 259–64.

J. C. GILBERT, 'The demand for money: the development of an economic concept', *J.P.E.*, vol. 61, April 1953, pp. 73–83.

D. LAIDLER, 'Some evidence on the demand for money', *J.P.E.*, vol. 74, February 1966, pp. 55–68.

T. H. LEE, 'Income, wealth and the demand for money: some evidence from cross-section data', *J.A.S.A.*, vol. 59, September 1964, pp. 746–62.

C. E. V. LESER, 'The consumer's demand for money', *Econometrica*, vol. 11, 1943, pp. 123–40.

H. F. LYDALL, 'Income assets and the demand for money', *R.E.Stats*, vol. 40, February 1958, pp. 1–14.

A. H. MELTZER, 'The demand for money: the evidence from the time series', *J.P.E.*, vol. 71, June 1963, pp. 219–46.

A. H. MELTZER, 'The demand for money: a cross-section study of business firms', *Q.J.E.*, vol. 71, August 1963, pp. 405–22.

H. L. MILLER, Jr, 'On "liquidity" and "transaction costs"', *S.E.J.*, vol. 32, July 1965, pp. 43–8.

B. P. PESEK, 'Determinants of the demand for money', *R.E. Stats*, vol. 45, November 1963, pp. 419–24.

J. SPRAOS, 'An Engel-type curve for cash', *Manchester School*, vol. 25, 1957, pp. 183–9.

J. TOBIN, 'The interest elasticity of transactions demand for cash', *R.E.Stats*, vol. 38, August 1956, pp. 241–7.

J. TOBIN, 'Liquidity preference as behaviour towards risk', *R.E.S.*, vol. 25, February 1958, pp. 65–86.

A. A. WALTERS, 'Professor Friedman on the demand for money', *J.P.E.*, vol. 73, October 1965, pp. 545–51.

The supply of money

K. BRUNNER, 'Some major problems in monetary theory', *A.E.R.*, vol. 51, May 1961, pp. 47–56.

K. BRUNNER, 'A scheme for the supply theory of money', *I.E.R.*, vol. 2, 1961, pp. 79–109.

P. CAGAN, 'The demand for currency relative to the total money supply', *J.P.E.*, vol. 66, August 1958, pp. 303–28.

D. J. COPPOCK and N. J. GIBSON, 'The volume of deposits and the cash and liquid assets ratios', *Manchester School*, vol. 31, 1963.

Further Reading

W. M. DACEY, 'Treasury bills and the money supply', *Lloyds Bank Review*, vol. 70, January 1960, pp. 1–16.

W. L. NEWLYN, 'The supply of money and its control', *E.J.*, vol. 74, June 1965, pp. 327–47.

Money and wealth

COMMITTEE ON THE WORKING OF THE MONETARY SYSTEM, *Radcliffe Report*, H.M.S.O., Cmd 827, 1959.

G. O. BIERWAG and M. A. GROVE, 'Indifference curves in asset analysis', *E.J.*, vol. 76, June 1966, pp. 337–43.

A. J. L. CATT, 'Idle balances and the motives for liquidity', *O.E.P.*, vol. 14, June 1962, pp. 124–38.

G. CLAYTON, 'British financial intermediaries in theory and practice', *E.J.*, vol. 72, December 1962, pp. 869–86.

A. B. CRAMP, 'Financial intermediaries and monetary policy', *Economica*, vol. 29, May 1962, pp. 143–51.

J. M. CULBERTSON, 'Intermediaries and monetary theory: a criticism of the Gurley–Shaw theory', *A.E.R.*, vol. 48, March 1958, pp. 119–31.

J. DUESENBERRY, 'The portfolio approach to the demand for money and other assets', *R.E.Stats* Supplement, vol. 45, February 1963, pp. 9–24.

L. E. GRAMLEY and S. B. CHASE, Jr, 'Time deposits in monetary analysis', *Federal Reserve Bulletin*, October 1965, pp. 1380–406.

H. W. GUTHRIE, 'Consumers' propensities to hold liquid assets', *J.A.S.A.*, vol. 55, Summer 1960, pp. 469–90.

S. E. HARRIS, J. W. ANGELL, W. FELLNER, A. H. HANSEN, J. TOBIN, A. G. HART, H. NEISSER, R. V. ROOSA, W. L. SMITH, W. THOMAS, S. WEINTRAUB and P. A. SAMUELSON, 'Controversial issues in recent monetary policy: a symposium', *R.E.Stats*, vol. 42, August 1960, pp. 245–82.

H. A. LATANÉ, 'Cash balances and the interest rate – a pragmatic approach', *R.E.Stats*, vol. 36, November 1954, pp. 456–60. Reprinted in R. S. THORN, *Monetary Theory and Policy.*

R. G. LIPSEY and F. P. R. BRECHLING, 'Trade credit and monetary policy', *E.J.*, vol. 73, December 1963, pp. 618–41.

L. A. METZLER, 'Wealth, saving and the rate of interest', *J.P.E.*, vol. 59, April 1951, pp. 93–116. Reprinted in R. S. THORN, *Monetary Theory and Policy.*

J. NIEHANS, 'Interest rates, forced saving and prices in the long run'. *R.E.S.*, vol. 32, October 1965, pp. 327–49.

D. PATINKIN, 'Financial intermediaries and the logical structure of monetary theory', *A.E.R.*, vol. 51, August 1963, pp. 347–62.

B. P. PESEK and T. R. SAVING, 'Monetary policy, taxes and the rate of interest', *J.P.E.*, vol. 71, August 1963, pp. 347–62.

J. TOBIN, 'Money capital and other stores of value', *A.E.R.* (Papers and Proc.), vol. 51, May 1961, pp. 26–37.

R. TURVEY, 'Consistency and consolidation in the theory of interest', *Economica*, vol. 21, November 1954, pp. 300–307.

The quantity theory of money

C. R. BARRETT and A. A. WALTERS, 'The relative stability of monetary and autonomous multipliers in the U.K.', *R.E. Stats*, vol. 58, November 1966, pp. 395–405.

R. W. CLOWER and M. L. BURSTEIN, 'The invariance of demand for money and other assets', *R.E.S.*, vol. 28, October 1960, pp. 32–6.

M. FRIEDMAN, 'The quantity theory of money – a restatement', M. Friedman (ed.), *Studies in the Quantity Theory of Money*, Chicago University Press, 1956, pp. 3–21.

T. NEGISHI, 'Conditions for neutral money', *R.E.S.*, vol. 31, April 1964, pp. 147–8.

B. OHLIN, 'The quantity theory in Swedish literature', *Economic History*, vol. 2, 1959, pp. 3–18.

M. K. RAKSHIT, 'Invariance of the demand for cash and other assets: a comment', *O.E.P.*, vol. 16, 1964, pp. 291–6.

A. A. WALTERS, 'Monetary multipliers in the U.K. 1880–1962', *O.E.P.*, vol. 18, 1966, no. 3, pp. 270–83.

The integration of monetary and value theory

G. C. ARCHIBALD and R. G. LIPSEY, 'Monetary and value theory: a critique of Lange and Patinkin', *R.E.S.*, vol. 26, October 1958, pp. 1–22.

W. J. BAUMOL, R. W. CLOWER, M. L. BURSTEIN, F. H. HAHN, R. J. BALL, R. BODKIN, G. C. ARCHIBALD and R. G. LIPSEY, 'A symposium on monetary policy', *R.E.S.*, vol. 28, October 1960, pp. 29–56.

G. S. BECKER and W. J. BAUMOL, 'The classical monetary theory: the outcome of the discussion', *Economica*, vol. 19, 1952, pp. 355–76.

K. BRUNNER, 'Inconsistency and indeterminacy in classical economics', *Econometrica*, vol. 19, April 1951, pp. 152–73.

R. W. CLOWER, 'Classical monetary theory revisited', *Economica*, vol. 30, May 1963, pp. 165–70.

R. W. CLOWER, 'Permanent income and transitory balances: Hahn's paradox', *O.E.P.*, vol. 15, July 1963, pp. 177–90.

R. W. CLOWER, 'A reconsideration of the microfoundations of monetary theory', *W.E.J.*, vol. 6, 1967, no. 1, pp. 1–9.

J. ENCARNACION, 'Consistency between Say's identity and the Cambridge equation', *E.J.*, vol. 67, 1958, pp. 827–30.

L. E. GALLAWAY and P. E. SMITH, 'Real balances and the permanent income hypothesis', *Q.J.E.*, vol. 75, 1961, pp. 302–13.

F. H. HAHN, 'The general equilibrium theory of money – a comment', *R.E.S.*, vol. 19, 1951–2, pp. 179–85.

F. H. HAHN, 'The rate of interest and general equilibrium analysis', *E.J.*, vol. 65, March 1955, pp. 52–66.

F. H. HAHN, 'Real balances and consumption', *O.E.P.*, vol. 14, June 1962, pp. 117–23.

F. H. HAHN, 'On some problems of proving the existence of an equilibrium in a monetary economy', F. H. Hahn and F. Brechling (eds.), *The Theory of Interest Rates*, Macmillan, 1965, pp. 126–35.

J. R. HICKS, 'A rehabilitation of "classical" economics?', *E.J.*, vol. 67, 1957, pp. 278–89.

R. E. KUENNE, 'Keynes' identity, Ricardian virtue, and the partial dichotomy', *Canadian Journal of Economics and Political Science*, vol. 27, August 1961, pp. 323–36.

O. LANGE, 'Say's law: a restatement and criticism', in O. Lange, F· McIntyre and T. O. Yntema (eds.), '*Studies in Mathematical Economics and Econometrics*', Chicago, 1942, pp. 49–68.

C. LLOYD, 'The real balance effect: *sine qua* what?', *O.E.P.*, October 1962, pp. 267–74.

C. LLOYD, 'The real balance effect and the Slutsky equation', *J.P.E.*, vol. 72, June 1964, pp. 295–9.

E. J. MISHAN, 'A fallacy in the interpretation of the cash balance effect', *Economica*, vol. 15, 1958, pp. 106–18.

F. MODIGLIANI, 'The monetary mechanism and its interaction with real phenomena', *R.E. Stats* Supplement, vol. 45, February 1963, pp. 79–107.

R. A. MUNDELL, 'The monetary dynamics of international adjustment under fixed and flexible exchange rates', *Q.J.E.*, vol. 74, 1960, pp. 249–340.

D. PATINKIN, 'The indeterminacy of absolute prices in classical economic theory', *Econometrica*, vol. 17, January 1949, pp. 1–27.

D. PATINKIN, 'Dichotomies of the pricing process in economic theory', *Economica*, vol. 21, May 1954, pp. 113–28.

M. K. RAKSHIT, 'Classical monetary theory revisited: a comment', *Economica*, vol. 32, February 1965, pp. 70–72.

P. A. SAMUELSON, 'What classical and neoclassical monetary theory really was', *Canadian Journal of Economics*, vol. 1, February 1968, no. 1, pp 1–15.

S. VALAVANIS, 'A denial of Patinkin's contradiction', *Kyklos*, vol. 4, 1955, pp. 351–68.

P. WONNACOTT, 'Neutral money in Patinkin's *Money, Interest and Prices*', *R.E.S.*, vol. 26, 1958, pp. 70–71.

Monetary theory and Keynesian economics

R. W. CLOWER, 'Productivity, thrift and the rate of interest', *E.J.*, vol. 64, March 1954, pp. 107–15.

R. W. CLOWER, 'The Keynesian counter-revolution: a theoretical appraisal', *Schweizerische Zeitschrift für Volkswirtschaft und Statistik*. March 1963, pp. 8–81 (in German). Reprinted in English in F. H. Hahn and F. Brechling (eds.), *The Theory of Interest Rates*, Macmillan, 1965, pp. 103–25.

W. FELLNER and H. M. SOMERS, 'Note on "stocks" and "flows" in monetary interest theory', *R. E. Stats*, vol. 31, May 1949, pp. 145–6, Reprinted in R. S. THORN (ed.), *Monetary Theory and Policy*.

J. F. FREEMAN, 'Liquidity preference *v.* loanable funds: a new approach to the problem', *E.J.*, vol. 73, December 1963, pp. 681–8.

J. R. HICKS, 'Mr Keynes and the Classics: a suggested interpretation', *Econometrica*, vol. 5, April 1937, pp. 147–59.

H. G. JOHNSON, 'Monetary theory and Keynesian economics', *Pakistan Economic Journal*, vol. 8, June 1958, no. 2, pp. 56–70.

H. G. JOHNSON, 'The general theory after twenty-five years', *A.E.R.* (Papers and Proc.), vol. 51, May 1961, pp. 1–17. Reprinted in H. G. JOHNSON, *Money, Trade and Economic Growth*, Allen & Unwin, 1962.

J. M. KEYNES, 'The general theory of employment', *Q.J.E.*, vol. 51, February 1937, pp. 209–23.

A. LEIJONHUFVUD, 'Keynes and the Keynesians: a suggested interpretation', *A.E.R.*, vol. 57, May 1967, no. 2, pp. 401–10.

C. L. LLOYD, 'The equivalence of the liquidity preference and loanable funds theories and the new stock flow analysis', *R.E.S.*, vol. 27, June 1960, pp. 206–9.

L. RITTER, 'The role of money in Keynesian theory', Carson (ed.), *Banking and Monetary Studies*, Irwin, 1963, pp. 134–50.

H. ROSE, 'Liquidity preference and loanable funds', *R.E.S.*, vol. 24, February 1957, pp. 111–19.

G. L. S. SHACKLE, 'Recent theories concerning the nature and role of interest', *E.J.*, vol. 71, June 1961, pp. 209–54. Reprinted in R. S. THORN, *Surveys of Economic Theory*, vol. 1.

S. C. TSIANG, 'Liquidity preference and loanable funds theories, multiplier and velocity analysis: a synthesis', *A.E.R.*, vol. 46, September 1956, pp. 539–64.

Money, growth and social welfare

A. C. ENTHOVEN, 'Monetary disequilibrium and the dynamics of inflation', *E.J.*, vol. 66, 1956, pp. 256–70.

B. HANSEN, *A Study in the Theory of Inflation*, Allen & Unwin, 1951.

H. G. JOHNSON, 'Money in a neo-classical, one-sector growth model', *Essays in Monetary Economics*, 1967, ch. 4, pp. 143–78.

H. G. JOHNSON, 'The neutrality of money in growth models: a reply', *Economica*, vol. 34, February 1967, pp. 73–4.

N. LIVIATAN, 'On the long-run theory of consumption and real balances', *O.E.P.*, vol. 17, 1965, pp. 205–18.

A. L. MARTY, 'Gurley and Shaw on money in a theory of finance', *J.P.E.*, vol. 69, February 1961, pp. 56–9.

R. A. MUNDELL, 'A fallacy in the interpretation of macroeconomic equilibrium', *J.P.E.*, vol. 73, 1965, pp. 61–6.

E. S. PHELPS, 'Anticipated inflation and economic welfare', *J.P.E.*, vol. 73, 1965, pp. 1–17.

A. W. PHILLIPS, 'A simple model of employment, money and prices in a growing economy', *Economica*, vol. 28, 1961, pp. 360–70.

M. SIDRAUSKI, 'Rational choice and patterns of growth in a monetary economy', *A.E.R.*, vol. 17, May 1967, pp. 534–44.

Further Reading

J. TOBIN, 'A dymamic aggregative model', *J.P.E.*, vol. 63, 1955, pp. 103–15.
J. TOBIN, 'Money and economic growth', *Econometrica*, vol. 33, October 1965, pp. 671–84.
J. TOBIN, 'The neutrality of money in growth models: a comment', *Economica*, vol. 34, February 1967, pp. 69–72.

Acknowledgements

Permission to reprint the papers published in this volume is acknowledged from the following sources:

Reading 2   Macmillan & Co. Ltd
Reading 3   *Kyklos*
Reading 4   Schenkman Publishing Company, Inc.
Reading 6   Macmillan & Co. Ltd
Reading 7   University of Chicago Press
Reading 8   Schenkman Publishing Company, Inc.
Reading 9   Harper & Row, Publishers, Inc.
Reading 10   G. C. Archibald, R. G. Lipsey and *The Review of Economic Studies*
Reading 11   M. L. Burstein and *The Review of Economic Studies*
Reading 12   P. A. Samuelson and *The Canadian Journal of Economics*
Reading 13   Macmillan & Co. Ltd
Reading 14   *Western Economic Journal*
Reading 15   Harvard University Press
Reading 16   *Pakistan Economic Journal*
Reading 17   The Macmillan Company, New York
Reading 18   The Clarendon Press, Oxford
Reading 19   Macmillan & Co. Ltd
Reading 20   A. Leijonhufvud and *American Economic Review*
Reading 21   University of Chicago Press
Reading 22   Harvard University Press

Author Index

Author Index

References to bibliographies are printed in italics

Subject Index

Subject Index

Penguin Modern Economics Readings

Volumes available

Economics of Education 1
Ed. M. Blaug

Public Enterprise
Ed. R. Turvey

The Labour Market
*Ed. B. J. McCormick and
E. Owen Smith*

Regional Analysis
Ed. L. Needleman

Managerial Economics
Ed. G. P. E. Clarkson

Transport
Ed. Denys Munby

Volumes recently published

Inflation
Edited by R. J. Ball and Peter Doyle

Since the Second World War our thinking about inflation has
changed considerably. Several different strains of the disease,
including 'creeping inflation', have been identified and the
literature on this topic, central to economists, politicians and
businessmen alike, is now enormous.

The feat of the editors of this key volume of Penguin Modern
Economics Readings is to make the interplay of theoretical and
applied thinking on inflation not only crystal clear but also a
fascinating story in its own right; they take the reader from Keynes
in 1940 ('There is no difficulty whatever in paying for the cost of
the war out of voluntary savings provided we put up with the
consequences') to the continuing controversies (*per* Machlup:
'The galloping inflation of literature on the creeping inflation of
price') focused on cost push and demand pull.

International Finance
Edited by R. N. Cooper

Balance-of-payments problems, their causes and remedies are
compelling and perennial issues. This volume starts with the
superb analysis of the specie-flow mechanism by David Hume
a tribute to the power of classical economics. Various forms of
balance-of-payments adjustment under fixed exchange rates are
then considered, followed by several selections on the consequences
of altering exchange rates. The difficulties of reconciling domestic
and foreign policies are explored, and the readings end with an
examination of international liquidity.

Monopoly and Competition
Edited by Alex Hunter

'People of the same trade', runs Adam Smith's famous remark,
'seldom meet together even for merriment and diversion but the
conversation ends in a conspiracy against the public or in some
contrivance to raise prices.' The problem is still with us in modern
dress. Indeed as the editor of this fascinating survey puts it: 'Not
only are we examining the phenomenon of monopoly, oligarchy
and merger from the wrong point of view, but the statutory tools
we employ are already obsolete.' In an area of thought in which
objectives of economic efficiency tangle consistently with value
judgements on the kind of society we wish to have, Dr Hunter is
a meticulous guide.

Part One indicates the progress of the more important developments
in theory. Part Two brings out the manipulative techniques of
economists. Part Three examines the particular difficulties of
applying efficiently economic and organizational concepts through
a process of law. Part Four quotes from judgements on problems
of competition and monopoly.

International Trade
Edited by Jagdish Bhagwati

The pure theory of international trade, one of the oldest branches of economics, deals with the causes of trade between nations, the gains from trade and the effects of commercial policy. The readings in this volume explore the theoretical foundations of the celebrated Hecksher Ohlin model and the associated empirical literature on the 'Leontief Paradox'. The gains from free trade and, more importantly, trade in the presence of tariffs and rigid wages also receive attention. The final section explores the inter-relations of trade and growth.

Economics of Education 2
Edited by M. Blaug

This second volume of readings in *Economics of Education* concentrates on the implications of the cost of education. Part One explores the international comparisons approach to planning, with particular relevance to the needs of developing countries. Part Two stresses the growing importance of mathematical models in planning and includes the 1964 Tinbergen and Bos development of the Correa–Tinbergen–Bos model. Professor Blaug includes in Part Three, 'International Migration of Human Skills', the leading article by Grubel and Scott (1966) that 'put the cat among the pigeons and altered the entire nature of the debate on "brain drain"'. Part Four deals with the problem of measuring the output of educational systems and 'educational vouchers' – a contentious issue that, Professor Blaug concludes,'virtually forces every reader to clarify his own values'.

Penguin Modern Economics Texts

A new series of short, original unit texts on various aspects of thought and research in important areas of economics. The series is under the general editorship of B. J. McCormick, Senior Lecturer in Economics, University of Sheffield.

The Economics of Agriculture
David Metcalf
Lecturer in Economics, London School of Economics

Balance-of-Payments Policy
B. J. Cohen
Assistant Professor of Economics, Princeton University

Elements of Regional Economics
Harry W. Richardson
Director for the Centre for Research in the Social Sciences
University of Kent at Canterbury

The International Monetary System
Herbert G. Grubel
Associate Professor, Wharton School of Finance and Commerce,
University of Pennsylvania

Wages
B. J. McCormick
Senior Lecturer in Economics at the University of Sheffield